WITH THE MASTER
IN HEAVENLY PLACES

*A Ladies' Bible Study
of Ephesians*

By
Susan J. Heck

With the Master in Heavenly Places
A Ladies' Bible Study of Ephesians
By Susan J. Heck

Cover design by Amelia Schussman

ISBN 978-1-936141-33-3

Printed in the United States of America

Dedication

To my friend and co-laborer in ministry,

Debbie Pendergraft

Your selfless sacrifice for the sake of the gospel is exemplary!

"For by grace you have been saved through faith, and that
not of yourselves; it is the gift of God, not of works, lest
anyone should boast. For we are His workmanship, created
in Christ Jesus for good works, which God prepared
beforehand that we should walk in them."
Ephesians 2:8-10

Also a special thank you to

The Believers Foundation

for their gracious grant which made the publishing
of this book possible.

Endorsements

Rarely do I commend theological books written by a woman because, quite frankly, most of today's popular female Bible teachers are not exactly known for their sound exposition of Scripture—which is one of the reasons for their popularity. Susan Heck is one of the very few notable exceptions to this. Susan has long been a careful exegete of Scripture and this work on Ephesians continues her faithful track record. Only the careful, deep, hermeneutically sound study of God's Word will bear true fruit in our lives. As a personal friend of Susan's I can tell you that not only does Susan teach sound doctrine, she lives it out. If you want a female Bible teacher to tickle your ears, turn on your television. If you want one to challenge and feed you, I commend to you With the Master in Heavenly Places.

Kathy Peters, wife of Justin Peters (Justinpeters.org)

Once again Susan Heck has done a masterful job of laying out the biblical truth of God's Word for women that want to follow the Master. We are so pleased to carry her weekly Bible study for ladies on our network and have heard from ladies all around the world that are benefiting from her accurate and consistent exposition of God's Word. Thank you Susan for your ministry both in print and audio.

Brannon Howse, WorldviewRadio.com

Table of Contents

Chapter 1

An Introduction to Ephesians

Ephesians 1:1-2

Several years ago the Los Angeles Times reported the story of an elderly man and wife who were found dead in their apartment. Autopsies revealed that both had died of severe malnutrition, although investigators found a total of $40,000 stored in paper bags in a closet.

For many years Hetty Green was called America's greatest miser. When she died in 1916, she left an estate valued at $100 million, an especially vast fortune for that day. But she was so miserly that she ate cold oatmeal in order to save the expense of heating the water. When her son had a severe leg injury, she took so long trying to find a free clinic to treat him that his leg had to be amputated because of advanced infection. It has been said that she hastened her own death by bringing on a fit of apoplexy while arguing the merits of skim milk because it was cheaper than whole milk.

The book of Ephesians is written to Christians who might be prone to treat their spiritual resources much like that miserly couple and Hetty Green treated their financial resources. Such believers are in danger of suffering from spiritual malnutrition, because they do not take advantage of the great storehouse of spiritual nourishment and resources that is at their disposal.[1]

As we begin our study of the Epistle to the Ephesians we should be struck with a sense of amazement, wonder, and humility as we consider the vast riches that are given to us by our Master

---

1   John F. MacArthur, *The MacArthur New Testament Commentary: Ephesians* (Chicago: Moody, 1986), vii.

in heavenly places. Throughout his brief letter, we see the apostle Paul emphasize this theme over and over again. In fact, he barely gets started writing to the church at Ephesus before he mentions this theme. In Ephesians 1:3, he says, "Blessed be the God and Father of our Lord Jesus Christ, who has blessed us with all spiritual blessings *in heavenly places* in Christ." Then, in Ephesians 1:20, he mentions it again: "Which He worked in Christ when He raised Him from the dead and seated Him at His right hand *in the heavenly places*." Also Ephesians 2:6, "and raised us up together, and made us sit together *in the heavenly places* in Christ Jesus." Then again in Ephesians 3:10, "to the intent that now the manifold wisdom of God might be made known by the church to the principalities and powers *in the heavenly places*." And even as Paul ends this letter, he is still contemplating the heavenly places as he says in Ephesians 6:12, "For we do not wrestle against flesh and blood, but against principalities, against powers, against the rulers of the darkness of this age, against spiritual hosts of wickedness *in the heavenly places*." Martyn Lloyd-Jones said, "Obviously the Apostle would not repeat this phrase unless it possessed some deep and real significance; and it is, I repeat, one of the most glorious representations of the Christian truth. If we could but see ourselves as we are in Christ in the heavenly places it would revolutionize our lives, and change our whole outlook."[2]

Before we dive into the first few verses, I'd like to go over some background information about the Epistle to the Ephesians by asking and answering several questions. First of all, *who wrote the Epistle to the Ephesians?*[3] We know Paul wrote it, as evidenced by

2 D. M. Lloyd-Jones, *God's Ultimate Purpose: An Exposition of Ephesians 1* (Grand Rapids: Baker, 1984), 70.

3 This study guide assumes the epistle was written to believers *at Ephesus* (1:1), although there are good reasons to suggest that this could have been a circular letter, (Peter T. O'Brien, *The Letter to the Ephesians* (Grand Rapids: Eerdmans, 1999), 86-87). For example, this is the most impersonal of all of Paul's epistles, lacking in personal greetings, although he ministered longer in Ephesus than in any other city of his missionary journeys (cf. Eph. 1:15). The words *at Ephesus* (Greek, en Epheso) are omitted from the earliest Greek manuscripts and the RSV. Marcion considered this epistle addressed to believers *in Laodicea,* perhaps being influenced by Col. 4:16. Those who suggest this was a circular letter hold that a blank was left and as copies were made at particular local churches the name was written in. However, it is questionable as to why no other manuscripts of this epistle offer other city names! It seems best to accept the traditional understanding, but to consider that Paul's intent was that this letter circulate among the

verse 1. Next, *where was Paul when he wrote this letter?* Paul was a prisoner in Rome. Ephesians is one of four letters that Paul wrote while in prison that are together referred to as the Prison Epistles; Colossians, Philippians, and Philemon being the other three. Paul's Epistle to the Colossians was written about the same time as his Epistle to the Ephesians, and both letters were probably delivered around the same time by the same person, Tychicus. Consider Ephesians 6:21, "But that you also may know my affairs and how I am doing, Tychicus, a beloved brother and faithful minister in the Lord, will make all things known to you." Also, Colossians 4:7, "Tychicus, a beloved brother, faithful minister, and fellow servant in the Lord, will tell you all the news about me." According to Acts 28, Tychicus was with Paul at this time, while Paul was under house arrest in Rome. Paul gave Tychicus these letters and had him deliver them to each of the churches. Colossians and Ephesians are known as sister epistles and share numerous similarities. Next, we should also ask, *when was this epistle written?* It is estimated that this epistle was written sometime between AD 60-62. It had been about five years since Paul had seen the church at Ephesus.

Probably the most important question for us to ask is, *why was this epistle written?* Paul seems to want to encourage the Ephesian believers in the things of Christ. He exalts Christ and emphasizes His sovereign plan and will. Interestingly, this letter to the Ephesians is one that has a positive tone; Paul isn't writing to rebuke the Ephesians, as he does the Galatians and the Corinthians. This does not mean there were no problems in the church of Ephesus, as no church is without problems. Ephesus had tensions between Jews and Greeks, and there were problems with the goddesses of the day which we will see in later lessons.

Paul spells out clearly not only the Ephesians' riches in Christ but their responsibilities in Christ as well. In the first part of the letter, he sets forth Christ, and in the latter part he sets forth their responsibilities in Christ. The first three chapters of Ephesians are doctrinal and the last three are practical. The first three chapters

---

fellowships of Asia Minor. Notice in Col. 4:16 he says *from* Laodicea, not *to* Laodicea, allowing that the epistle may have just been at Laodicea. Also, internal evidence is implied in the mission of *Tychicus* sent to Ephesus (cf. Eph. 6:21-22), who, according to 2 Tim. 4:12, was later sent to the same city.

deal with what we should believe, and the last three tell us how we should behave. Some of you might be thinking, "Well, let's get into the practical stuff; I don't care much for doctrine." Well, my friend, what you believe dictates how you behave. What you believe about God determines how you will live for God. What you believe about the Holy Spirit will decide how you respond to the Holy Spirit. What you believe about heaven will determine if you will live for the life to come. What you believe about sin will determine how determined you'll be to repent of it. What you believe about your brothers and sisters in Christ will determine how you love them. It's a sad day in which we live when all we want is application and no doctrine. In his letter to Timothy, Paul tells us that will happen: "For the time will come when they will not endure sound doctrine, but according to their own desires, because they have itching ears, they will heap up for themselves teachers; and they will turn their ears away from the truth, and be turned aside to fables" (2 Timothy 4:3-4).

Let's consider some other interesting facts about the Epistle to the Ephesians. It was John Calvin's favorite! It is the only book in the Bible that contains a complete description of the believer's armor. It also contains the seven "ones" in Ephesians 4:4-6: one body, one Spirit, one hope, one Lord, one faith, one baptism, one God. Did you also know that Ephesians has the favorite verse of every married woman?! Here it is! Ephesians 5:25 says, "Husbands, love your wives, just as Christ also loved the church and gave Himself for her." Martyn Lloyd-Jones said of this epistle, "But the peculiar feature and characteristic of the Epistle to the Ephesians is that here the Apostle seems to be, as he puts it himself, in 'the heavenly places,' and he is looking down at the great panorama of salvation and redemption from that particular aspect."[4] Lloyd-Jones also states in his commentary, "Luther says of the Epistle to the Romans that it is 'the most important document in the New Testament, the gospel in its purest expression,' and in many ways I agree that there is no purer, plainer statement of the gospel than in the Epistle to the Romans. Accepting that as true I would venture to add that if the Epistle to the Romans is the purest expression of the

---

4   Ibid, 11-12.

gospel, the Epistle to the Ephesians is the sublimest and the most majestic expression of it." [5]

Some of the things we will be considering together as we study this great letter from Paul include: the doctrine of election, which comes up several times; forgiveness of sins, which also comes up several times; our inheritance in heaven; Paul's wonderful prayers for the church at Ephesus, of which there are two in this letter; the way to get to heaven; the importance of walking in unity; our role in the body; spiritual gifts; putting off the old man and putting on the new man (e.g., putting off lying, putting on truth; putting off corrupt communication, putting on edifying communication); fornication; coveting; removing ourselves from sinning, professing believers; redeeming our time; the danger of drunkenness and the blessing of being filled with the Spirit instead; grieving the Spirit; husband and wife roles; children/parent roles; slave/master roles; the believer's armor; our responsibility to the gospel; and much more.

Let's begin our study by looking at the first two verses of Ephesians. As we do, we will also look at some more helpful information about this book, which will aid us in our study of Ephesians.

Ephesians 1:1-2

> Paul, an apostle of Jesus Christ by the will of God, to the saints who are in Ephesus, and faithful in Christ Jesus: [2] Grace to you and peace from God our Father and the Lord Jesus Christ (Ephesians 1:1-2).

In this chapter, we'll use the following outline: *The Writer and Three Facts about Him*, (v 1a); *The Receivers and Three Facts about Them*, (v 1b); and *The Greeting and Three Facts about It*, (v 2). Let's begin by looking at the writer to the Ephesians, in verse 1.

---

5   Ibid, 12.

Ephesians 1:1a

The Writer and Three Facts about Him

Paul, an apostle of Jesus Christ by the will of God
(Ephesians 1:1a).

The first question we might have as we look at verse 1 is, who is *Paul*? Paul, we know, was formerly called Saul. He was born a Roman citizen. He was not physically impressive, nor was he a very dynamic speaker (1 Corinthians 2:1 and 2 Corinthians 10:10; 11:6). He had a sister and a nephew (Acts 23:16) and was educated in Jerusalem under the famous Jewish teacher Gamaliel (Acts 22:3). He was a Pharisee (Acts 26:5) and a tentmaker (Acts 18:3), and he participated in the stoning of Stephen, the first of the Christian martyrs (Acts 7:58). Paul wrote the most books of the New Testament, and his conversion to Christ is among the most well-known in church history. We know from Acts 9 that the Lord saved him on the Damascus road while he was on his way to persecute the Christians of that city. I don't think Paul ever got over his conversion, as he has the following to say regarding himself in 1 Corinthians 15:9, which is quite a contrast to our self-esteem-promoting generation: "For I am the least of the apostles, who am not worthy to be called an apostle, because I persecuted the church of God." And in 1 Timothy 1:12-13, he says, "And I thank Christ Jesus our Lord who has enabled me, because He counted me faithful, putting me into the ministry, although I was formerly a blasphemer, a persecutor, and an insolent man; but I obtained mercy because I did it ignorantly in unbelief." No wonder Paul says, in 1 Timothy 1:15, "This is a faithful saying and worthy of all acceptance, that Christ Jesus came into the world to save sinners, of whom I am chief." He established himself as an apostle.

What is an apostle? The word *apostle* in the Greek is apostollos, meaning "one sent forth" as an ambassador of the Gospel. An apostle is a minister sent directly by God to do a specific work. An apostle would be one who is sent by another—in this case, the

Lord Jesus—and who bears the authority of the sender. Paul goes on to say not only that he was sent forth to be an apostle *of Jesus Christ*, but that it was *by the will of God*. The will of God would mean that God willed for Paul to be an apostle. It is the same for us; God has willed that we do certain things for His kingdom and glory. So what are the facts about the writer of this epistle? His name was Paul; he was an apostle of Jesus Christ; and it was the will of God that he be an apostle. Next, let's look at the recipients of this letter and three facts about them.

Ephesians 1:1b
The Recipients and Three Facts about Them

> To the saints who are in Ephesus, and faithful in Christ Jesus (Ephesians 1:1b).

Now Paul is not writing this letter to a specific local church in the city of Ephesus but to all of the Christians in this city. Using a modern-day parallel, it would be as though he were writing not to your specific church you attend but to all the Christians in your city. The history of Christianity at Ephesus began about AD 50, perhaps as a result of the efforts of Priscilla and Aquila. Paul came to Ephesus in about AD 52, and was there for about three years, founding the church of Ephesus as part of his second missionary journey.

Paul writes this epistle *to the saints*. What is a saint? A saint is one who is set apart; set apart from the world and for the purpose of serving the Lord. The term saint (Greek, <u>hagios</u>) refers to someone set apart by God for His service and separated from sin. Theologically, a saint refers to one who is cleansed by the blood of Christ, and by the renewing of the Holy Spirit, and is thus separated from the world and consecrated unto God. In the New Testament, this refers to all believers, regardless of their maturity in Christ (See 1 Corinthians 1:2) [6]. The term is used quite often in the Scriptures:

---

6   Roman Catholic dogma teaches that *saints* are solemnly proclaimed such because of heroic virtue and having performed at least two recognized miracles; as such, they are models and intercessors for the church. cf. *Catechism of the Catholic Church* (<u>Libreria</u>

34 times in the Old Testament and 64 times in the New Testament.

The term saint would be very important to the group of believers in Ephesus, because their city was filled with goddesses, Diana being one of them. They were called to separate themselves from the world, from these idolatrous practices. Ladies, there is nothing new under the sun, as our world today is also filled with many things from which we must separate ourselves. We must ask ourselves regularly, "Is this activity becoming to a daughter of God? Am I separated from the world and unto Christ?" This separation is borne out of a desire to be separated from the world, not because we're obligated to do so. This was one of the things I noticed after I came to faith in Christ. I thought I knew God and was doing things because I knew it was what Christians did, but I never had a heart of obedience. I was wicked. But after the Lord saved me, my heart changed so that I longed to do the will of God. It became my delight.

Paul is writing to the saints *in Ephesus*. Ephesus was a city in Asia Minor, located near the Aegean Sea. It was a city known for its splendor and riches. It was the largest city in the area, with a population of 300,000. The Ephesians worshiped the goddess Artemis, or Diana, whose temple was one of the Seven Wonders of the World. (Artemis was the Greek name and Diana was the Latin name.) Diana was known as the moon goddess, the goddess of hunting, and the patroness of young girls. The temple at Ephesus housed the multi-breasted image of Artemis, which was said to have come directly from Zeus. Consider Acts 19:35, "And when the city clerk had quieted the crowd, he said: 'Men of Ephesus, what man is there who does not know that the city of the Ephesians is temple guardian of the great goddess Diana, and of the image which fell down from Zeus?'" This temple had columns that were sixty feet high. "The influence of this goddess and the cult attached to her permeated every area of life for those who lived in this city. The temple was the major banking center for the city, her image adorned the coinage, a month of the year was named after her, Olympic-style

---

Editrice Vaticana, 1994), 219. Such teaching is not supported by NT Scriptures.

games were held in her honor (called the Artemisia), and she was trusted as the guardian and protector of the city."[7] She was not the only goddess worshiped in the city of Ephesus; it has been said that there were about 50 others goddesses worshiped there. Even though we don't put up huge statues, we worship the gods of self, pleasure, money, success, and more.

Not only did the city worship goddesses, it was also involved in sorcery. Let's look at Acts 19:13-20. (Note that verse 1 of Acts 19 indicates that they were in Ephesus.)

> Then some of the itinerant Jewish exorcists took it upon themselves to call the name of the Lord Jesus over those who had evil spirits, saying, "We exorcise you by the Jesus whom Paul preaches." Also there were seven sons of Sceva, a Jewish chief priest, who did so. And the evil spirit answered and said, "Jesus I know, and Paul I know; but who are you?"
> Then the man in whom the evil spirit was leaped on them, overpowered them, and prevailed against them, so that they fled out of that house naked and wounded. This became known both to all Jews and Greeks dwelling in Ephesus; and fear fell on them all, and the name of the Lord Jesus was magnified. And many who had believed came confessing and telling their deeds. Also, many of those who had practiced magic brought their books together and burned them in the sight of all. And they counted up the value of them, and it totaled fifty thousand pieces of silver. So the word of the Lord grew mightily and prevailed (Acts 19:13-20).[7]

Evidently, Sceva and his sons wanted to add Jesus to their exorcism. When they attempted to do this, the demon-possessed man leaped on them and overpowered them. This caused fear to come upon the people in Ephesus, which caused many to repent and believe and to burn their books about magic. The value today of those books would have been 50,000 days wages. That's a lot of money! When one repents, the grace of God compels them, no matter what it might cost them!

---

7   Clinton E. Arnold, *Exegetical Commentary on the New Testament: Ephesians* (Grand Rapids: Zondervan, 2010), 31.

As we learned before, Paul spent three years in Ephesus, and it ended abruptly after a dramatic scene recorded in Acts 19:23-41. Let's read it together.

And about that time there arose a great commotion about the Way. For a certain man named Demetrius, a silversmith, who made silver shrines of Diana, brought no small profit to the craftsmen. He called them together with the workers of similar occupation, and said: "Men, you know that we have our prosperity by this trade. Moreover you see and hear that not only at Ephesus, but throughout almost all Asia, this Paul has persuaded and turned away many people, saying that they are not gods which are made with hands. So not only is this trade of ours in danger of falling into disrepute, but also the temple of the great goddess Diana may be despised and her magnificence destroyed, whom all Asia and the world worship."

And when they heard this, they were full of wrath and cried out, saying, "Great is Diana of the Ephesians!" So the whole city was filled with confusion, and rushed into the theater with one accord, having seized Gaius and Aristarchus, Macedonians, Paul's travel companions. And when Paul wanted to go in to the people, the disciples would not allow him. Then some of the officials of Asia, who were his friends, sent to him pleading that he would not venture into the theater. Some therefore cried one thing and some another, for the assembly was confused, and most of them did not know why they had come together. And they drew Alexander out of the multitude, the Jews putting him forward. And Alexander motioned with his hand, and wanted to make his defense to the people. But when they found out that he was a Jew, all with one voice cried out for about two hours, "Great is Diana of the Ephesians!"

And when the city clerk had quieted the crowd, he said: "Men of Ephesus, what man is there who does not know that the city of the Ephesians is temple guardian of the great goddess Diana, and of the image which fell down from Zeus? Therefore, since these things cannot be denied, you ought to be quiet and do nothing rashly. For you have brought these men here who are neither robbers of temples nor blasphemers of your goddess. Therefore, if Demetrius and his fellow craftsmen have a case against anyone, the courts are open and there are proconsuls.

Let them bring charges against one another. But if you have any other inquiry to make, it shall be determined in the lawful assembly. For we are in danger of being called in question for today's uproar, there being no reason which we may give to account for this disorderly gathering." And when he had said these things, he dismissed the assembly (Acts 19:23-41).

Paul's ministry was so influential in Ephesus that the silversmiths who fashioned the souvenirs of the temple feared that the preaching of the gospel would undermine the great temple of Artemis. As a result, one of the silversmiths, a man named Demetrius, stirred up a riot against Paul.

After this, Paul says goodbye to the Ephesians, in Acts 20:1, "After the uproar had ceased, Paul called the disciples to himself, embraced them, and departed to go to Macedonia." Later on, we see him return to Ephesus, in Acts 20:17-38, where he has a final, tearful goodbye with the elders of the church.

From Miletus he sent to Ephesus and called for the elders of the church. And when they had come to him, he said to them: "You know, from the first day that I came to Asia, in what manner I always lived among you, serving the Lord with all humility, with many tears and trials which happened to me by the plotting of the Jews; how I kept back nothing that was helpful, but proclaimed it to you, and taught you publicly and from house to house, testifying to Jews, and also to Greeks, repentance toward God and faith toward our Lord Jesus Christ. And see, now I go bound in the spirit to Jerusalem, not knowing the things that will happen to me there, except that the Holy Spirit testifies in every city, saying that chains and tribulations await me. But none of these things move me; nor do I count my life dear to myself, so that I may finish my race with joy, and the ministry which I received from the Lord Jesus, to testify to the gospel of the grace of God.

"And indeed, now I know that you all, among whom I have gone preaching the kingdom of God, will see my face no more. Therefore I testify to you this day that I am innocent of the blood of all men. For I have not shunned to declare to you the whole counsel of God. Therefore take heed to yourselves and to all the flock, among which the Holy Spirit has made you overseers, to shepherd the church of God which He purchased with His own blood. For I know this, that after my departure savage wolves will come in among you, not sparing the flock. Also from among yourselves men will rise up, speaking perverse things, to draw away the disciples after themselves. Therefore watch, and remember that for three years I did not cease to warn everyone night and day with tears.

So now, brethren, I commend you to God and to the word of His grace, which is able to build you up and give you an inheritance among all those who are sanctified. I have coveted no one's silver or gold or apparel. Yes, you yourselves know that these hands have provided for my necessities, and for those who were with me. I have shown you in every way, by laboring like this, that you must support the weak. And remember the words of the Lord Jesus, that He said, 'It is more blessed to give than to receive.'"

And when he had said these things, he knelt down and prayed with them all. Then they all wept freely, and fell on Paul's neck and kissed him, sorrowing most of all for the words which he spoke, that they would see his face no more. And they accompanied him to the ship (Acts 20:17-38).

After Paul departed from Ephesus, Timothy remained behind to combat the false teaching that would later arise there (1 Timothy 1:3; 2 Timothy 4:3; Acts 20:29).

It is interesting to note that the apostle John lived and ministered in Ephesus toward the end of the first century. In his vision from the island of Patmos, off the coast of Asia Minor, John dictated Jesus' evaluation of the Ephesian church, describing it as flourishing, though troubled with false teachers and having lost its first love (Revelation 2:1-7). Simply put, idolatry results in lost love for Christ. John also wrote his first epistle from the city of Ephesus, and it's likely that he had Diana and other goddesses in mind when he closed that book with, "Little children, keep yourselves from idols. Amen" (1 John 5:21).

Paul not only calls the Ephesian believers saints, but he calls them *faithful*. What does faithful mean? It means that they are believing. Paul is addressing believers in this epistle, those who are the faithful ones of God. "It means that we keep the faith, that we hold to the faith, that we are constant in the faith, and loyal to the faith, and ready with Paul to defend the faith, and to contend earnestly for it."[8] And he says they are faithful *in Christ Jesus*, which means they belong to Him, which is why they are faithful to Him. These three words are found 27 times in Ephesians, emphasizing our position in Christ. The Ephesians are saints and they are faithful because they are in Christ Jesus. So who are the receivers of this letter? They are saints, they are in Ephesus, and they are faithful. Let's move on to the greeting and the three facts about it.

Ephesians 1:2
The Greeting and Three Facts about It

> Grace to you and peace from God our Father and the Lord Jesus Christ (Ephesians 1:2).

Paul begins with a greeting that is similar to most of his epistles, *grace ... and peace*. In fact, a similar greeting can be found in seven of his epistles: Romans, 1 and 2 Corinthians, Galatians, Philippians, 2 Thessalonians, and Philemon. These two things, grace and peace, are certainly needed in our walk with the Lord. What is *grace*? It is the free, undeserved favor and mercy of God. Grace not only comes as a result of the gospel, but it is the gospel. It is the grace of God that saves any of us. Paul actually mentions the word grace 95 times in his epistles. What is *peace*? Peace would be rest, spiritual prosperity, completeness. And, this grace and peace come *from God our Father and the Lord Jesus Christ*. Ladies, you can try to muster up grace and peace all you want and you won't obtain it. These gifts come only from a relationship with God the Father through His Son Jesus Christ. So what are the three facts about the greeting? Paul sends a greeting of grace, a greeting of peace, and affirms that these come from God the Father and the Lord Jesus Christ.

---

8   Lloyd-Jones, 30.

Summary

In this first lesson in our study of Paul's Epistle to the Ephesians, we have seen: *The Writer and Three Facts about Him*, (v 1a): His name is Paul; he is an apostle of Jesus Christ; and it was the will of God that he was an apostle. *The Recipients and Three Facts about Them*, (v 1b): They are saints; they are in Ephesus; and they are faithful. *The Greeting and Three Facts about It*, (v 2): Paul sends a greeting of grace, a greeting of peace, and affirms that these come from God the Father and the Lord Jesus Christ.

My dear sister, do you know the grace and peace of which Paul speaks? If you don't, why not embrace Him today as your Lord? Are you one of the saints and faithful sisters of our Lord? If not, why not bow your knee to Him today? For those of you who know the grace and peace of which Paul speaks, for those of you who are saints and faithful sisters of our Lord, hold on tight, as Ephesians promises to be an exciting study, as we lay hold of our Master in heavenly places!

Questions to Consider

An Introduction to Ephesians
Ephesians 1:1-2

1. (a) Read the entire Epistle to the Ephesians and list ten key words or phrases that you think Paul gives importance to, along with any reasons for their importance. (b) Memorize Ephesians 1:1.

2. What are some facts you already know about the Epistle to the Ephesians?

3. (a) Read over Acts 19 and 20, and list any further facts you glean about the city of Ephesus and the Ephesians. (b) How might these facts influence Paul's letter to them?

4. What are the similarities in Paul's opening remarks in Ephesians 1:1-2 and his closing remarks in Ephesians 6:23-24?

5. Paul addresses the believers at Ephesus as "saints" and "faithful in Christ Jesus." How would you describe the believers in your church if you were addressing them in a letter?

6. What do you personally hope to gain from this study in Ephesians? Why not pause right now and ask the Lord to help you with the desire of your heart?

7. Have you experienced the grace of God that Paul speaks of in Ephesians 1:2? Do you have a living relationship with God our Father and His Son, the Lord Jesus Christ? If so, write a praise of thanksgiving, to be shared with your group, for what this amazing grace means in your life!

Chapter 2

The Believer's Blessings in Christ! (Part 1)

Ephesians 1:3-9

In the six months prior to writing this study of Ephesians, the Lord allowed me to go through some of the most difficult trials of my life. In fact, in just the week before I wrote this lesson, I felt somewhat like Paul, when he said he was hard pressed on every side (2 Corinthians 4:8). Of course, Paul also says that even though he was hard pressed on every side, he was not crushed. In God's providence during this "pressing" time, I was also reading in Psalm 88. I found verses like verse 1: "O LORD, God of my salvation, I have cried out day and night before You." Verse 3: "For my soul is full of troubles, and my life draws near to the grave." Verses 6 and 7: "You have laid me in the lowest pit, in darkness, in the depths. Your wrath lies heavy upon me, and You have afflicted me with all Your waves. Selah." And verse 14: "LORD, why do You cast off my soul? Why do You hide Your face from me?" I thought to myself, "This is exactly how I feel. Lord, are there no answers?!" My eyes began to read the next psalm, Psalm 89, and in the first verse the answer came: "I will sing of the mercies of the LORD forever; with my mouth will I make known Your faithfulness to all generations." And then I said, "O Lord, this is the cure, this is the help I need. I must sing of your mercies, O Lord!" And so I began to sing and praise the Lord throughout the day and began to change my mindset to think of my blessings instead of my troubles. Did my circumstances change? No, but my attitude did.

Why do I say all of this? Because, as we come to our second lesson in Ephesians, we find the apostle Paul bursting forth, telling the Ephesian believers of their many blessings in Christ. And remember, these words are coming from a man who is in prison! My dear friends, there are so many of these blessings that we will need two lessons to cover them all! In this lesson, we will discover 8 blessings and in the next lesson we will discover 4 more. And I trust that the Lord will encourage your heart through each one of them. Let's read verses 3-14, as it really is one expanding thought. Actually, it is one long sentence composed of 202 words. This is the longest sentence in the New Testament, although the NASV and NIV translations break the paragraph into numerous sentences.[9] In this paragraph, the apostle Paul outlines the blessings of our salvation by the Triune God, showing us the blessing of God the Father in our past election, the blessing of God the Son in our present redemption, and the blessing of God the Spirit in our future inheritance.

Ephesians 1:3-14

Blessed be the God and Father of our Lord Jesus Christ, who has blessed us with every spiritual blessing in the heavenly places in Christ, [4]just as He chose us in Him before the foundation of the world, that we should be holy and without blame before Him in love, [5]having predestined us to adoption as sons by Jesus Christ to Himself, according to the good pleasure of His will, [6]to the praise of the glory of His grace, by which He has made us accepted in the Beloved. [7]In Him we have redemption through His blood, the forgiveness of sins, according to the riches of His grace [8]which He made to abound toward us in all wisdom and prudence, [9]having made known to us the mystery of His will, according to His good pleasure which He purposed in Himself, [10]that in the dispensation of the fullness of the times He might gather together in one all things in Christ, both which are in heaven and which are on earth—in Him. [11]In Him also we have obtained an inheritance, being predestined according to the purpose of Him who works all things according to the counsel of His will, [12]that we who first trusted in Christ should

---

9   In the Greek, verses 3-14 comprise one doxology sentence (202 words) and encompass the past, present, and future of God's eternal purpose for the Church. It is Paul's outline of God's master plan for salvation. In verses 3-6a we are shown the past aspect, election; in verses 6b-11 we are shown the present aspect, redemption; and in verses 12-14 we are shown the future aspect, inheritance. The passage can also be divided into three sections, each of which focuses on a different Person of the Trinity: verses 3-6a center on the Father, verses 6b-12 center on the Son, and verses 13-14 center on the Holy Spirit. cf. MacArthur, 5. Usually Paul begins with a thanksgiving, but a doxology introduction is also found in 2 Corinthians. First Peter also begins with a doxology.

be to the praise of His glory. [13] In Him you also trusted, after you heard the word of truth, the gospel of your salvation; in whom also, having believed, you were sealed with the Holy Spirit of promise, [14]who is the guarantee of our inheritance until the redemption of the purchased possession, to the praise of His glory (Ephesians 1:3-14).

In this lesson we'll look at eight of the believer's blessings in Christ[10]:

> 1. *He has Chosen Us in Him before the Foundation of the World,* (v 4a)
>
> 2. *He has Made Us Holy and Blameless before Him,* (v 4b)
>
> 3. *He has Predestined Us to be His Adopted Sons,* (v 5-6a)
>
> 4. *He has Made Us Accepted in the Beloved,* (v 6b)
>
> 5. *He has Given Us Redemption through His Blood,* (v 7a)
>
> 6. *He has Forgiven Us of Our Sins,* (v 7b)
>
> 7. *He has Given Us Wisdom and Prudence,* (v 8)
>
> 8. *He has Made Known to Us the Mystery of His Will,* (v 9)

We'll take two lessons to cover this passage because Paul mentions so many blessings in verses 3-14. As Proverbs 28:20a states, "A faithful man will abound with blessings," and we will see that to be true in this lesson. Before we look at the blessings themselves, let's begin by looking at the giver of these astounding blessings! Where do these blessing come from?

Ephesians 1:3

Blessed be the God and Father of our Lord Jesus Christ, who has blessed us with every spiritual blessing in the heavenly places in Christ (Ephesians 1:3).

---

10 Remember, the phrase *in Christ* or *in Christ Jesus,* is found 27 times in Ephesians and is the basis for all our distinctive blessings, either positional or practical. "Christ is the golden string on which all the pearls of this doxology are strung." cf. R. C. H. Lenski, *The Interpretation of St. Paul's Epistles to the Galatians, to the Ephesians and to the Philippians* (Minneapolis: Augsburg, 1961), 350.

Paul begins by saying *blessed be the God and Father of our Lord Jesus Christ*. The word *blessed* means to speak well of, to eulogize. When we go to a funeral there is usually a eulogy given and it is a time when the person is spoken well of, hopefully. Paul is bursting forth with a eulogy like no other because it is about God! It is interesting that the phrase "Blessed be God" was a customary phrase which was repeated by the Jews three times a day. A good example of this would can be found in Daniel 6:10, where we see Daniel kneeling three times a day and praying and giving thanks to God! This might be a great habit for all of us to get into. My fear is that most of us don't bless God once a day, much less three times a day! Notice that the speaking well of, or blessing, is of *the God and Father of our Lord Jesus Christ*. One man helps us with this phrase: "What is striking in this berakah (or benediction) from a Jewish point of view is the description of God as the Father of our Lord Jesus Christ. Paul thereby stresses that the God of Israel has a close father-son relationship with Jesus of Nazareth, the Messiah of Israel, who has come to bring redemption."[11]

Now what is it that He *has blessed us with*? Paul says, *every spiritual blessing in the heavenly places in Christ*. Ladies, these blessings are spiritual; they are supernatural. They are not fleshly, they are not material, and they are not from this world. They are spiritual, and may I say, if your heart is set on this world and all it has to offer then these blessings will seem boring and insignificant to you. But to the genuine believer they are utterly amazing and humbling! God blessing *us* with spiritual blessings?!

Now what does Paul mean when he says these blessings are *in the heavenly places in Christ*? Paul is referring to the spiritual realm and not the earthly realm. Paul repeats this phrase in Ephesians 1:20, 2:6, 3:10 and 6:12. His repetition of this phrase means it is of importance and we would do well to take heed. Because this is a phrase we take as a theme for the Epistle to the Ephesians, we should understand it as we start our journey through Ephesians. My husband has a helpful note of commentary for us (See Footnote 12).

---

11 Arnold, 78.

There is a question as to what the *heavenly places* refers to. There are only five occurrences of this combination of terms in the New Testament and each of them occurs in the Epistle to the Ephesians (1:20; 2:6; 3:10; 6:12). And in three of those passages (1:20; 2:6; 3:10), possibly four (4:12), the sense is local, which strongly suggests this is the sense here. This may refer to the entire supernatural realm of God, His full domain and extent of His sovereign operations, anywhere and everywhere in the universe, involving all events under the providence of God. In this case, the *heavenly places* may be within the believer, (as Lightfoot, Alford and Ellicott commend). Others assume this to be a non-experiential but positional blessing, as if we already exist in heaven in our spirit but not yet bodily. However, this view is difficult to support in Scripture. We do not experience a divided being, with one part of our being on heaven and the other part on earth. The best view, perhaps, is a combination of the above two ideas, while viewing us *in Christ Jesus,* i.e.,, as the Lord Jesus Christ manifests Himself in a special location in the heavenly places so we share in that sphere of exaltation by reason of our union with Him. Ephesians 2:6 says that God has "raised us up with Him, and seated us with Him in the *heavenly places* in Christ Jesus." And this despite our never practically experiencing this rising and seating in heaven! We also wrestle with principalities and powers *in heavenly places* (6:12), although in practice this is non-experiential. Hence, by the sovereign operations of God, He positions us even in the heavenly places because of our union with Christ! And because of this vital union in Christ, we are blessed, among other ways, with the Father's election, the Son's redemption and the Spirit's inheritance, all of which were blessings received from heaven itself.[12] This non-experiential but vital union with Christ is the principle spiritual blessing which Paul prays the Ephesian believers will understand (Ephesians 1:15-23).

You know my friend, if we would really view ourselves as in the heavenlies, we would not be so bogged down with this world. If we would see our citizenship as in heaven, if we would see ourselves as just passing through, if we would set our affection on things above

---

12 In 2 Cor. 12:2, Paul speaks of the same *heavenly places,* translated by most English versions as "the third heaven." cf. NASV, KJV, ASV, NIV. This is the abode where God manifests His distinctive glory. cf. A. T. Lincoln, *A Reexamination of the Heavenlies in Ephesians*, New Testament Studies, 19 [July, 1973], 471.

and not on this earth, then we would fully understand what Paul is saying here. Also, it goes without saying, that if we would see ourselves in the heavenly realm, it would make our earthly troubles seem insignificant. In light of eternity nothing that happens here really matters.

Notice before we go on that these blessings are *in Christ*. He is the One who is the giver of all blessings! Without Him, none of these things that we will look at in this lesson would be possible. So now that we have seen who the giver is of these blessings, let's begin by looking at blessing number one for the believer.

Blessing #1
He has Chosen Us in Him before the Foundation of the World
Ephesians 1:4a

> just as He chose us in Him before the foundation of the world (Ephesians 1:4a).

The first blessing that should knock your socks off is that *He chose us in Him* before the foundation of the world. Isn't it interesting that our blessings are in Christ, but also we were chosen *in Him*? It's all about Him; it is not about us![13] He chose us; we did not choose Him. We may like to think we did, but we were dead in our sins before Christ (Ephesians 2:5) and unable to do anything. Only God can make alive someone who is dead! Jesus makes this choosing of us clear in John 15:16: "You did not choose Me, but I chose you and appointed you that you should go and bear fruit, and that your fruit should remain, that whatever you ask the Father in My name He may give you."

When did this choosing take place? Paul says, *before the foundation of the world*. What does this mean? It means we were not

---

13 The verb is <u>eklego</u>, in the emphatic position, and because the voice is middle, it has a reflexive sense, i.e.,, the Father elected us by Himself and for Himself. This is central: the primary purpose of the electing work of God is His own glory! cf. 1:6, 12, 14. Only secondarily is election for the good of the elect ones.

an afterthought, but before the world was even formed God chose us.

Blessing #2
He has Made Us Holy and Without Blame before Him
Ephesians 1:4b

that we should be holy and without blame before Him in love (Ephesians 1:4).

You might say, well, why would God choose us? Paul says it was so *that we would be holy and without blame before Him*. This is the second blessing of the believer, and it refers to the reality of what we are now in Christ: we stand before Him holy and blameless. We call that justification. Some people use the phrase, "it's just as if I'd never sinned," to define the term justified. But Paul is also referring to our sanctification. In other words, we grow in holiness after the moment of our salvation; we strive to be blameless. It is very similar to what Peter says in 1 Peter 1:15-16: "but as He who called you is holy, you also be holy in all your conduct, because it is written, 'Be holy, for I am holy.'" To be holy and blameless is not only the reality of every believer; it should also be the goal and desire of every believer. What does it mean to be *holy and without blame*? What is the difference? The term *holy* denotes an inward state of purity, while the term *blameless* denotes the outward state of purity. God is concerned about both. You can look holy outwardly and still be a hypocrite in your heart. God looks on the heart and wants both heart and body to be pure. Paul then adds the words *in love*. This phrase could be referring to the fact that we should be holy and blameless coupled with love. In other words, we are holy and blameless because of our love for God and our love for others. Or it could be that the phrase is in reference to the next verse, *in love He predestined us*. In my opinion, this is the probable interpretation, as only the love of God could predestinate any of us!

Blessing #3
He has Predestined Us to be His Adopted Sons
Ephesians 1:5-6

> having predestined us to adoption as sons by Jesus Christ to
> Himself, according to the good pleasure of His will, to the
> praise of the glory of His grace (Ephesians 1:5-6a).

Here we have the third blessing of every believer, that He
predestined us to adoption as sons! What does it mean to *predestine*?
It means that God, in eternity past, destined a certain group of people
to be adopted into His family. He predestined us to be adopted as
His sons! We who are Gentiles are now called sons of God. In the
Roman world and under their law, when a child was adopted, they
were given all the legal rights of a natural-born child, much as it is
in our world today. They were given the name of their new family,
along with all the privileges of that family: food, shelter, security,
protection, and even an inheritance. I have four grandchildren
adopted from Africa. They were much like we were before Christ,
in that they were without hope in this world, destined to be orphans.
But when my daughter and her husband legally adopted them, the
children took their legal name along with all the rights of being their
children. This is what God did for us. He saw us as without hope,
orphans in this world, and adopted us into His family, giving us
His name. We are children of God, with full inheritance rights (see
verse 11).

Paul goes on to say that this adoption was *by Jesus Christ to
Himself.* In other words, this is the purpose for the predestination:
for Himself, for His purposes. You might ask, "Why would He do
that?" Paul says *according to the good pleasure of His will.* God took
pleasure in choosing us as His children; it brought Him great delight.
Paul tells us another reason why, in Romans 8:29: "For whom He
foreknew, He also predestined to be conformed to the image of His
Son, that He might be the firstborn among many brethren." God did
this so that we would be conformed to His image. It is very similar

to what Paul has said here in Ephesians about being chosen to be holy and blameless (conformed to His image).

Not only was our predestination for the good pleasure of His will, but it was also *to the praise of the glory of His grace*, as Paul says in verse 6. God's predestinating us as His sons was for His praise, not ours,[14] all for the praise of *His* glory of *His* grace! It puts Him on display, not us! This is the ultimate motive behind the predestination: that the glory of His grace would be put on display by those whom He's chosen. This is a far cry from what we see proclaimed by some of God's children today. In fact, just recently, I taught a ladies' conference and was horrified when someone handed me some literature written by a member of their church, which stated the following: "Lord, You found me. Lord, You anoint me. Lord, You need me. Lord, You exalt me. Lord, You serve me." The writer of this material certainly put us on display, but not Him. Many are now making God into some image of their own evil imagination; but, my friend, that is not the God of the Bible.

Blessing #4
He has Made Us Accepted in the Beloved
Ephesians 1:6b

by which He has made us accepted in the Beloved
(Ephesians 1:6b)

Paul briefly mentions a fourth blessing of being His child, that *He has made us accepted in the Beloved*. What does this mean? The word *accepted* means highly favored. We are highly favored in the *Beloved*, a term which means Son of His love. As God's children,

---

14 The Arminian position is that we are elected and predestined because God *foresaw* that *we* would exercise faith, if given the chance to believe. This they try to support by Romans 8:29 and 1 Peter 1:2, which base the election of God on His *foreknowledge*, ignoring the fact that the biblical definition of foreknowledge is more than simply a pre-knowing. Ephesians 1:3-6a states we were chosen *according to the good pleasure of His will,* i.e.,, independent of anything in man! We were not chosen because we believe the Gospel; we believe the Gospel because we were chosen! cf. 2 Thess. 2:13-14.

we are the objects of God's love, and, my friend, it is an everlasting love which cannot be taken away! This is an amazing and humbling truth! And if that isn't enough, Paul goes on to yet another incredible blessing in verse 7.

Blessing #5
He has Given Us Redemption through His Blood
Ephesians 1:7a

In Him we have redemption through His blood (Ephesians 1:7a).

The fifth blessing is that *we have redemption through His blood*. Notice that it is *in Him*, in the beloved, that we have redemption. Only through Him do we have redemption. Redemption is the full payment of a ransom price. The price that was paid for our redemption was costly; it was the blood of Christ. The apostle Peter makes this very clear in 1 Peter 1:18-19: "knowing that you were not redeemed with corruptible things, like silver or gold, from your aimless conduct received by tradition from your fathers, but with the precious blood of Christ, as of a lamb without blemish and without spot." Ladies, the Beloved redeemed you, He paid the price in full, by shedding His precious blood! Only His blood can wash away our sins. And this brings us to the sixth amazing blessing: He forgives our sins.

Blessing #6
He has Forgiven Us of Our Sins
Ephesians 1:7b

the forgiveness of sins, according to the riches of His grace (Ephesians 1:7b).

Forgiveness means to loose something from someone which is binding him. That's what our sins do; they bind us. Without forgiveness, we are bound in darkness and sin. *Forgiveness* also means to send away, and it is like the scapegoat upon whose head

26

Aaron would confess all the sins of the children of Israel, and then send it away into the wilderness, never to be seen again (Leviticus 16:10). It is like the Psalmist says in Psalm 103:12: "As far as the east is from the west, so far has He removed our transgressions from us." This is amazing! You cannot measure the east from the west! If you start going east you just keep going; it never ends. If you start traveling west, the same thing happens; it never ends. However, if you go north, you stop going north at the North Pole, and if you continue on you begin to go south. If you go south, you eventually reach the South Pole, and continuing on from there you actually begin going north. This isn't the case with the east and the west. Our sins are sent so far away from us by God that they are removed forever. Are you shouting "Hallelujah!" yet? Paul ends this powerful thought by saying it is *according to the riches of His grace*. This is very similar to what he said in verse 5, that it was for the glory of His grace. Once again, it is all for Him and because of Him. The riches of His grace have been showered upon us! Paul continues on with God's abundant blessings in verse 8.

Blessing #7
He Made Wisdom and Prudence Abound toward Us
Ephesians 1:8

> which He made to abound toward us in all wisdom and prudence (Ephesians 1:8).

Paul now gives another, the seventh, blessing of being adopted into God's family, *wisdom and prudence. Wisdom* is the Greek word <u>sophia</u> and pertains to knowledge which can see into the heart of things. *Prudence* is the understanding and discernment that leads to right action. "God's lavish grace not only provides redemption but also supplies, along with this, all necessary wisdom and insight to understand and live in the light of what He has done."[15] John MacArthur says, "God not only forgives us—taking

---

15   Andrew T. Lincoln, *Word Biblical Commentary: Ephesians* (n.p.: Word, Incorporated, 1990), 29.

away the sin that corrupts and distorts our lives—but also gives us all the necessary equipment to understand Him and to walk through the world day by day in a way that reflects His will and is pleasing to Him. He generously gives us the wherewithal both to understand His Word and to know how to obey it."[16] The wisdom and prudence seem to be in connection with knowing the mystery of His will, which Paul mentions in the next verse. Without this wisdom and prudence we would not understand the mystery of His will. It is similar to what Paul says in 1 Corinthians 2:14-16: "But the natural man does not receive the things of the Spirit of God, for they are foolishness to him; nor can he know them, because they are spiritually discerned. But he who is spiritual judges all things, yet he himself is rightly judged by no one. For 'who has known the mind of the Lord that he may instruct Him?' But we have the mind of Christ." A natural man cannot understand the mystery of the gospel, but God's adopted children can, for we have the mind of Christ. We have wisdom and prudence, and because of this, we have the ability to know the mystery of His will, as Paul mentions in verse 9.

Blessing #8
He Made Known to Us the Mystery of His Will
Ephesians 1:9

> having made known to us the mystery of His will, according to His good pleasure which He purposed in Himself (Ephesians 1:9).

This is the eighth blessing of the believer. He *made known to us the mystery of His will*. What does that mean? A *mystery* is a truth that was once hidden but is now made known. God made known His redemptive plan to His people. God made known to us the gospel! But without a supernatural understanding and enabling we would not be able to understand such a mystery!

Once again, even this is *according to His good pleasure which He purposed in Himself.* (This is very similar to what he

---

16 MacArthur, 25.

said in verse 5.) God purposed, God set before Himself, what the redemptive plan would be, and it was all according to His good pleasure! How can we not echo with the hymn writer, John Newton, "Amazing grace, how sweet the sound, that saved a wretch like me! I once was lost but now am found, was blind but now I see!"?!

Summary

What are the eight blessings for the believer? 1. *He has Chosen Us in Him before the Foundation of the World*, (v 4a); 2. *He has Made Us Holy and Blameless before Him*, (v 4b); 3. *He has Predestined Us to be His Adopted Sons*, (v 5-6a); 4. *He has Made Us Accepted in the Beloved*, (v 6b); 5. *He has Given Us Redemption through His Blood*, (v 7a); 6. *He has Forgiven Us of Our Sins*, (v 7b); 7. *He has Given Us Wisdom and Prudence*, (v 8); and 8. *He has Made Known to Us the Mystery of His Will*, (v 9). (By the way, did you notice all the times the terms *we* and *us* are used in this passage?!) He did this for us, not because we are something special, but because *He* loved us, and because of *His* amazing grace which is poured out on *us!* How can we not shout "Hallelujah!" to the King of the Heavens who chose us, predestinated us, adopted us, sanctifies us, forgives us, loves us, justifies us, and blesses us?!

So do the trials of life have you discouraged this day? Are your friends forsaking you? Is your family persecuting you? Are you wondering if you or your husband might lose a job? Are your kids sick—again? Do you wonder how you are going to pay your bills this month? Do you feel pressed on every side? My dear sister, why not take some time this week and meditate on this passage? No matter what difficulties you are having in this life, I am confident our Father will use them to lift your heart to rejoice that you have such wonderful spiritual blessings in heavenly places in Christ!

Questions to Consider

The Believer's Blessings in Christ! (Part 1)
Ephesians 1:3-9

1. (a) What are the spiritual blessings that Paul mentions in Ephesians 1:3-9? (b) How have you personally been blessed by these things? (c) What is your response to these gracious gifts from God? (d) Memorize Ephesians 1:3.

2. (a) Paul states in Ephesians 1:5 that we are adopted sons of God. What are some of the privileges we have as God's adopted children, according to Romans 8:14-31; 2 Corinthians 6:18; Galatians 4:5-7; Hebrews 12:5-9; 1 John 3:1-2; and Revelation 21:7? (b) What are some of the privileges that adopted children have in the physical world? (c) How do these compare with the privileges that spiritual children have in Christ?

3. (a) Paul states in Ephesians 1:9 that God made known to us the mystery of His will. What is Paul referring to, according to verses 10-14, along with Ephesians 3:3-12 and Ephesians 6:19-20? (b) If you were a Gentile sitting in the worship service at the church of Ephesus, and heard the minister read these words, what do you think your response would be? (c) As a Gentile (unless you are a Jew) what is your response to this today?

4. (a) How could you use these verses in Ephesians 1:3-9 to encourage someone who is going through difficult times? (b) How could you use these verses to admonish someone who is proud about their spirituality or spiritual achievements?

5. What blessing from Ephesians 1:3-9 is the most outstanding to you personally and why?

6. As you consider question three, write out a praise to God for the privileges He has granted you as His daughter!

Chapter 3

The Believer's Blessings in Christ! (Part 2)

Ephesians 1:10-14

In the past few years, the world we know seems to have gone on a spiraling journey downward so fast that my head spins at times. Same-sex marriage, increasing government control, fewer religious freedoms, America no longer a Christian nation, natural disasters of record proportion, and many other things that are going on have many of us wondering, "What is happening to our world?" I take great comfort, however, in knowing that there is nothing that is happening worldwide, or even in my own personal life, that is outside of the good pleasure of the Father's will or His glorious purpose. I also take great joy in knowing that He is working all things according to His will and He purposed that each of these events would take place in His providence. It is mind-boggling to think that one day He will gather everything together and time as we know it here on earth will end. These truths, along with the blessings we have as believers, are the joy we have before us as we study this lesson. Let's listen in on what the apostle Paul has to say. As we did in our last lesson, let's read the whole sentence of 202 words as one complete thought.

Ephesians 1:3-14

Blessed be the God and Father of our Lord Jesus Christ, who has blessed us with every spiritual blessing in the heavenly places in Christ, ⁴just as He chose us in Him before the foundation of the world, that we should be holy and without blame before Him in love, ⁵having predestined us to adoption as sons by Jesus Christ to Himself, according to the good pleasure of His will, ⁶to the praise of the glory of His grace, by which He has made us accepted in the Beloved. ⁷In Him we have redemption through His blood, the forgiveness of sins, according to the riches of His grace ⁸which He made to abound toward us in all wisdom and prudence, ⁹having made known to us the mystery of His will, according to His good pleasure which He purposed in Himself, ¹⁰that in the dispensation of the fullness of the times He might gather together in one all things in Christ, both which are in heaven and which are on earth—in Him. ¹¹In Him also we have obtained an inheritance, being predestined according to the purpose of Him who works all things according to the counsel of His will, ¹²that we who first trusted in Christ should be to the praise of His glory. ¹³In Him you also trusted, after you heard the word of truth, the gospel of your salvation; in whom also, having believed, you were sealed with the Holy Spirit of promise, ¹⁴who is the guarantee of our inheritance until the redemption of the purchased possession, to the praise of His glory (Ephesians 1:3-14).

In our last lesson, we began to look at the believer's blessings from verses 3-9 and discovered eight of them. In this lesson, we'll discover four more blessings for the believer, which will make twelve blessings in all:

9. *He has Obtained for Us an Inheritance, (v 11)*

10. *He has Enabled Us to Trust Christ, (v 13a)*

11. *He has Sealed Us with His Holy Spirit, (v 13b)*

12. *He has Guaranteed Our Inheritance by His Holy Spirit, (v 14).*

Ephesians 1:10

that in the dispensation of the fullness of the times He might gather together in one all things in Christ, both which are in heaven and which are on earth—in Him (Ephesians 1:10).

In this statement is the crux of what we learned last time; here we find the reason God has done all those things we saw in verses 3-9. He has done all of them, in order that one day He will gather together in one all things in Christ. The word *dispensation* means the management of household affairs; stewardship or administration; an arrangement of things; a scheme or plan. God has planned each event in time past and time present. One day time will end as we know it and God will gather everything together and make a new heaven and a new earth. When this age is over, after Christ has established His earthly kingdom and after He has reigned for 1,000 years, after the final judgment, and then when eternity itself is ushered in, this is the sum of it all, that God will bring all things together in Him.

Bible scholars have offered many different translations for the Greek term <u>oikonomia</u>, which we read as *dispensation* in the New King James Version of the Bible.[17] One commentator, Henry Alford, expresses frustration in trying find an English synonym for this term; he says, "After long and careful search, I am unable to find a word which will express the full meaning of <u>oikonomia</u>."[18] He settles for the term *economy*, because he views the *fullness of the times* as the filling up or completing of the appointed seasons under the Gospel age. A. T. Robertson agrees with the use of the term *economy*, but John Eadie translates it as *dispensation* or *arrangement*.[19] Another commentator helpfully summarizes the idea of <u>oikonomia</u> as "that of a great household of which God is the Master and which has a certain system of management wisely ordered by Him."[20]

When the times and seasons are fully completed, when all the periods of time are passed, when God deems, then He will gather together in one all things. God planned all this before the foundation of the world; He knew in eternity past that when the times are completed He will gather all things together. What does it mean that *He might gather together in one all things in Christ*? Some people

---

17 KJV, NKJV and ASV translate *dispensation;* NASB translates *administration;* and the NIV omits completely a translation of the term.

18 cf. Henry Alford, *The Greek Testament: Ephesians* (Chicago: Moody, 1958), 76.

19 cf. John Eadie, *A Commentary on the Greek Text of the Epistle of Paul to the Ephesians* (Grand Rapids: Baker, 1979), 50. Eadie also calls attention to Martin Luther's departure, who referred to <u>oikonomia</u> as *preaching* or the disclosing of the mystery of the Gospel. Ibid., 50.

20 cf. W. Robertson Nicoll, *The Expositor's Greek Testament: the Epistle to the Ephesians* (Grand Rapids: Eerdmans, 1979), 259. Cf. Charles Hodge, *Commentary on the Epistle to the Ephesians* (Grand Rapids: Eerdmans, 1994), 47-48. The fact that God is the administrator of this economy is obvious from the context of His sovereignty.

will say this verse can be used to prove that all will be saved. But that is ludicrous! We know from other Scriptures that not all will be saved! Revelation 20:15 would be one good example of that truth: "And anyone not found written in the Book of Life was cast into the lake of fire." Notice that Paul gives the qualifier of the *all things* as *in Christ*. Also, Paul doesn't say anything about things in hell, but only things *which are in heaven and which are on earth*, and he adds *in Him*. Martyn Lloyd-Jones says, "The perfect harmony that will be restored will be harmony in man, and between men. Harmony on the earth and in the brute creation! Harmony in heaven, and all under this blessed Lord Jesus Christ, who will be the Head of all! Everything will again be united in Him. And wonder of wonders, marvelous beyond compare, when all this happens it will never be undone again. All will be re-united in Him to all eternity. This is the message; that is God's plan. That is the mystery which has been revealed to us."[21]

Blessing #9
He has Obtained for Us an Inheritance
Ephesians 1:11

> In Him also we have obtained an inheritance, being predestined according to the purpose of Him who works all things according to the counsel of His will (Ephesians 1:11).

Paul goes on to mention another blessing for the believer; this is blessing #9 as we continue on from our last lesson. He says, *in Him also we have an obtained an inheritance*. The Greek rendering of this phrase is such that this is a certain thing that cannot fail to happen and has already occurred. So what is this thing that cannot fail? What is our *inheritance*? Some think that Paul is speaking regarding our inheritance in heaven, which Peter also speaks of in 1 Peter 1:3-4, when he says, "Blessed be the God and Father of our Lord Jesus Christ, who according to His abundant mercy has begotten us again to a living hope through the resurrection of Jesus

---

21 Lloyd-Jones, 207.

Christ from the dead, to an inheritance incorruptible and undefiled and that does not fade away, reserved in heaven for you." However, there is another opinion which says this *inheritance* is referring to the fact that we are Christ's inheritance. Jesus often spoke of those whom the Father had given Him (John 17:6, 9). Everyone whom God has chosen is His adopted child and therefore is His inheritance. Both of these interpretations could be true.

Paul does let us know, however, how we received this inheritance. It wasn't due to anything we did, but it was all, again, because of God. He *predestined* it! Paul has already mentioned this in verse 5 and now he mentions it here again. The word means pre-determined. "What can be greater or more staggering than this, that God thought of me, thought of you, there in the counsel of His own will! He not only conceived the plan, He saw us in it."[22] Paul makes this clear again in Romans 8:29-31: "For whom He foreknew, He also predestined to be conformed to the image of His Son, that He might be the firstborn among many brethren. Moreover whom He predestined, these He also called; whom He called, these He also justified; and whom He justified, these He also glorified. What then shall we say to these things? If God is for us, who can be against us?"

This predestination was *according to the purpose of Him who works all things according to the counsel of His will*. What does this mean? It means that there is nothing that God does that is not in His will. My plans fail all the time, but what God purposes and plans that He does! Albert Barnes helps us here: "He may have the highest and best reasons for what he does, but he does not choose to make them known to others, or to consult others. So it may be of God, and so we should presume it to be. It may be added, that we ought to have such confidence in him as to believe that he will do all things well. The best possible evidence that anything is done in perfect wisdom and goodness, is the fact that God does it. When we have ascertained that, we should be satisfied that all is right."[23] In

22 Ibid, 228.
23 Albert Barnes, *Notes on the New Testament: Ephesians, Philippians, and Colossians*

thinking about the fact that God works things out according to His will, Paul moves on to speak of something that was God's will from the beginning, that is, the order in which men and women would believe in Him.

Ephesians 1:12

that we who first trusted in Christ should be to the praise of His glory (Ephesians 1:12)

Who are they *who first trusted in Christ?* This would be the Jews who recognized Jesus as Messiah. Paul makes this clear in Romans 1:16: "For I am not ashamed of the gospel of Christ, for it is the power of God to salvation for everyone who believes, for the Jew first and also for the Greek." It's interesting that here in Ephesians Paul includes himself in the *we*, as Paul was a Jew. Listen to his commentary on himself in Philippians 3:5-6: "Circumcised the eighth day, of the stock of Israel, of the tribe of Benjamin, a Hebrew of the Hebrews; concerning the law, a Pharisee; concerning zeal, persecuting the church; concerning the righteousness which is in the law, blameless." The Jews were the ones who first trusted in Christ. In all fairness, Paul also could be referring to the fact that he and the ones with him first trusted in Christ and then those at the church he founded in Ephesus trusted in Christ, but more weight should be given to the first interpretation, since we can't be dogmatic as to the order of salvation in those he is writing to here. But we do know that the gospel was first offered to the Jews and then to the Greeks. Regardless of the interpretation, Paul says something astonishing next.

Paul says that our belief in Christ *is to the praise of His glory!* My dear friend, God redeemed you so that you might be to the praise of His glory, that you might glorify Him! Paul tells us in Romans that we glorify Him with our minds and our mouths! Consider Romans 15:6: "That you may with one mind and one mouth glorify the God

(Grand Rapids: Baker, 1972), 28.

and Father of our Lord Jesus Christ." He also says in 1 Corinthians 6:20 that we glorify God in our body and spirit: "For you were bought at a price; therefore glorify God in your body and in your spirit, which are God's." Do you glorify God in these ways, with your mind, mouth, body and spirit? Does your mind glorify God by the things you think about during the day? Or is it cluttered with ungodly and unkind thoughts? Is it cluttered with too much social networking? Is your mind clear to worship and pray during the day? What about your mouth? (What comes out of our mouths is what is in our hearts, by the way.) Is your mouth glorifying God by praising Him, being kind and tender in your speech toward others, or is your mind filled with angry and unkind words? And then there is the body. Does your body glorify God? Do you give it enough rest, exercise and proper energy? Last, but certainly not least, is our spirit. Do you feed your spirit the pure milk of the Word of God or are you gorging your spirit with internet, TV and entertainment? Do you realize you are His purchased possession and that He predestinated you so that you might bring Him glory? It is not about us; it is about Him! Let us use our whole being to glorify the one who saved us.

Blessing #10
He has Enabled Us to Trust Christ
Ephesians 1:13a

> In Him you also trusted, after you heard the word of truth, the gospel of your salvation (Ephesians 1:13a).

Paul goes on to give another class of people besides the Jews that were granted the invitation to the gospel, that being the Gentiles, when he says *you also*. In verse 12 he used the words *we who first trusted*. And now he says *in Him you also trusted*, referring to the Gentiles. The gospel was first offered to the Jews and then to the Gentiles. Now you might be wondering, "If we were predestined, if we were chosen, then why do we have to believe or trust? Why, the whole thing seems like we have no choice in this matter of salvation!" We do—and that's the point! But salvation *is* all of God and it is God who gives us the ability to understand the gospel, as we've already seen in verse 8, and He is the one who grants us the faith to believe or to trust in Him. Jesus makes this clear to Peter in Matthew 16:13-17: "When Jesus came into the region of Caesarea Philippi, He asked His disciples, saying, 'Who do men say that I, the Son of Man, am?' So they said, 'Some say John the Baptist, some Elijah, and others Jeremiah or one of the prophets.' He said to them, 'But who do you say that I am?' Simon Peter answered and said, 'You are the Christ, the Son of the living God.' Jesus answered and said to him, 'Blessed are you, Simon Bar-Jonah, for flesh and blood has not revealed this to you, but My Father who is in heaven.'" Jesus makes it clear to Peter that only the Father can reveal to any of us that Jesus is the Christ, the Savior of the world. We cannot conjure this up on our own. In our unredeemed state, none of us would seek after God. Paul makes this clear in Romans 3:9-12: "What then? Are we better than they? Not at all. For we have previously charged both Jews and Greeks that they are all under sin. As it is written: 'There is none righteous, no, not one; There is none who understands; there is none who seeks after God. They have all turned aside; they have together become unprofitable; there is none who does good, no, not one.'" It has been said that "Faith is the response to God's elective purpose. God's choice of men is election; men's choice of God is faith. In election God gives His promises, and by faith men receive them."[24]

This is the tenth blessing for the believer: God gave us the ability to trust in Christ. Notice how Paul is very clear in communicating that no one can trust Christ unless they have heard the word of truth, the gospel of salvation. Paul makes this unmistakably clear in Romans 10:13-15: "For 'whoever calls on the name of the Lord shall be saved.' How then shall they call on Him in whom they have not believed? And how shall they believe in Him of whom they have not heard? And how shall they hear without a preacher? And how shall they preach unless they are sent? As it is written: 'How beautiful are the feet of those who preach the gospel of peace, who

---

24 MacArthur, 33.

bring glad tidings of good things!'" Just think back to your own experience of embracing the gospel. How did you hear? Someone had to share the amazing gospel with you. It may have been a series of seeds which were planted, but someone shared the word of truth. We can't know the gospel without hearing it. This should give us motivation to share the gospel with lost men and women who are on their way to hell, because someone has to open their mouth and tell them the good news.

Blessing #11
He has Sealed Us with His Holy Spirit
Ephesians 1:13b

> in whom also, having believed, you were sealed with the Holy
> Spirit of promise (Ephesians 1:13b)

One of the incredible things that takes place when we believe or trust in Christ is a sealing of the Spirit. This is the eleventh blessing for the believer: We are *sealed with the Holy Spirit of promise*. What does this mean? Sealing has a couple of meanings. First of all, it was used in reference to an official mark that was put on a letter or important document. The seal was made with hot wax and then pressed with some type of ring. In fact, all documents that were important were marked with a seal. Esther 8:8 refers to this: "You yourselves write a decree for the Jews, as you please, in the king's name, and seal it with the king's signet ring; for a letter which is written in the king's name and sealed with the king's signet ring no one can revoke." So we understand that this type of seal was used for the purpose of securing important documents. Secondly, a seal was used for marking animals. We call this practice "branding" in our day. This seal was used as a mark of ownership. When we put the two ideas together, we can conclude that our sealing by the Holy Spirit is for the purpose of marking our security in Christ and as a sign of His ownership of us. As believers, we are secure—praise God!—but we also are owned by Someone other than ourselves, that being our wonderful Master. We are sealed with the Holy Spirit of Promise by the authority of God and nothing can take that away. He owns us. We are His. It is interesting to me that the Spirit is called *the Holy Spirit of Promise*. The translation actually reads: "You were sealed with that Spirit of that promise that holy." As this is a promise that cannot be broken. We are His! Amen! Even so, come Lord Jesus! And just as we are sealed with the Spirit, He is also the guarantee of our inheritance, the last of the blessings we'll see in this passage.[25]

Blessing #12
He has Guaranteed Our Inheritance by His Holy Spirit
Ephesians 1:14

> who is the guarantee of our inheritance until the redemption of the purchased possession, to the praise of His glory (Ephesians 1:14).

This is the twelfth blessing for the believer: The Holy Spirit is the *guarantee of our inheritance*. He is the down payment of our inheritance. In biblical times, this would be pledge money, which would be part of the process of completing the payment in due time. I remember when I was growing up that my Mom would purchase something and put it in "lay-away." That is, she would purchase an item, like an appliance, and pay a little bit of down payment. Then as she was able, she would pay a little at a time, until the item was paid for and the item was hers! She made a down payment for an item she would soon own.

This word, *guarantee*, was also used to describe an engagement ring. As women, we understand this concept, as an

---

25 Many have asked, is the sealing ministry of the Spirit experiential or non-experiential? Does it happen subsequent to salvation or at the moment of salvation? Grammatically, the participle could suggest either possibility, i.e.,, *after* or *when*. Representatives of those seeing the sealing of the Holy Spirit as experiential and subsequent to salvation include: Thomas Goodwin, John Owen, John Wesley, George Whitefield, Charles Simeon, Charles Hodge, John Eadie and Martyn Lloyd-Jones. Those representatives of the non-experiential-at-salvation view include: Lewis S. Chafer, John F. Walvoord, John MacArthur, E. K. Simpson, F. F. Bruce, G. R. Beasley-Murray, Andrew T. Lincoln and Charles Ryrie. The KJV translators suggested the sealing to be after or *subsequent to salvation* and if the sense is to confirm the promise, then His ministry is *experiential*. cf. Rom. 8:14-17.

engagement ring is a pledge from a man that one day he will marry the woman to whom he gives the ring. It is the same way with the Holy Spirit: He is our guarantee, the pledge we receive, until the redemption of the purchased possession. When the Lord draws all things to a close He will then redeem those who are His purchased possession. "The Spirit received is the first installment and guarantee of the inheritance of the age to come that awaits God's sons and daughters."[26] A day is coming when our very bodies will be delivered entirely from sin. And the guarantee of that blessing is the presence of the Spirit within our bodies now. It is because of the Spirit present within me that I know my body is destined someday to be delivered once and for all from sin's presence.[27]

Paul ends this 202 word sentence with a grandiose thought: *to the praise of His glory*. It's all to the praise of *His glory*! It is not about us; it is about our great God!

Summary

My dear sister, no matter what things are going on in our world today, or even in your personal world, you can bank on these twelve blessings for your life! But remember, as you count these blessings, to consider that they are all for the glory of our God! Meditate and think on this as you read these beautiful words:

To the Praise of His Glorious Grace

What astonishing mercy and power:
In accord with his pleasure and will
He created each planet, each flower,
Every galaxy, microbe, and hill.
He suspended the planet in space
To the praise of his glorious grace.

---

26 O'Brien, 121.
27 Lloyd-Jones, 307.

With despicable self-love and rage,
We rebelled and fell under the curse.
Yet God did not rip out the page
And destroy all who love the perverse.
No, he chose us to make a new race,
To the praise of his glorious grace.

Providentially ruling all things
To conform to the end he designed,
He mysteriously governs, and brings
His eternal wise plans into time.
He works out every step, every trace,
To the praise of his glorious grace.

Long before the creation began,
He foreknew those he'd ransom in Christ;
Long before time's cold hour-glass ran,
He ordained the supreme sacrifice.
In the cross he removed our disgrace,
To the praise of his glorious grace.

We were blessed in the heavenly realms
Long before being included in Christ.
Since we heard the good news, overwhelmed,
We reach forward to seize Paradise.
We shall see him ourselves, face to face,
To the praise of his glorious grace.[28]

---

28 *To the Praise of His Glorious Grace*, words by D. A. Carson.

Questions to Consider

The Believer's Blessings in Christ! (Part 2)
Ephesians 1:10-14

1. (a) Read Ephesians 1:10-14 and list all the blessings that you see for the believer. (b) Who is the giver of these blessings? (c) Why are we given these blessings? (d) Memorize Ephesians 1:13-14.

2. As you read over Ephesians 1:3-14, write down the places and the context in which Paul mentions that something is for God's glory, God's pleasure, or God's grace. What things do you observe? What does this tell you about God? About His glory? About His pleasure? About His grace?

3. Paul says in Ephesians 1:12 that there were some who first trusted in Christ, and then in verse 13 he indicates that there was another group who trusted in Christ. Read over Acts 10-11 to see another account in which there were some who first trusted in Christ and then there was a second group of people who trusted in Christ. Write down any observations or truths from Acts that help you to better understand what Paul is saying in Ephesians 1:13-14.

4. How could you use verses 10-14, especially verse 11, to encourage someone (or yourself) who is going through troubling times?

5. Which blessing from Ephesians 1:10-14 is especially meaningful to you and why?

6. Is there someone you are praying for who has not yet trusted in Christ and been sealed with Holy Spirit of Promise? Please write a prayer request for their salvation.

Chapter 4

Paul's First Prayer for the Church at Ephesus

Ephesians 1:15-23

In the weeks during which I was studying for this lesson, the church my husband pastors had been called to fast and pray for numerous needs in our body. We had been asked to participate each week whenever we were able. This "call to fast" for our church caused me to start thinking about how we should pray for our church, or any church of Jesus Christ, for that matter. What should our prayers consist of when we think of praying for our individual churches or even the church of Jesus Christ worldwide? Too often, we pray only for physical needs or material needs, though they are important. But are they the best things we can be praying about for the body of Christ? The apostle Paul helps us with this very question, as he gives us a glimpse into what he prays for the church at Ephesus. What do his prayers consist of? Let's listen in and find out as Paul prays:

Ephesians 1:15-23

> Therefore I also, after I heard of your faith in the Lord Jesus and your love for all the saints, [16]do not cease to give thanks for you, making mention of you in my prayers: [17]that the God of our Lord Jesus Christ, the Father of glory, may give to you the spirit of wisdom and revelation in the knowledge of Him, [18]the eyes of your understanding being enlightened; that you may know what is the hope of His calling, what are the riches of the glory of His inheritance in the saints, [19]and what is the exceeding greatness of His power toward us who believe, according to the working of His mighty power [20]which He worked in Christ when He raised Him from the dead and seated Him at His right hand in the heavenly places, [21]far above all principality and power and might and dominion, and every name that is named, not only in this age but also in that which is to come. [22]And He put all things under His feet, and gave Him to be head over all things

to the church, [23]which is His body, the fullness of Him who fills all in all (Ephesians 1:15-23).

In our past two lessons, we have considered twelve blessings that Paul tells us are for believers in Jesus Christ. In this lesson, as we look at verses 15-23, we'll see Paul's prayer for the church at Ephesus, and it's two-fold:

Paul's Prayers for the Church, (vv 17-19)

Paul's Praises for Christ, (vv 20-22)

Evidently the blessings of verses 4-14 cause Paul to break out in prayer for the church at Ephesus, and a glorious one it is! Having completed his doxology of the blessings in Christ to the Ephesian believers, the apostle Paul now pauses to pray for their understanding of these great truths.[29] This is the second longest prayer in the New Testament.[30] It is also one big long sentence, just like the previous one. However, this sentence is only 169 words compared to the previous one of 202 words. For you who are grammar students, I am sure this verse is a grammatical nightmare! I, for one, am thankful that God doesn't care about our proper use of grammar as much as He cares about us using our words for His

29 The order in the Ephesian epistle is basic: a summary of *our position* in Christ (1:3-14) leading to a prayer that they would *understand* those truths deeply (1:15-23); a second summary of *our position* in Christ (2:1-3:13) leading to a prayer that they would *understand* those truths deeply (3:14-21). Then from 4:1ff., he appeals to practically apply their lives to the resources they have and understand deeply. A deep understanding of who we are in our position is the foundation of right behavior practically! This is the *primary motive* for Christian ethics in the Epistle to the Ephesians. We are in the process of becoming who we are! cf. 2 Peter 1:3-8; Col. 1:12 with 2:8-10, 16-19.

30 The longest prayer in the NT is from Jesus. cf. John 17:1-26. The apostle Paul records 27 specific prayers of his own: Rom. 1:8-12; 15:5-7; 15:13; 15:33; 16:20-27; 1 Cor. 1:4-7; 2 Cor. 1:2-5; 2 Cor. 12:7-10; 13:14; Eph. 1:3; 1:15-23; 3:14-21; Phil. 1:2-11; Col. 1:1-12; 1 Thess. 1:1-3; 3:11-13; 1 Thess. 5:23-24; 2 Thess. 1:3, 11-12; 2:16-17; 3:5; 1 Tim. 1:17; 6:15-16; 2 Tim. 1:2-7, 6-18; 4:14-18; Philemon 4-6. Add to these his 8 further appeals for prayer or teaching about prayer: Rom. 8:15-27; 10:1; 11:26; Eph. 6:18-19; Phil. 4:6-7, 19-23; Col. 4:2-6; 2 Thess. 3:1-4. cf. Arthur W. Pink, *Gleanings from Paul* (Chicago: Moody, 1967), is an excellent commentary on most of the prayers of the apostle.

glory. In fact, it was once said that D. L. Moody was pretty poor as a public speaker, especially as it pertained to his grammar. One of his deacons even said he would do better if he just kept quiet. Another man who was especially critical of his public speaking told him, "You make too many mistakes in grammar." It was said that D.L. Moody responded by saying, "I know I make mistakes, and I lack many things, but I'm doing the best I can with what I've got." He then said to his critic, "Look here, friend, you've got grammar enough—what are you doing with it for the Master?" Well, let's begin this one long sentence of prayer for the glory of our Master!

Ephesians 1:15-16

> Therefore I also, after I heard of your faith in the Lord Jesus and your love for all the saints, do not cease to give thanks for you, making mention of you in my prayers (Ephesians 1:15-16).

When we come across the term *therefore* in Scripture, it's always a good idea to ask, "What is the therefore, there for?" In this case, the *therefore* pertains to all that Paul has just written in verses 3-14. I mean, think about it: When you reflect on the richness of what Paul has already said, it causes you to break forth in prayer and praise. Now, you might be wondering how Paul heard of their *faith* and *love*? Evidently, someone had informed Paul, while he was there in prison, about the church at Ephesus and how they were doing spiritually. It had been about 4-6 years since he had seen them, and this must have been a special encouragement to Paul as he heard about their faith and love, as these are two essential signs of a genuine believer. Consider Galatians 5:6, where Paul says, "For in Christ Jesus neither circumcision nor uncircumcision avails anything, but faith working through love." Or 2 Thessalonians 1:3, where Paul states, "We are bound to thank God always for you, brethren, as it is fitting, because your faith grows exceedingly, and the love of every one of you all abounds toward each other." Even John the apostle echoes this in 1 John 4:7-8: "Beloved, let us love one another, for love is of God; and everyone who loves is born of God and knows God. He who does not love does not know God, for God is love."

John and Paul both convey that faith and love are characteristics of God's children (see also Colossians 1:3-4 and Philemon 1:5).

Notice, dear friend that this faith is *in the Lord Jesus*. It is imperative when we think of this great salvation that has been provided for us, that we realize that we are not putting our trust in some religion but in the person of our Lord Jesus Christ. This means He is now our owner, our Lord. We are not our own; we have been bought with a price.

Genuine believers not only have faith in the Lord Jesus Christ, but they also have *love for all the saints*, and Paul says *all* the saints. Love for the brethren would include laying down one's life; being patient, kind, not rude or puffed up; not envious or rejoicing in evil, but rejoicing in the truth. It is a love that is willing to confront other believers who are in sin; a love that endures to the end and remains steadfast even though it might be difficult. This is a sign of a genuine believer: love for God and love for others. Isn't that what Jesus said in Matthew 22:37-40? "You shall love the Lord your God with all your heart, with all your soul, and with all your mind. This is the first and great commandment. And the second is like it: You shall love your neighbor as yourself. On these two commandments hang all the Law and the Prophets."

This hearing of their faith and love for the brethren causes Paul to break out in thanksgiving and prayer for the church at Ephesus. He goes on to say, *I ... do not cease to give thanks for you, making mention of you in my prayers. Cease* means to quit. Paul says, I don't stop praying for you. There are many things and many people we don't stop praying for. In fact, there are many things and people we pray for on a daily basis. Now Paul says that this unceasing praying is that of *giving thanks*. This is a rebuke to many of us who lack thanksgiving in our prayers. As we petition the Lord for certain individuals we should incorporate giving thanks to God for them, even if they are people whom we might be having struggles with. This means that Paul is thankful for them, and this thanksgiving for them causes him to burst forth in prayer and praise. What does he pray for them? Well, let's consider his requests:

Paul's Prayers for the Church
Ephesians 1:17-19

> that the God of our Lord Jesus Christ, the Father of glory, may give to you the spirit of wisdom and revelation in the knowledge of Him, the eyes of your understanding being enlightened; that you may know what is the hope of His calling, what are the riches of the glory of His inheritance in the saints, and what is the exceeding greatness of His power toward us who believe, according to the working of His mighty power (Ephesians 1:17-19).

Isn't it interesting that as we have been studying the first chapter of Ephesians we have been learning that all is for the praise and glory of our God, to the praise of His glorious grace, and now we see Paul here calling God *the Father of glory*. Oh, He is indeed! He is the Father of glory! Here is Paul's first request for the Ephesians (and for us!): *that God would give them the spirit of wisdom and revelation in the knowledge of Him.* What is *the spirit of wisdom and revelation*? *Revelation* is insight and discernment that the Holy Spirit reveals regarding truth. *Wisdom* is the ability to use that knowledge that is given to us by the Spirit. *Knowledge* is the Greek word epignosis, which is a full knowledge that we obtain by a personal acquaintance.[31] For example, the Holy Spirit might reveal through

31 The function of the prepositional prefix epi-, according to Lightfoot, is to intensify and hence it indicates "a larger and more thorough knowledge" (Lightfoot, 138; Eadie, 85) than gnosis. Robinson, in disagreeing with Lightfoot, thinks the epi is not intensive but directive, and hence, whereas gnosis signifies breadth and looks at knowledge in the full and abstract sense, "epignosis is knowledge directed toward a particular object, perceiving, directing, recognizing. This latter idea seems to be the correct assessment of the word and it fits well with this context. ... Therefore, Paul prays that God would give the Holy Spirit's insight and disclosure in the sphere or area of the knowledge of God Himself" (Harold W. Hoehner, *Ephesians: An Exegetical* Commentary (Grand Rapids: Baker Academic, 2002), 258-259). "The word [Greek, epignosis] occurs in Romans 3:20, which will enable the average reader to better perceive its force. *By the law is the knowledge* (or full knowledge) *of sin.* A man knows something of what sin is by the light of nature; but only as sin is viewed and measured in the light of the authority, the spirituality, the strictness of the divine law, does he obtain a full and adequate

His word in these verses that we are studying, in this particular lesson, the unbelievable mighty working of the power of God which raised Christ from the dead. I might obtain a fuller understanding of that concept through this passage. Wisdom, then, will take that revelation that is revealed to me from this portion of Scripture and use that in my life or the lives of others. It might look something like this: "Susan, Paul is speaking here of the amazing power that God has. If that power is able to raise Christ from the dead, then there is no need for you to be concerned about this particular situation in your life right now. God is able to work it out according to His will by His power." Isn't it interesting that in verse 8 Paul spoke of the wisdom and prudence we have as it relates to understanding the gospel, and now he prays that we would have wisdom and revelation as it pertains to our living? Notice, also, that this revelation is in the knowledge *of Him*. The purpose of the wisdom and revelation is so that we might have knowledge of Him. This is a prayer for a theological deepening. A young Charles H. Spurgeon insightfully commented:

> The highest science, the loftiest speculation, the mightiest philosophy, which can ever engage the attention of the child of God, is the name, the nature, the person, the work, the doings, and the existence of the great God whom he calls his Father... when we come to this master science, finding that our plumb-line cannot sound its depth, and that our eagle eye cannot see its height, we turn away with the thought that vain man would be wise, but he is like a wild ass's colt; and with solemn exclamation, "I am but of yesterday, and know nothing." No subject of contemplation will tend more to humble the mind, than thoughts of God...But while the subject humbles the mind, it also expands it...Nothing will so enlarge the intellect, nothing so magnify the whole soul of man, as a devout, earnest, continued investigation of the great subject of the Deity...Then go, plunge yourself in the Godhead's deepest sea; be lost in

knowledge of the sinfulness of sin. Thus something more than a bare, fragmentary inchoate acquaintance with God was here prayed for—a full knowledge of Him. Not a perfect knowledge, but a firsthand, well-rounded, intimate, and thorough knowledge of His person, his character, His perfections, especially as He is revealed in and by Christ" (Pink, 106-7).

his immensity; and you shall come forth as from a couch of rest, refreshed and invigorated. I know nothing which can so comfort the soul; so calm the swelling billows of grief; so speak peace to the winds of trial, as a devout musing upon the subject of the Godhead.[32]

Paul continues on with his second request: *that the eyes of their understanding would be enlightened.* What does Paul mean when he says *the eyes of their understanding?* In the human realm, our physical eyes allow us to see by the light that enters in through the pupil. That is how our eyes see light. The *eyes,* as Paul mentions here, would be used as a metaphor to describe the means by which light flows to the understanding of the heart. The word *enlightened* means illuminated, or to shed rays of light upon. Paul is praying that our spiritual eyes would see truth. We know that left in our unredeemed state our spiritual eyes are blind. We must receive sight in the spiritual sense (see Isaiah 42:7 and Matthew 13:15). In fact, we know that God specifically commissioned Paul for this very purpose, after he saved him on the Damascus road. Consider Acts 26:18: "to open their eyes, in order to turn them from darkness to light, and from the power of Satan to God, that they may receive forgiveness of sins and an inheritance among those who are sanctified by faith in Me." After we are saved, we still need our eyes opened to understand truth. The Psalmist puts it well in Psalm 119:18: "Open my eyes, that I may see wondrous things from Your law." So when Paul prays that the eyes of their understanding would be enlightened, he is praying that the church at Ephesus would have a greater understanding of the truth of God's Word and of God Himself. Would you say this is true about you? Do you have a deeper knowledge of God and His word today than you did a year ago?

There is a reason behind why Paul prays that their eyes would be enlightened and that is his third prayer request: *that they would know what is the hope of His calling.* Paul is saying, I am praying that you will understand that God has called you (which he

32 These words were preached by Charles H. Spurgeon at the New Park Street Chapel on January 7, 1855, when he was only 20 years old. cf. James I. Packer, *Knowing God* (Downer's Grove: InterVarsity Press, 1973), 13-14.

has clearly set forth in the first part of chapter one) to this glorious hope. Ladies, we have an eternal destiny with Christ in heaven. This is our hope! The early church would often speak of that glorious hope to one another and I think we would do well to remind each other of that, as it sets our focus upward and not on this world.

There is yet another reason that Paul wants the eyes of their understanding enlightened eternally, and that is so that they would know *what are the riches of the glory of His inheritance in the saints*. This is Paul's fourth request for the church: *that they would know the riches of the glory of His inheritance in the saints*. Paul has already mentioned this inheritance in verses 11 and 14. Now what is Paul speaking of here? He wants the church at Ephesus to understand what he says in another epistle, in 1 Corinthians 2:9: "Eye has not seen, nor ear heard, nor have entered into the heart of man the things which God has prepared for those who love Him." My friend, our Lord has gone to prepare a place for us, according to John 14:1-3. In fact, He is preparing a room for each of us in His kingdom. We know that there are glories untold! We need to open our eyes of understanding to this glorious truth and let it sink into our inner-most being.

Paul ends the request portion of his prayer for the church at Ephesus in verse 19. His fifth request for the church is: *that they would know the exceeding greatness of His power toward those who believe*. What is *the exceeding greatness of His power*? It is God's power—the term from which we derive our English word for dynamite—it is dynamite power! And notice that this power is only toward those who believe. Our salvation—past, present and future—is all because of the greatness of his mighty power. The word for *working* here refers to an energizing force. We were saved by His power, we are being saved today because of His power, and we will be saved in the future because of His power. It is His power that enables us to live for Him. Without Him we can do nothing.[33] It

---

33 Should believers pray for more power? Of the 142 times the English term *power* is used in the NT, there is never a reference to a believer praying for more power, nor a

is impossible for us to fully understand the power of our God, but Paul prays that we will, and he tries to convey this in the next verse. Thinking of the mighty power of God causes Paul to now break forth with praise and exaltation for the wondrous working of Christ. This is the praise portion of his prayer.

Paul's Praises for Christ
Ephesians 1:20-22

> which He worked in Christ when He raised Him from the dead and seated Him at His right hand in the heavenly places, far above all principality and power and might and dominion, and every name that is named, not only in this age but also in that which is to come. And He put all things under His feet, and gave Him to be head over all things to the church, (Ephesians 1:20-22).

God's power is shown in many ways, and the apostle Paul shares those ways with the Ephesians in the form of praises to Christ. The first of Paul's praises, and the first way that Paul says God's power is shown, is: *for the power which raised Christ from the dead.* In his commentary, Albert Barnes helps us to get the depth of this comment Paul makes: "The 'power' which was then exerted was as great as that of creation. It was imparting life to a cold and 'mangled' frame. It was to open again the arteries and veins, and teach the heart to beat and the lungs to heave. It was to diffuse vital warmth through the rigid muscles, and to communicate to the body the active functions of life. It is impossible to conceive of a more direct exertion of 'power' than in raising up the dead; and there is no more striking illustration of the nature of conversion than in such a resurrection."[34] Now ladies that is power! Only a dynamite, supernatural power can raise anyone from the dead!

---

command that we do so. Rather, the believer already has the great power of God. cf. Acts 1:8, with examples of 4:7, 33; 6:8, etc. and 1 Cor. 4:19-20; Eph. 3:20; 2 Tim. 1:7; Simeon was rebuked for trying to buy it in Acts 8:14. Unbelievers deny it in the sense of lacking it (cf. 2 Tim. 3:5). Believers already have all the power they need but need to experience it (Greek, epiginosko) in their lives. cf. Phil. 1:10.

34 Barnes, 32.

The second demonstration of God's power, and Paul's second praise, is: *For the power which set Christ at God's right hand in the heavenly places.* He not only raised Christ *from the dead,* but then God's power raised Christ to the heavens and *seated Him* at God's right hand. The *right hand* is significant, in that it indicates honor, authority, friendship and favor. God's power raised Jesus to sit with Him at His right hand! Once again, Paul mentions this is *in the heavenly places,* which is an indication that this is in heaven.

Not only does Paul give forth praise for God's amazing power which raised Christ from the dead and seated Him at His right hand, but he then praises Him for His preeminence. Yet another demonstration of God's power, praise number three is: *for the power that set Christ far above all principality, power, might, dominion, and every name that has ever been.* The Lord is above any authority, any power, which would include any angels or demons or anything or anyone. He is also over any might or dominion, which would be anyone in authority. He is over any president, any ruler, and any government. He is far above any creature of any rank. You can think of anyone in any position of authority, and He is above all of them. Paul says this includes *every name that is named.* This would include any ruler there has ever been, any movie star, any sports figure, any political figure, any family member, any friend, anyone. He is above everyone. Paul tells us this in a passage that is familiar to many of us, Philippians 2:9-11: "Therefore God also has highly exalted Him and given Him the name which is above every name, that at the name of Jesus every knee should bow, of those in heaven, and of those on earth, and of those under the earth, and that every tongue should confess that Jesus Christ is Lord, to the glory of God the Father." He is above all!

This power also enables God to make all things subject to Christ, as evidenced in verse 22. Paul's fourth praise, and the fourth way in which God's power is made known, is: *for the power that put all things under His feet.* Christ is not only above everything, as seen in verse 21, but *all things are under His feet.* There is nothing that is not under His subjection. Paul puts it well in 1 Corinthians 15:24-28: "Then comes the end, when He delivers the kingdom to God the Father, when He puts an end to all rule and all authority and power. For He must reign till He has put all enemies under His feet. The last enemy that will be destroyed is death. For 'He has put all things under His feet.' But when He says 'all things are put under Him,' it is evident that He who put all things under Him is excepted. Now when all things are made subject to Him, then the Son Himself will also be subject to Him who put all things under Him that God may be all in all." Christ will reign, having all things under His feet, until that last enemy, death, is destroyed. Then Christ Himself will be subject to God in order that God may reign supreme over all.

Paul ends with the fifth and final praise of His prayer, and the fifth way that God's power is shown: *for the power that God gave Him to be head over all things to the church*. Christ is not only above all things and all things are subject to Him, but He also is *head over all things to the church*. When we think of what Paul is saying here it is staggering, because in the human realm our brain controls all the functions going on in our bodies. We can't do anything without our head. I have a great-nephew who has cerebral palsy, and he is unable to walk or sit or do many other physical tasks because his brain does not function normally. This same concept describes the relationship between Christ and His church. He is our head and we cannot do anything without Him. He controls every aspect of His church, His body. This is a good reminder to us: we're not detached from our head in the physical sense; and we should not be detached from our Head in the spiritual sense. Paul goes on to speak of what the church is in verse 23.

Ephesians 1:23

which is His body, the fullness of Him who fills all in all (Ephesians 1:23).

The church is Christ's *body*. Paul will elaborate on this concept later on in his letter to the Ephesians. But for now, consider Ephesians 4:15-16: "but, speaking the truth in love, [we] may grow up in all things into Him who is the head—Christ—from whom the whole body, joined and knit together by what every joint supplies, according to the effective working by which every part does its

share, causes growth of the body for the edifying of itself in love."
The church is His body.

Paul ends with a mysterious phrase as he ends his prayer: *the
fullness of Him who fills all in all*. You might be saying to yourself,
as I did, "Say, what?!" There are three possible interpretations
of this puzzling phrase. It could mean: 1. The church is filled by
Christ, and Christ fills the world completely through the church; or
2. The church is filled by Christ, who, in turn, is filled completely by
God; or, lastly, 3. The church is the completion (or, complement) of
Christ, who is being completely filled (as more and more members
are incorporated into His body).[35]

Summary

Let's review *Paul's Prayers for the Church*, (vv 17-19):
1. That God would give them the spirit of wisdom
and revelation in the knowledge of Him
2. That the eyes of their understanding would be
enlightened
3. That they would know what is the hope of His
calling
4. That they would know the riches of the glory of
His inheritance in the saints
5. That they would know the exceeding greatness of
His power toward us who believe.

Let's also review *Paul's Praises for Christ*, (vv 20-22):
1. for the power which raised Christ from the dead
2. for the power which set Christ at God's right hand
in the heavenly places
3. for the power that set Christ far above all
principality, power, might, dominion, and every
name that has ever been
4. for the power that put all things under His feet

35   Arnold, 119.

5. for the power that God gave Him to be head over
   all things to the church.

My dear sister, these are amazing prayers to consider! I trust that, even today, we may be the answers to these requests of Paul, though they were requests for a church that was in existence many centuries ago: that we would have that wisdom and revelation in the knowledge of Him, to understand our hope in heaven with unbelievable riches, and the power that is at work in us each day; that we would grasp the depth of our Father's power in raising Christ from the dead, seating Him at His right hand, putting Him above all things, even the church, and putting all things under Him. If we really believed these truths, I think it would radically change our daily living. I would encourage you to use these prayers in your own personal prayer life, as well as for the church that you attend. It will lift your heart to the Master and to the heavenly places in Christ!

Questions to Consider

Paul's Prayer for the Church at Ephesus
Ephesians 1:15-23

1. Read Ephesians 1:15-23. (a) What do these verses tell you about Paul's prayer life? (b) What do they tell you about God's power? (c) What do they tell you about the needs in the life of a believer? (d) Memorize Ephesians 1:19.

2. (a) Paul mentions in verse 16 that He gives thanks for the church at Ephesus. What other churches does Paul give thanks for, according to Romans 1:8-9; 1 Corinthians 1:4-6; Philippians 1:3-4; Colossians 1:3-4, 1 Thessalonians 1:2-4; 2 Thessalonians 1:3-4; Philemon 1:4-6? Also, if it is mentioned in the text, what does he give thanks for regarding each of these churches? (b) What things are you thankful for regarding your own church?

3. (a) Paul prays for the church, in verse 17, that God would give them "the spirit of wisdom and revelation in the knowledge of Him." What does God's wisdom look like, according to James 3:13-18? (b) How do these verses help you to know if the wisdom you possess comes from God or not?

4. (a) Paul tells us that Christ is the head over the church, which is His body, in Ephesians 1:22-23. Skim over 1 Corinthians 12 and write down some things that should characterize the body of Christ. (b) Do these things characterize the body you worship with? Are you doing your part?

5. (a) As you reflect on Ephesians 1:19-23, which pertains to the mighty power of God, what thoughts come to your mind regarding God's power? (b) If we seriously contemplated the amazing power of God on a daily basis, how do you think it would affect our living?

6. Write a prayer for your church that includes petitions and praises.

Chapter 5

From Death to Life!

Ephesians 2:1-10

Since my conversion, the Lord in His kindness has allowed me to participate in several evangelism training programs, from which I have benefitted greatly. They have been used by God to help me be more effective in my sharing of the gospel with lost people. One of the passages of Scripture that is almost a "given" in any evangelism program is Ephesians 2:8-9, which states, "For by grace you have been saved through faith, and that not of yourselves; it is the gift of God, not of works, lest anyone should boast." In fact, most believers can quote Ephesians 2:8-9 like they can John 3:16. These are powerful verses to contemplate when thinking of our salvation. However, right before Ephesians 2:8-9 comes Ephesians 2:1-7, a passage that, in my humble opinion, should also be included when sharing the gospel because it gives the very bad news regarding our unregenerate state and then sets forth the great news of God's grace in Ephesians 2:8-9. What is that bad news and what is the good news? Paul sets forth the answer to those questions in this lesson. Let's read along with Paul as he writes to the church at Ephesus about what it means to pass from death to life.

Ephesians 2:1-10

And you He made alive, who were dead in trespasses and sins, [2]in which you once walked according to the course of this world, according to the prince of the power of the air, the spirit who now works in the sons of disobedience, [3]among whom also we all once conducted ourselves in the lusts of our flesh, fulfilling the desires of the flesh and of the mind, and were by nature children of wrath, just as the others. [4]But God, who is rich in mercy, because of His great love with which He loved us, [5]even when we were dead in trespasses, made us alive together with Christ (by grace you have been saved), [6]and raised us up together, and made us sit together in the heavenly places in Christ Jesus, [7]that in the ages to come He might show the exceeding riches of His grace in His kindness toward us in Christ Jesus. [8]For by grace you have been saved through faith, and that not of yourselves; it is the gift of God, [9]not of works, lest anyone should boast. [10]For we are His workmanship, created in Christ Jesus for good works, which God prepared beforehand that we should walk in them (Ephesians 2:1-10).

In our last lesson we looked at Paul's prayer for the church at Ephesus and we noted five prayers and five praises in that prayer. In this lesson, we'll consider our transition from death to life:

Our Life without Christ, (vv 1-3)

Our Life with Christ, (vv 4-10)

As we do, we will see five amazing contrasts! Let's begin with first verse of chapter two, where we will note the first characteristic of our lives before Christ.

Our Life without Christ
Ephesians 2:1-3

And you He made alive, who were dead in trespasses and sins, in which you once walked according to the course of this world, according to the prince of the power of the air, the spirit who now works in the sons of disobedience, among whom also we all once conducted ourselves in the lusts of our flesh, fulfilling the desires of the flesh and of the mind, and were by nature children of wrath, just as the others (Ephesians 2:1-3).

The words *and you* seem to be used by Paul for emphasis: *you*, who were dead ... *you*, who were sons of disobedience ... *you*, who were children of wrath ... *you*, who walked according to the course of this world ... *you*, who were fulfilling your lusts and desires of the flesh. Here, Paul says *you He made alive*! When we consider all that *you* entails we have to say "Amen, Paul! I was a wretch!" He made us alive—we *who were dead*! *Dead* means we were spiritually dead; we were separated from God; we had no life, spiritually-speaking. When someone we love is dead, we are separated from them; they are dead to us, and they have no life. Someone who is dead cannot respond in any way. They don't communicate; they don't breathe; they don't live; they don't eat; they don't do anything. At the time of this writing, my mother had been gone five years from this life. And I can go to her gravesite all I want and hope there might be some life that will come out of the ground, but it will never happen in this life. She is dead. There is no life. That is how we were before Christ. We were dead to any spiritual life. We could not be aroused to any spiritual life on our own. In fact, we were walking around not even knowing we were dead. Paul says we were dead in our *trespasses and sins*. *Trespasses* are things that cause us to stumble or go a wrong direction. *Sins* are indicators that we are missing the mark or falling short.[36] Someone who is dead in their sins and trespasses cannot respond spiritually. The first characteristic of our life before Christ is that *we were dead in our trespasses and sins*.

Paul goes on to give us two more characteristics of our life before Christ, in verse 2. He says, *in which you once walked according to the course of this world, according to the prince of the power of the air, the spirit who now works in the sons of disobedience.* Paul points out the second characteristic of our lives without Christ: that *we walked according to the course of this world. Walk* here is a word for a lifestyle or a pattern of life. John tells us in 1 John 2:16 that a lifestyle that looks like the world would include the lust of the flesh, the lust of the eyes and the pride of life. This is the way we walked before Christ. We acted just like the world and we thought just like

---

36 Various views have been suggested: 1.) *trespasses* (Greek, <u>paraptoma</u> is to fall by the side; go in the wrong direction) as sins of commission or something we do but shouldn't, and *sins* (Greek, <u>harmartia</u> is to miss the mark; not reaching the goal) as sin of omission or something we should do but don't. cf. S. Lewis Johnson, *Tyndale Theological Seminary, Lecture on Ephesians 1-3, Tape 3* (Fort Worth); 2.) *trespasses* as sinful actions and *sins* as the sinful movements of the soul in inclinations and words; 3.) *trespasses* is an emphatic reference to Jewish disobedience and *sins* to Gentile transgressions; 4.) *trespasses* as spiritual errors and *sins* as moral sins and faults; 5.) *trespasses* and *sins* are basically synonymous. cf. Eadie, 119.

the world. And you know why? Because we were of the *world*. This term is speaking of the world around us, in all its subtle and direct influences of ungodliness, secularism, humanism and selfishness. Sometimes it is referred to as "the spirit of the age." Of course, after coming to Christ for salvation, we know that we walk differently than the world. In fact, in 1 John 2:6, the apostle John says, "He who says he abides in Him ought himself also to walk just as He walked."

The third characteristic of our lives without Christ, Paul says in verse 2, is that *we walked according to the prince of the power of the air*. The progression here makes sense, as those who are dead in their sins and living like the world are controlled by none other than Satan himself, *the prince of the power of the air*. At the time Paul was writing this letter, people believed the air to be the dwelling place of evil spirits. What Paul is saying in this verse is that before we knew Christ we were under the influence and control of Satan. Jesus calls Satan the ruler of this world in John 12:31, 14:30 and 16:11. Ladies, nothing better describes the evil one than that he rules this world. Just pick up a newspaper or look at the evening news, or read it online, and you will see this to be true. Evil men are becoming worse and worse, and they are energized by none other than the ruler of this world, the prince of the power of the air, Satan himself. And this was also our state before Christ! Paul even goes on to say that Satan is *the spirit who now works in the sons of disobedience*. That's what he does; he works in the hearts of those without Christ and leads them down paths of rebellion, disobedience and destruction. Such was our life before God had mercy on us!

If all this isn't horrible enough, Paul goes on to give us a fourth and a fifth characteristic of our lives before Christ. (You might be saying, "When are we going to get to the good news?!" We'll get there, I promise!) In verse 3, he says of us that *we all once conducted ourselves in the lusts of our flesh, fulfilling the desires of the flesh and of the mind*. The word for *lusts* here would include any strong desire of any sort and is not always sexual. It might be lust for money, or entertainment, or fame. *Desires* is a word which means a strong wanting or seeking of something with diligence. Let's say you had a lust for money, but then you go deeper by stealing or cheating to get it. The desire takes over and you do whatever you can to have the thing you desire. If it's sexual desire, you will fornicate or commit adultery to satisfy it. If it's fame, you'll run over the person ahead of you or lie or slander about them, so you'll be pushed to the front of the success ladder. If its entertainment you lust after, you will neglect your household responsibilities and even spend money you don't have in order to be entertained. And Paul says it's not just our *flesh*, but our *mind*, as well. This would mean deliberately choosing things that go against God's will. Before we knew Christ we were uncontrolled with our passions, our lusts and our thoughts. What a sad commentary on our life before Christ! This is Paul's fourth characteristic of our life before Christ: *We fulfilled the desires of our flesh and our mind.*

Paul goes on to say we *were by nature children of wrath, just as the others*. This is Paul's fifth description of our life before Christ: *we were by nature children of wrath*. We were sons of disobedience, as he says in verse 2, or *children of wrath*. Now, I know we might not like to think of ourselves this way, but it is true nonetheless. The Psalmist says in Psalm 58:3, "The wicked are estranged from the womb; they go astray as soon as they are born, speaking lies." And because of this we are under the wrath of God. Paul speaks of this in Romans 1:18, where he says, "For the wrath of God is revealed from heaven against all ungodliness and unrighteousness of men, who suppress the truth in unrighteousness." Even John, the apostle of love, says in John 3:36, "He who believes in the Son has everlasting life; and he who does not believe the Son shall not see life, but the wrath of God abides on him."

Paul says we were children of wrath, *just as the others*. Just in case we might seem to think we deserve this great mercy of God, Paul says no, this was all of us before Christ. You and I were children of wrath just like the rest of mankind. You and I aren't any more special than the next person. And just in case the Ephesian believers are having such thoughts, Paul reminds them, in verses 4-10, as to how they as children of wrath became children of His love. He shifts from the bad news to the good news, from our life without Christ to our life with Christ, from death to life!

Our Life with Christ
Ephesians 2:4-10

> But God, who is rich in mercy, because of His great love with which He loved us, even when we were dead in trespasses, made us alive together with Christ (by grace you have been saved), and raised us up together, and made us sit together in the heavenly places in Christ Jesus, that in the ages to come He might show the exceeding riches of His grace in His kindness toward us in Christ Jesus. For by grace you have been saved through faith, and that not of yourselves; it is the gift of God, not of works, lest anyone should boast. For we are His workmanship, created in Christ Jesus for good works, which God prepared beforehand that we should walk in them (Ephesians 2:4-10).

But God ... oh my friend, *but God*! In contrast with our wretched self, we have *God*. Who is this God? We just saw from Paul's prayer that this God has an amazing power, but He is also *rich in mercy*, which means He has an abundance of compassion. You almost wonder if Paul is thinking of this mercy in his own personal life when he says in 1 Timothy 1:13-16, "... I was formerly a blasphemer, a persecutor, and an insolent man; but I obtained mercy because I did it ignorantly in unbelief. And the grace of our Lord was exceedingly abundant, with faith and love which are in Christ Jesus. This is a faithful saying and worthy of all acceptance, that Christ Jesus came into the world to save sinners, of whom I am chief. However, for this reason I obtained mercy, that in me first Jesus Christ might show all longsuffering, as a pattern to those who are going to believe on Him for everlasting life." Paul was once a child of wrath, but he obtained mercy.

Not only is God's mercy rich, but Paul goes on to say it is *because of His great love with which He loved us.* We who were once children under His wrath are now children under His love. This is the first distinction of those who are in Christ: *we are the recipients of His great love!* It was His love that saw us in our wretched condition and had compassion to give us life. And my dear friend, this love was shown to us *even when we were dead in trespasses,* verse 5. He loved us even when we were dead in our sins! Amazing!

And Paul says God *made us alive together with Christ.* We who were once dead are now alive together with Christ. This means that we are now vitally connected with him. We who were without Christ, disconnected, are now united with Christ, connected, alive together with Him. Most of us, by now, in the age of technology, know what it means to be disconnected. I mean, if our cell phones, computers or tablets should lose power, we think it's a catastrophe! But once we get reconnected we're back in business. This is a minute illustration of what Paul is saying: we who were once like a dead cell phone are now connected by the mercy and power and grace of God. And ladies, we are always alive together with Him! We don't have to fear being dead again in our sins because we are sealed unto the day of redemption, as Paul has already said in Ephesians 1:13-14. This is the second characteristic of our new life in Christ: *we have been made alive together with Christ.*

Paul inserts the phrase *by grace you have been saved.* This section of Paul's epistle to the Ephesians, 2:4-8, contains the most concentrated usage of the term *grace.* This Greek term, <u>charis,</u> means more than simply undeserved favor. It also expresses God's goodness, mercy, love, strength, provision and all the spiritual blessings having to do with salvation. *Grace* is the all-comprehensive provision of salvation which flows from the unmerited favor of God toward the believer in Jesus Christ. This explains why Paul, the apostle of grace, was captured by this truth and desired so passionately to share it with others.[37]

---

37 L. B. Smedes says that Paul's usage of <u>charis</u> is used "as shorthand to describe the motive and manner of the whole program of redemption, from the beginning to the end,

And if that isn't enough, Paul goes on to say that God not only made us alive, but He has *raised us up together with Christ*. The power that raised Jesus from the dead physically raised us up from the dead spiritually. This is the third description of those who are in Christ: *we are raised together with Christ*. We have been raised from death in sin to life in Christ. Paul writes similar thoughts to the Colossians, in Colossians 2:12-13: "buried with Him in baptism, in which you also were raised with Him through faith in the working of God, who raised Him from the dead. And you, being dead in your trespasses and the uncircumcision of your flesh, He has made alive together with Him, having forgiven you all trespasses."

Not only were we raised up with Christ, but the fourth characteristic of our new relationship with Christ is that *we were made to sit together in the heavenly places in Christ*. The words *heavenly places* are favorite terms of Paul's in Ephesians. "We are here on this earth, yes, but we are in the heavenly places also—a truth we shall see him working out in this second chapter. But all the blessings that we are enjoying are spiritual blessings. The lot of the Christian in this world is sometimes a difficult one; he is surrounded by problems and trials and tribulations; but he is 'blessed with all spiritual blessings in heavenly places.' And if he realizes this and dwells there, and sets his affections on things above, not on things on the earth, he will rejoice with a joy unspeakable and full of glory."[38] The word *sit* is in the aorist tense in the Greek, which means this has already taken place. It's as if we are already seated with Christ in heavenly places. Why would He do all of this? Not for us, but for Him, as we see in verse 7.

Paul says the reason for God saving us is to *show the exceeding riches of His grace in His kindness toward us*! Lenski says regarding the word *show*, "The verb means that God intends to make such a grand display of His wondrous grace before all the angels and the

---

even where the word itself had not yet been put into Christian service. cf. Geoffrey W. Bomiley, General Editor. *The International Standard Bible Encyclopedia*, Vol 2 (Grand Rapids: Eerdmans, 1982), 552.

38 D. M. Lloyd-Jones, *God's Way of Reconciliation* (Grand Rapids: Baker Book House, 1984), 4.

saints in heaven that all may see, admire and glorify."[39] Throughout all eternity God's grace and glory will be on display as seen through the salvation of depraved men and women. Ladies, this is truly an incredible statement!

Paul has now shown us four characteristics of God which caused Him to act on our behalf—His mercy, His love, His grace, and now His kindness. Without these attributes of God, we would all be lost and under His wrath. But in verse 8, Paul elaborates on how we have obtained this great salvation we so richly enjoy. He says *for by grace you have been saved through faith, and that not of yourselves; it is the gift of God.* It is by *grace,* or God's unmerited favor, that we have been saved. And we are saved through *faith!* Faith is the act of believing. Believing is not a mental assent but a commitment to the person of Jesus and who He is. If faith were a mental assent alone, then the demons would enter into heaven; but we know they will not be in heaven, according to Revelation 20. At least they have enough sense to believe and tremble, which most of mankind does not! (See James 2:19.) Paul is quick to say *and that not of yourselves; it is the gift of God.* We cannot save ourselves, even though many teach that. How can we who are dead do anything? It doesn't make sense! All of salvation is a *gift of God.* The gift of grace, the gift of faith, the entire package of salvation, is a gift. Lenski says, "Poor sinners are not even in a condition to go to God and to beg the gift from Him; God devised all the means for appropriating the gift. Everything about us is a gift."[40]

---

39 R. C. H. Lenski, 421.

40 Ibid., 424. What precisely is the *gift of God* here? There are two major views: Some see the gift of God is faith. It has been suggested that the pronoun touto, translated *that,* refers to the act of believing, which would exclude the demand for the pronoun to have the same gender as faith. Those who hold that *faith* is the gift of God are: Chrysostom, Theodoret, Jerome, Beza, Grotius, Bengel, Charles Hodge, A. Kuyper, William Hendriksen and John MacArthur. Many Calvinistic interpreters have been attracted to this view, pointing out that *faith* is not generated by fallen man. cf. 2 Pet. 1:1; Phil. 1:29; Acts 3:16, etc. The second view suggests that the pronoun touto refers to the concept of *grace-by-faith salvation,* which is the preferred biblical view, because a demonstrative pronoun regularly takes a conceptual antecedent. Representatives of this view include: John Calvin, H. A. W. Meyer, Henry Alford, Charles J. Ellicott, John Eadie, A. T. Robertson, R. C. H. Lenski, Hoehner, O'Brien. Because the noun and the pronoun have differing genders, this second broader aspect of the gift of God is the better option.

In case some still think salvation is of themselves, Paul says in verse 9, *not of works, lest anyone should boast.* Our faith is not of works; we cannot do enough good deeds to enter into heaven. Why? Because Isaiah says, "But we are all like an unclean thing, and all our righteousnesses are like filthy rags; we all fade as a leaf, and our iniquities, like the wind, have taken us away" (Isaiah 64:6). Even our best works, our best days, Isaiah says, are like dirty menstrual cloths!

Another reason we cannot work our way to heaven is because we would *boast.* We would claim we have saved ourselves. We'd think we did it! No one is good enough; not one of us! Salvation is all of the Lord. Paul says in Romans 3:27-28, "Where is boasting then? It is excluded. By what law? Of works? No, but by the law of faith. Therefore we conclude that a man is justified by faith apart from the deeds of the law."

Now, Paul makes it clear in the next verse that even though we are not saved by our good works, it is expected that after salvation we will produce good works. As James says, in James 2:26, faith without works is nothing more than a dead faith. But we who were once dead are now alive to serve our loving Lord by our acts of gratitude. Paul says in verse 10, *for we are His workmanship.* *Workmanship* means a poem, a piece of literary workmanship. We are God's poem, His work of art! And my friend, God's poems and art work are not like any we can imagine. They are more superb than Rembrandt, Leonardo da Vinci; William Shakespeare, Elizabeth Barrett Browning. They are created by the Master Artist, who created the heavens and earth!

Paul says God created us for good works, which God prepared beforehand that we should walk in them. In his epistle to Titus, Paul is clear about this: "who gave Himself for us, that He might redeem us from every lawless deed and purify for Himself His own special people, zealous for good works" (Titus 2:14). Jesus makes this clear, as well, in John 15:16: "You did not choose Me, but I chose you and appointed you that you should go and bear fruit, and that your fruit should remain, that whatever you ask the Father in My name He may give you." So the fifth description of those who are in Christ is that *we are His workmanship, created to do good works*.

Summary

Ladies, the contrasts in what Paul is saying in this passage are absolutely amazing! As we draw this lesson to a close, let your mind wrap around these amazing truths, will you?

We were once *Dead in Our Sins*, (v 1), but we have been *Made Alive in Christ*, (v 5): Can you confidently say that you are alive in Christ? Are you connected to Him in a vital way?

We were once *Walking According to the Course of this World*, (v 2a), but we have been *Raised Together with Christ*, (v 6a): Is your life filled with earthly passions, or is it filled with heavenly passions?

We were once *Walking According to the Prince of the Power of the Air*, (v 2b), but we are now *Seated with Christ in the Heavenly Places*, (v 6b): Is your life influenced by Satan, or is it controlled by Christ, Who is in heaven?

We were once *Fulfilling the Lusts of our Flesh*, (v3a), in our life and mind, but we are now *Fulfilling the Good Works which God Designed for Us*, (v 10b): Are your days consumed with carrying out evil passions, or are you consumed with serving God with the gifts He's given you?

We were once *Children of Disobedience, Children of Wrath*, (v 3b), but we now are *His Workmanship*, (v 10a), the *Recipients of His Great Love*, (v 4): Are you walking through life with a heart to obey, praising God that you are a chosen daughter—a recipient of His great love?

Questions to Consider

From Death to Life!
Ephesians 2:1-10

1. (a) Read Ephesians 2:1-10 and write down what Paul says about what we were like before we were in Christ and also what Paul says we are now like in Christ. (b) What does this tell you about your former life? (c) What do these verses tell you about your current life and your life to come? (d) Memorize Ephesians 2:8-9.

2. (a) In Ephesians 2:1-10 Paul mentions that before we were in Christ we were fulfilling the lusts of our flesh (verse 3), but after salvation we do good works (verse 10). According to Galatians 5:17-26 what are some of the ways we demonstrated those lusts of our flesh before salvation and what are some of the things our life should produce after salvation? (b) What are some other passages that deal with our life before Christ and our life after Christ? (c) Are you doing the good works that God has ordained you to do?

3. According to the following passages, what are the dangers of boasting in our good works? Matthew 6:1-18; Matthew 19:16-26; Matthew 23; Luke 18:9-14.

4. (a) How could you use Ephesians 2:8-9 to help someone who thinks they can earn their way to heaven by their works? (b) What other passages could you use? (c) Do you think someone who believes that salvation is by works can be genuinely saved? Prove your answer from Scripture.

5. (a) How would you describe your own life before salvation? (b) How would you describe your life now, after salvation?

6. Either write a praise to God for bringing you out of darkness into light, or write a prayer request for someone who is still dead to God and needs to be awakened to eternal life.

Chapter 6

From Hopeless to Hopeful!
Ephesians 2:11-18

Some time ago, I was sitting in the back of the sanctuary of my church, and as I was looking around I noticed men and women of different ethnic groups: Hispanic, African American, Caucasian, Native American, European and Asian. There are people from different races and different countries that attend our church. And yet, because of the cross of Christ, there is no distinction between any of these races because we are all one in Christ Jesus. This is the reminder that Paul sets forth to the church at Ephesus as he continues to write to them. The church at Ephesus was like all the New Testament churches during biblical times, in that they were divided into two groups, Jews and Gentiles. You might say, "So, what's the problem with that?" Well, there were a lot of problems, but they all stemmed from the fact that the Jews and the Gentiles despised each other.

In the beginning, God set His love upon a people who were called His own, the nation of Israel, the Jews. God intended for the Jewish people, His chosen people, to represent Him to the world, to act like Him. He gave them laws and ordinances so that they would resemble Him. But, instead of resembling Him, some became prideful and arrogant and hypocritical and pharisaical. They looked down upon all others who were not of the Jewish race, and referred to them as Gentiles. The Jews considered the Gentiles nothing more than dogs, fuel for hell. The Jews could not believe that God loved anyone but them alone. In fact, during biblical times Jewish women refused to help Gentile women during the birthing process because they wanted no part of bringing a Gentile child into the world. When a Jew would come back into the land of Israel, they would shake the dust off their feet in case their feet had been contaminated with Gentile dust. Jews would not eat with Gentiles, nor be seen walking with them. They had no dealings with Gentiles, socially or religiously. We could spend much time rehearsing all the ways in which these two groups despised one another. I would encourage you to do some study on just how awful this division was, because it will enhance your understanding of this passage, along with many other parts of the Scriptures. With these cultural conditions in mind, Paul writes to his Ephesian brothers and sisters,

Ephesians 2:11-18

Therefore remember that you, once Gentiles in the flesh—who are called Uncircumcision by what is called the Circumcision made in the flesh by hands—[12]that at that time you were without Christ, being aliens from the commonwealth of Israel and strangers from the covenants of promise, having no hope and without God in the world. [13]But now in Christ Jesus you who once were far off have been brought near by the blood of Christ. [14]For He Himself is our peace, who has made both one, and has broken down the middle wall of separation, [15]having abolished in His flesh the enmity, that is, the law of commandments contained in ordinances, so as to create in Himself one new man from the two, thus making peace, [16]and that He might reconcile them both to God in one body through the cross, thereby putting to death the enmity. [17]And He came and preached peace to you who were afar off and to those who were near. [18]For through Him we both have access by one Spirit to the Father (Ephesians 2:11-18).

In our last lesson, we saw some amazing contrasts of our lives before Christ and after Christ. Paul continues to reflect on life before Christ and after Christ, but he moves on to focus specifically on the Gentiles and their lives before and after Christ. As we look at this passage we will discover that for the Gentiles, they went from hopeless to hopeful! As an outline for our lesson, we'll consider *The Hopeless State of the Gentiles without Christ*, (vv 11-13a), and see six descriptions of that state. We'll also consider *The Hopeful State of the Gentiles with Christ*, (vv 13b-18), and see six descriptions of it, as well. Let's begin by looking first of all at the hopeless state of the Gentiles before their conversion.

The Hopeless State of the Gentiles without Christ
Ephesians 2:11-13

Therefore remember that you, once Gentiles in the flesh—who are called Uncircumcision by what is called the Circumcision made in the flesh by hands—that at that time you were without Christ, being aliens from the commonwealth of Israel and strangers from the covenants of promise, having no hope and without God in the world. But now in Christ Jesus you who once were far off have been brought near by the blood of Christ (Ephesians 2:11-13).

Paul begins by saying, *therefore remember that you ... Therefore* is there because of what has been said in the previous verse 1-10. Because of the wonderful fact that those who were dead in trespasses and sins are now made alive in Christ, Paul says, "You Gentiles, remember this!" *Remember* this—don't dwell on your past disadvantages, but dwell on the fact of what God has now done in your life because of Christ.[41] You Gentiles now have the same privileges of God's chosen people.

He then goes on to say that they were *once Gentiles in the flesh—who are called Uncircumcision by what is called the Circumcision made in the flesh by hands*. What is Paul saying here? The Jewish people, who were circumcised, looked at the Gentiles as inferior because they were not circumcised. Calling themselves the *circumcision*, the Jews referred to the Gentiles as the *uncircumcision*, or *Gentiles in the flesh*. When a Jew was circumcised it showed that they were in a covenant relationship with God. Gentiles, on the other hand, because they were not circumcised, showed that they were estranged from God. It has been said that Gentiles would even laugh at the fact that the Jews were circumcised. They thought it was ridiculous. And of course, the Jews thought the Gentiles were disgusting because they weren't circumcised.[42] It was so ridiculous

---

41 There is great spiritual benefit in often recalling what we were before we were saved, for it deepens our humility and incites continued thankfulness for God's grace. Six times in Paul's epistles he requests his readers to remember: that the Corinthians *remember* him in all things and keep the ordinances (cf. 1 Cor. 11:2); that the Colossians *remember* his bonds (cf. Col. 4:18); that the Thessalonians *remember* his labor and travail in ministry among them (cf. 1 Thess. 2:5) and his teaching (cf. 2 Thess. 2:5); and that Timothy *remember* Jesus Christ, of the seed of David, was raised from the dead, as an encouragement to sufferings (cf. 2 Tim. 2:8).

42 The term *uncircumcised* is used 39 times in the Bible and most often to reproach or point out some sort of spiritual or ethnic lack. e.g.,, Gen. 34:14; Exod. 6:12, 30; 12:48; Judg. 14:3; 1 Sam. 14:6; 17:26, 36; 31:4; Isa. 52:1; Jer. 9:25-26; Ezek. 32:19-32; 44:7-9, etc. It is interesting that *circumcision* is not used figuratively in the 22 usages in the OT, but *uncircumcision* is often used figuratively, i.e.,, in a third of the 34 usages.

that even when Paul met Timothy, who was a Gentile believer, he took Timothy and had him circumcised, even though Timothy was an adult! Consider the following passage, Acts 16:1-3: "Then he came to Derbe and Lystra. And behold, a certain disciple was there, named Timothy, the son of a certain Jewish woman who believed, but his father was Greek. He was well spoken of by the brethren who were at Lystra and Iconium. Paul wanted to have him go on with him. And he took him and circumcised him because of the Jews who were in that region, for they all knew that his father was Greek."

We know from other places in the Word of God that being circumcised or uncircumcised does not prove one is in a living relationship with Christ. Paul says in Galatians 5:6, "For in Christ Jesus neither circumcision nor uncircumcision avails anything, but faith working through love." And in Colossians 2:11, Paul says, "In Him you were also circumcised with the circumcision made without hands, by putting off the body of the sins of the flesh, by the circumcision of Christ." And even to the church at Philippi, Paul says, "For we are the circumcision, who worship God in the Spirit, rejoice in Christ Jesus, and have no confidence in the flesh" (Philippians 3:3). Circumcision without a relationship with Christ is nothing but an outward show of religion. God is not interested in an outward show, as the Jews sought, but the inward circumcision of the heart, not of the flesh.

In our culture, we don't use circumcision as a gauge of spirituality, but we do wrongly measure one another's spirituality by things like the way one schools their children, what translation of the Bible one uses, if one wears a head covering in church or not, if one wears makeup, jewelry or pants, and so on. These things, like circumcision, are never areas by which God commands us to judge one another. Paul does, however, go on in verse 12 to explain the six ways in which the Gentiles were hopeless before Christ. He says, *at that time you were without Christ, being aliens from the commonwealth of Israel and strangers from the covenants of promise, having no hope and without God in the world.*

---

cf. T. K. Abbott, *The International Critical Commentary: Ephesians and Colossians*, (Edinburgh: T. & T. Clark, 1985), 56-57.

The first hopeless state of the Gentiles is that they were without Christ. This means they were separate from Christ. They knew nothing about the Messiah, their Savior. As Gentiles, they would not have had the same privileges of God's chosen people, the Jews. Ladies, we too, when we were dead in our sins, were without Christ. Let us never forget this—we, too, were in a hopeless state!

The second hopeless state of the Gentiles is that they were aliens from the commonwealth of Israel. The Gentiles were not Jews, thus they were strangers to the community of God's chosen people. They were strangers to all the privileges, both civil and religious, of the Jewish people.

Third, the Gentiles were hopeless because they were strangers from the covenants of promise. Being Gentiles, they were outside the covenant promises God shared with His chosen people. They had no part in the covenants God made with His chosen people, Israel, the covenants He made with Abraham, Isaac or Jacob, or any of the other patriarchs.[43]

Fourth, the Gentiles had no foundation for hope. As the songwriter says, "Our hope is built on nothing less than Jesus' blood and righteousness."[44] I was speaking with a gal at lunch recently and she was sharing how her husband did not want to live anymore,

---

43 *The Abrahamic Covenant.* cf. Genesis 12:1-3, 6-7; 13:14-17; 15:1-21; 17:1-14; 22:15-18. This covenant promised special blessings, a land, a kingdom, and first distinguished the Jews from Gentiles, as it was reaffirmed through Isaac and, especially, Jacob. *The Mosaic Covenant.* cf. Exodus 19:5-8; 20:1-17ff. Deut. 5:1-25. This covenant provided distinctive laws, statutes, and ordinances concerning the government, personal life, and religious worship of the people of God, which the Abrahamic covenant implied, but which the Gentiles lacked. *The Palestinian Covenant.* cf. Deut. 30:1-10; Gen. 17:7-8. This covenant elaborated the promise of the land given to the Jews, contained in the Abrahamic covenant, which the Gentiles lacked. *The Davidic Covenant.* cf. 2 Samuel 7:12-16; Ps. 89:3-4; Jer. 33:14-22, 25-26. This covenant elaborated the promise of coming kings (cf. Gen. 17:6) given in the Abrahamic covenant, which, of course, the Gentiles lacked. *The New Covenant.* cf. Jer. 31:31-34; 32:37-42; Ezek. 36:24-32. This covenant especially elaborates the blessings of God upon His people and the unique special relationship He has with them, which the Gentiles lacked. That the Abrahamic covenant acts as a *foundation* to the other major covenants is affirmed by Moses in Exodus 2:24-25 and 32:12-13; David in 1 Chron. 16:8-18; Isaiah in Isa. 41:8-10; Jeremiah in 31:35-36; Nehemiah in Nehemiah 9:7-8, etc.

44 Words by Edward Mote, 1797-1874.

how he had even talked about suicide. I mentioned to her how sad that was, but it made sense to me, since this man wasn't a believer in Jesus Christ. He didn't believe he had a purpose for living. Life without Christ is hopeless. But, praise the Lord, that hopeless state did not remain for the Gentiles, as Paul says in Colossians 1:27: "To them God willed to make known what are the riches of the glory of this mystery among the Gentiles: which is Christ in you, the hope of glory."

The fifth hopeless condition of the Gentiles before Christ is that they were without God in the world. This means they had no knowledge of the true God. The Gentiles worshiped, but they did not worship the true God. In fact, when Paul went into Athens and preached his famous sermon on Mars Hill, he made this statement in Acts 17:22-23: "Men of Athens, I perceive that in all things you are very religious; for as I was passing through and considering the objects of your worship, I even found an altar with this inscription: TO THE UNKNOWN GOD. Therefore, the One whom you worship without knowing, Him I proclaim to you." It wasn't that the Gentiles were atheists; they believed in gods, but they did not believe in the one true God who made heaven and earth and could save them from their sins. My dear friends, this too, was our life before Christ. We worshiped many gods—the gods of self, pleasure, and fame—but we did not know God. Thanks be to God who revealed Himself to us through His Son, Jesus Christ!

Before he moves on to focus on the hopeful state of the Gentiles since coming to Christ, Paul shares one more description of the hopeless state of the Gentiles when they were without Christ. He says, *but now in Christ Jesus you who once were far off have been brought near by the blood of Christ.* This means they were *far* away, a great way *off* from the true God and from His people. *This is the sixth hopeless state of Gentiles: that they were far off.* And this, too, was our condition before salvation. If you would think about your life before conversion, you would have to admit that you were about as far off—as far away—as you could get from God.

The Hopeful State of the Gentiles with Christ
Ephesians 2:13-18

> But now in Christ Jesus you who once were far off have been brought near by the blood of Christ. For He Himself is our peace, who has made both one, and has broken down the middle wall of separation, having abolished in His flesh the enmity, that is, the law of commandments contained in ordinances, so as to create in Himself one new man from the two, thus making peace, and that He might reconcile them both to God in one body through the cross, thereby putting to death the enmity. And He came and preached peace to you who were afar off and to those who were near. For through Him we both have access by one Spirit to the Father (Ephesians 2:13-18).

But now, Paul says, *in Christ Jesus you ... have been brought near by the blood of Christ*. This *but now* is very similar to what we saw in verse 4, when Paul said, "but God." The Gentiles' helpless, hopeless condition is now a happy, hopeful condition—all because of *Christ Jesus*. Praise be to God, Paul says, *you have been brought near by the blood of Christ*. As Paul says in 1 Timothy 2:5-6, "there is one God and one Mediator between God and men, the Man Christ Jesus, who gave Himself a ransom for all, to be testified in due time." Christ Jesus is the ransom for all, Jew and Gentile. *This is the first hopeful condition of the Gentiles, now that they are in Christ: Christ has brought them near*. And this bringing near is only made possible through the blood of Christ. There is no other way. Without the shedding of blood there is no remission of sins.

The second hopeful state of the Gentiles in Christ is that Christ has become their peace. Paul continues to write about the hopeful conditions for the Gentiles when he says in verse 14: *for He Himself is our peace, who has made both one, and has broken down the middle wall of separation*. The blessing of *peace* that belonged to the Jewish people now belongs to the Gentiles as well. This is interesting because there is a blessing that the Lord conveys to Moses in Numbers 6:23-26, "Speak to Aaron and his sons, saying, 'This is the way you shall bless the children of Israel. Say to them: The LORD bless you and keep you; the LORD make His face shine upon you, and be gracious to you; the LORD lift up His countenance upon you, and give you peace.'" This was for the Jewish people. But now, because of Christ's shed blood, all of His children have the gift of peace. Even Christ, in the Upper Room, left his disciples with the wonderful promise of peace: "Peace I leave with you, My peace I give to you; not as the world gives do I give to you. Let not your heart be troubled, neither let it be afraid" (John 14:27). This is such a wonderful gift that comes after salvation; we have peace, peace with God, peace in this troubled world. Just the day before I wrote this lesson, I had some surgery done on my face and I was awake for the whole procedure. Even though my face was deadened I could sense the pulling and cutting and stitching. I shut my eyes and quoted more than once, "You will keep him in perfect peace, whose mind is stayed on You, because he trusts in You" (Isaiah 26:3). I was at peace. This is a gift that comes from knowing God, which the world knows nothing about.

The third hopeful state of the converted Gentile is that Christ has made both one. Paul says of Christ, he *has made both one.* This means there is no division now between Jew and Greek, as we are all *one* in Christ Jesus. There is no more hatred, no more prejudice; but there is reconciliation between Jew and Greek, as they are now one. As Paul says in Galatians 3:28, "There is neither Jew nor Greek, there is neither slave nor free, there is neither male nor female; for you are all one in Christ Jesus." Or as Paul says in Romans 10:12, "there is no distinction between Jew and Greek, for the same Lord over all is rich to all who call upon Him."

Fourth, believing Gentiles have hope because Christ has broken down the wall of separation. John MacArthur helps us here: "The barrier of the dividing wall alludes to the separation of the Court of the Gentiles from the rest of the Temple. Between that court and the Court of the Israelites was a sign that read, 'No Gentile may enter within the barricade which surrounds the sanctuary and enclosure. Anyone who is caught doing so will have himself to blame for his ensuing death.' This physical barrier illustrated the barrier of hostility and hate that also separated the two groups."[45]

---

45 MacArthur, 77. Because the issue is alienation, the author offers a helpful comment: "The root cause of strife, discord, antagonism, enmity, hate, bitterness, fighting, war, conflict and every other form of disunity and division is sin...The only solution for divisions among men is the removal of sin, which Jesus Christ accomplished by the

(See Acts 21:17-30 for a good example of this.) Because the wall is broken down, the Gentile now has the same access to God as the Jew does. There is no more hostility. What hope! What joy!

Paul goes on to give yet another hopeful state the Gentiles find themselves in after embracing the Lordship of Christ. He says, *having abolished in His flesh the enmity, that is, the law of commandments contained in ordinances, so as to create in Himself one new man from the two, thus making peace.* In verse 15, *Paul gives us the fifth hopeful condition of the Gentiles: that Christ has abolished in His flesh the enmity.* In other words, Christ destroyed or abolished the hostility between the Jews and Gentiles. There is now a new covenant, which has been established because of Christ's death. The Jews prided themselves on keeping the ceremonial law; the Gentiles regarded those laws as ridiculous. By His death, Christ came and abolished the ceremonial law. The Mosaic covenant is history; the new covenant is current. Now, the moral law is still in effect, and Paul emphasizes that in Ephesians 4-6, but the ceremonial law is no longer in effect. That was the problem Paul addressed in his epistle to the Galatians, as they were trying to implement the Mosaic Law within the church, and Paul rebuked them many times for trying to go back to keeping the law. He even goes so far as to say that he seriously doubts they know God, that he's afraid he has ministered to them in vain, and he calls them foolish!

Paul goes on to give the reason why Christ abolished the law: *so as to create in Himself one new man from the two, thus making peace.* This means that now Jew and Gentile are one person, meaning they are united spiritually. Two races who were at odds are now one new man. They now live in harmony with each other. Paul gives us help here with the word *new*, in 2 Corinthians 5:17; he says, "Therefore, if anyone is in Christ, he is a new creation; old things have passed away; behold, all things have become new." Or, as Paul says in Galatians 6:15, "For in Christ Jesus neither circumcision nor <u>uncircumcision</u> avails anything, but a new creation."

shedding of His own blood. Those who trust in His atoning work are freed from sin now in their new nature and will be practically and permanently freed from sin in their new bodies, when they meet the Lord. The cleansing value of the blood of Christ immediately washes away the penalty of sin and ultimately washes away even its presence. Because in Christ the great foundational barrier of sin has been removed, every other barrier has been removed as well." cf. Ibid., 75.

The result of this new harmony is peace, as Paul says, *thus making peace*. This is the second time *peace* is mentioned. When Christ comes into the lives of two people, no matter who they are, even though they might be at odds, the result is peace. I think one of the most beautiful illustrations we have of this is in the story of Elisabeth Elliot. You may know that her first husband, Jim, was martyred by the Auca Indians in January of 1956. He was one of five missionaries that were speared to death. Three years after the death of her husband, Elisabeth and her three year old daughter, Valerie, returned to the jungle, along with one of the other widows whose husband was killed. The linguistic work of these women brought the message of salvation to the tribe that had killed their husbands. Elisabeth Elliot courageously introduced the Aucas, her husband's murderers, to Christ. Ladies, this is the result of the gospel; two who are at odds are now at peace. In Christ, Jew and Gentile are at peace; in Christ, the American and the Auca Indian are now at peace.

Paul goes on to share about this reconciliation between Jew and Gentile by saying, in verse 16, *that He might reconcile them both to God in one body through the cross, thereby putting to death the enmity*. The word *reconcile* means to turn from hostility to friendship. Jews and Gentiles who once were hostile toward one another are now friends. They are in one body, the body of Jesus Christ. Paul brings out again, as he did in verse 13, that it is only because of the cross, only because of the blood of Jesus that those who were at war can now be at peace. He has put *to death the enmity*. We are now at peace with man and at peace with God.

Speaking of peace, Paul goes on to say, verse 17: *And He came and preached peace to you who were afar off and to those who were near*. This is the third mention of *peace*. Christ came and preached peace both to those who were afar off, the Gentiles, and to those who were near, the Jews. We, who were at war with God, are now at peace with Him because of the reconciling work of Christ done on the cross. Paul will write later in this epistle concerning the importance of sharing the gospel of peace, when he mentions it as part of the believers' armor in Ephesians 6:15: "having shod your feet with the preparation of the gospel of peace."

In verse 18, *Paul ends with the sixth hopeful state of the converted Gentile, that Christ has given them access to the Father.* He says, *through Him we both have access by one Spirit to the Father.* Paul says in 1 Corinthians 12:13, "For by one Spirit we were all baptized into one body—whether Jews or Greeks, whether slaves or free—and have all been made to drink into one Spirit." Both Jew and Greek have access to the Father. Ladies, we have admission to the Father; we have the ability to approach His throne of grace at any time for any need. Because of the work on the cross the veil has been torn in two and we can boldly approach Him. Paul puts it beautifully in 1 Timothy 2:5, "For there is one God and one Mediator between God and men, the Man Christ Jesus."

Summary

In this lesson, we have considered *The Hopeless State of the Gentiles without Christ*, (vv 11-13a):
1. They were without Christ.
2. They were aliens from the commonwealth of Israel.
3. They were strangers from the covenants of promise.
4. They were without hope.
5. They were without God in the world
6. They were far off.

We have also learned of *The Hopeful State of the Gentiles with Christ*, (vv 13b-18
1. Christ has brought them near.
2. Christ has become their peace.
3. Christ has made both one.
4. Christ has broken down the middle wall of separation.
5. Christ has abolished in His flesh the enmity.
6. Christ has given them access to the Father.

Today, our world is much larger than two people groups, Jews and Greeks. There are more than 248 nations in our world today, which only seems to gives us more cause for prejudice and hostility. Maybe you think you have some sort of privilege because you were born in America, raised in a Christian home, raised in a country with plenty to eat, have a good job, have an air-conditioned home and car. Maybe you look down on others in your country and other countries who are of a different ethnicity or social status than you. In the church of Jesus Christ, there is no room for this type of sinful attitude, as God is no respecter of persons and He expects the same of His children (see James 2:1-9).

When you and I are tempted to look down upon others because of race, school choices, food choices, clothing choices, or any other choices that are not spelled out as sinful in the Word of God, we need to take ourselves to this passage in Ephesians. Remember, you and I once were without Christ; you and I had no hope; and remember that you and I were without God in the world. But because of Jesus' blood, you and I have been brought near. God has called men and women from every tribe and tongue and people and nation together in one, thus making peace, that we one day might sit with Him in heavenly places, to the praise of the glory of His grace!

Questions to Consider

From Hopeless to Hopeful!
Ephesians 2:11-18

1. (a) Read Ephesians 2:11-18 and list all the disadvantages the Gentiles had before coming to Christ, as well as the advantages they received after coming to Christ. (b) How did you and do you find these to be true in your own life? (c) What are some other disadvantages you had before your salvation, and what are some other advantages you have now because of your salvation? (d) Memorize Ephesians 2:18.

2. (a) Several times in Ephesians 2:11-18 Paul mentions that Jews and Gentiles both have the same privileges in Christ because of the blood of Christ. According to the following verses, what are some of those privileges we both have? Romans 3:21-30; 1 Corinthians 12:13; Galatians 3:26-29; Ephesians 3:6. (b) According to the following passages, what will take place in the future when both Jews and Gentiles have been gathered together in one? Revelation 7:9-17; Revelation 21:24-27.

3. (a) Paul mentions in Ephesians 2:18 that those who are redeemed have access to the Father. According to Romans 5:2, how do we obtain this access? (b) What are the blessings of having access to the Father, according to Hebrews 4:15-16; Hebrews 10:19-20; and 1 John 2:1-2? (c) What are some personal blessings you have experienced by having access to the Father?

4. (a) What are some ways in which you think Christians today show partiality to those who are of different ethnicity or social status? (b) Do you look down upon those who are not like you or who you think are not as privileged as you are? (c) What do you think Christ would say to this? (You can use the passage we studied in this lesson in Ephesians or other passages to remind yourself of what God thinks of this.)

5. (a) Paul mentions three times in these verses that Christ is our peace (Ephesians 2:14-15, 17). Do you have this peace that comes from knowing the Savior? (b) Is there something that is robbing you of your peace today? Why not cast it on the blessed Savior?! Write your need in the form of a prayer request.

Chapter 7

Citizens of the Household of God!

Ephesians 2:19-22

Most of you reading this Bible study have had the privilege of being born in the United States of America and being citizens of this country. There are, however, countless individuals from all over the world who have desired to become citizens of the United States, and some of them have been able to actually do that! What is it like to become a citizen of the United States? For those of us who were born United States citizens, it is something we often take for granted. But I'd like to let you in on what it is like to *become* a citizen of the United States, by giving you some thoughts written by those who have actually gone through that process. One person wrote, "For me being an American citizen means freedom of expression and to live and work in a free country ... and not having to be afraid of being arrested or harassed because of owning common books or pictures. I also feel a sense of responsibly to my adopted country."[46] Another wrote, "To be an American is not just a great honor, but also an obligation to do more and reach higher. I'm thankful for the opportunity to stay, study and work [in the U.S.], but it was not free by any means. ... The process was a nightmare that never ended: thousands of dollars and many years of fear and hopelessness."[47] Still another shared these thoughts:

> Some people have asked me what it means to be a U.S. Citizen; have wondered what's different in my life now. I don't think there's any real way to convey the advantages of being a citizen without talking about what it's like to live in the U.S. *without* citizenship. I'm guessing many of you reading this probably don't think too often about the fact that you are U.S. citizens. And why would you? There are many words that I think sum up what citizenship means to a former non-citizen, but the ones I

---

46 Emoke Barabas.
47 Imania.

keep returning to are *opportunity* and *freedom*. What do I mean by those words? Opportunity means never having to worry about how your job is going to pay you, and never being deprived of your hard-earned pay because you didn't have the right government forms. It means never having to get paid "under the table" (unless you want to). It means never needing to worry about being "eligible" for financial aid, when you apply to college or graduate school. Perhaps, more importantly, opportunity is having the option to vote in local and national elections, to engage in our collective polity, and to do your part to shape our country and the world. It is the chance to make a difference, to take control, to take ownership of your fate, and the fate of the place that you live. It is self-determination in its purest form. Freedom is the ability to leave the United States without having any fear of not being able to get back in. It means escaping the fate of my father, whose freshly expired visa prevented him from going back home when *his* father died in Taiwan many years ago. It means never having to give up amazing, incredible opportunities abroad due to complications with your immigrant status. It means being able to settle down here, to live here, to have a home here, without worrying that one day you'll be asked to leave this place you have contributed so much to. In the end, freedom is, perhaps counter-intuitively, a sense of permanence. The one thing I can safely say I feel is "relief," an emotion I'm sure is shared by hundreds of the others who joined me in taking the Oath today. Filing out of the hall, the mood was jubilant everywhere. People hugged their loved ones. Families took countless photos. As I wrote on my twitter account, it was like leaving a wedding, except 900 people got married ... to the United States of America. Truly a special day that I'll remember for the rest of my life. Theodore Roosevelt once said, "Nothing in the world is worth having or worth doing unless it means effort, pain, difficulty." So I say again: Today I am a citizen of the United States of America. And it means everything.[48]

As wonderful as these testimonies are, they are nothing in comparison to the testimonies of those who have been made citizens

48 David Chen.

of the household of God. As we finish with chapter two of Ephesians, Paul has some amazing things to say about those who are citizens not of the United States of America but of the heavenly kingdom. Let's listen in to what he has to say.

Ephesians 2:19-22

> Now, therefore, you are no longer strangers and foreigners, but fellow citizens with the saints and members of the household of God, [20]having been built on the foundation of the apostles and prophets, Jesus Christ Himself being the chief cornerstone, [21]in whom the whole building, being fitted together, grows into a holy temple in the Lord, [22]in whom you also are being built together for a dwelling place of God in the Spirit (Ephesians 2:19-22).

In our previous lesson, we considered *The Hopeless State of the Gentiles without Christ,* (vv 11-13a). We also learned of *The Hopeful State of the Gentiles with Christ,* (vv 13b-18). Christ has brought them near, become their peace, made the Jews and Gentiles one, broken down the middle wall of separation, abolished in His flesh the enmity, and given them access to the Father.

In this lesson, we'll consider what it means to be citizens of the household of God. Our outline will include:

The Citizen's Heritage, (v 19);

The Citizen's Head, (v 20);

The Citizen's House, (v 21); and

The Citizen's Heart, (v 22).

Ephesians 2:19-22
The Citizen's Heritage

> Now, therefore, you are no longer strangers and foreigners, but fellow citizens with the saints and members of the household of God, (Ephesians 2:19).

Paul starts out again by saying *now therefore*. Why does he use these words? The term *therefore* points us back to everything Paul has already mentioned. Because you, who were dead in trespasses and sins, who were Gentiles and far off, have been granted salvation, because of this, you are no longer strangers and foreigners. Before salvation, the Gentiles were strangers and foreigners. They had no rights to the kingdom of God; they had no rights to citizenship. It's just like someone who is not a U.S. citizen; they have no rights to the privileges of this country. But that all changed after salvation, and, my friend, it all changed for you as well. Paul says that the Gentiles are now *fellow citizens with the saints and members of the household of God*. They used to be strangers from the covenant of promise (verse 12), but they are no longer. Paul says, you are now a native of the same town; you are now a relative of the household of God! This metaphor Paul uses, the *household of God*, is used to describe a family. It would indicate the closeness and unity we have as brothers and sisters. It is often true that our spiritual family is much closer to us than our physical family because of the bond we have in Christ and the fact that we are members of His household, which is eternal. The citizen's heritage is that of belonging to the household of God. One man says, "But the readers are no longer completely without a homeland; they are no longer even second-class citizens in someone else's homeland. They now have full citizenship in and belong firmly to a commonwealth, for they are fellow citizens with the holy ones."[49] Paul puts it well in his epistle to the Philippians: "For our citizenship is in heaven, from which we also eagerly wait for the Savior, the Lord Jesus Christ" (Philippians 3:20).

When we think of being a member of a household in the human realm, we think of protection, warmth, food, clothing, security, a place of refuge, a place where we belong. So it is in the spiritual realm. We, who are now daughters of God, are a part of His house in the heavenly places, a place of security, refuge, and belonging. It is a place that John speaks of in Revelation 21:4, where he says, "And God will wipe away every tear from their eyes; there shall be no more death, nor sorrow, nor crying. There shall be no more pain, for the former things have passed away." He also says in Revelation 22:3, "And there shall be no more curse, but the throne of God and of the Lamb shall be in it, and His servants shall serve Him."

49 Lincoln, *Word Biblical Commentary*, 150.

So we see that the citizen's heritage is that of belonging to the household of God. When we think of a household, we think also of someone who is in charge. So we move from the citizen's heritage in verse 19 to the citizen's head in verse 20. Who is it? Paul says,

Ephesians 2:20
The Citizen's Head

> having been built on the foundation of the apostles and prophets, Jesus Christ Himself being the chief cornerstone, (Ephesians 2:20).

The citizen's head is *Jesus Christ*, who is *the chief cornerstone*. Now, this is an interesting verse, because Paul has just mentioned in verse 14 that Christ has broken down that middle wall of separation. The old is out; the new structure is in! The wall has been broken down between Jew and Gentile and now there is a new foundation being built that joins the two together. What does it mean that it has been *built on the foundation of the apostles and prophets*? The *apostles* would be the twelve disciples plus any other apostles who had personally seen the resurrected Christ (See 1 Corinthian 9:1). The *prophets* would be those who Paul speaks of in Ephesians 4:11, where he says, "And He Himself gave some to be apostles, some prophets, some evangelists, and some pastors and teachers." Prophets are those who herald the truth of God's Word. (See also 1 Corinthians 12:29 and 1 Corinthians 14:37-38). The *apostles and prophets* were the foundation of the established church, and they are an important part of the building of Jesus Christ.[50] But they are not the most important part, as there is one who is the head of all citizens, Jesus Christ, the chief cornerstone.

Now you might be wondering what Paul means when he says that Jesus is the *chief cornerstone*. Some think this means He is the capstone, the tip of the angle. This would be the stone that would hold all the other stones together. It would bind all the other stones as well as the wall and hold it all in place. This describes the

---

50 Wayne Grudem seeks to explain that the *prophets* here could refer to OT prophets. The obvious weakness is that the order should then be "the prophets and the apostles," but that is not the case. Grudem realizes this issue is a challenge to his view and gives an extensive dealing in answer but is not convincing.

binding stone that would hold an entire structure together. However, others think that the chief cornerstone would be at the foundation of the building. "Paul is here referring to the cornerstone—the most significant part of the foundation of the temple. This large stone bore much of the weight of the building and tied the walls firmly together. In the early 1990's, archaeologists discovered five enormous stones that helped form the foundation of the Jerusalem temple. The largest stone measures 55 ft. long, 11 ft. high, 14 ft. wide and is estimated to weigh 500 tons."[51] Now that's a big cornerstone! It had to be exact and it had to be strong, because if it wasn't the entire building would crumble and fall. Now, I think there are possibilities with both of these interpretations. The capstone would be worth considering because of the connection of the stones, Jew and Gentile, into one building. The cornerstone, meaning the large stone laid before the others, would give weight to Christ being the only one exact and strong enough to bring Jew and Gentile together. Regardless of which view you take, the citizen's head is Jesus Christ, the chief cornerstone. We who are citizens of God's household need a house to live in, a family to live with, right? That's why Paul goes on to talk about the citizen's house in verse 21.

Ephesians 2:21
The Citizen's House

in whom the whole building, being fitted together, grows into a
holy temple in the Lord, (Ephesians 2:21).

When Paul mentions *the whole building* he is referring to the entire body of Christ, which would include both Jew and Gentile. With the chief cornerstone, the whole building, the body of Christ, is *fitted together*. In other words, every piece of the building fits perfectly together. There is nothing out of place, or faulty. But what does it mean that we are fitted together? The English Standard Version and the New International Version of the Bible translate this phrase as "joined together." When we think of being joined together we think of what the minister says at a wedding: "What God has joined together, let no man put asunder." We think of a man and wife being joined together. The two become one flesh. But that is not what

---

51 Arnold, 171.

Paul is referring to here. Being joined or fitted together has the idea of being fit together like stitches that bind or sew a wound together. This is so vivid to me, because while I was in the process of writing this lesson I had several stitches in my face that were binding a wound together. After several days, the stitches were removed and the wound had closed up completely. And it wasn't long before the wound was completely healed. The stitches had bound my wound together. In the same way, Paul is saying that every piece of the building fits together, there is nothing out of place, like a puzzle with all the pieces tightly fitting together.

Paul goes on to say that this building *grows into a holy temple in the Lord.* What does he mean by this? The building, God's family, *grows* because the building is not yet complete; there are still people who are being saved. Christ mentions this in John 10:16 when He says, "And other sheep I have which are not of this fold; them also I must bring, and they will hear My voice; and there will be one flock and one shepherd." We know that one day that last person will be saved and the building will be complete as the last stone is laid. I have often wondered who that last person will be who will be brought into the household of God.

Before we go on to the next verse, notice that Paul mentions that this *temple*, this building, is *holy*. Hasn't he already said that holiness should be our calling in life? Remember Ephesians 1:4? "Just as He chose us in Him before the foundation of the world, that we should be holy and without blame before Him in love." Paul also says in Romans 6:22, "But now having been set free from sin, and having become slaves of God, you have your fruit to holiness, and the end, everlasting life." The apostle Peter echoes this in 1 Peter 1:15-16: "but as He who called you is holy, you also be holy in all your conduct, because it is written, 'Be holy, for I am holy.'" It is also interesting that Paul uses the word holy to describe the temple because in Ephesus, remember, there was another temple that was not holy, the temple of Artemis, which was a pagan temple. A citizen of God's household has a new heritage, a new head, a new house, but they also have a new heart, as seen in verse 22.

Ephesians 2:22
The Citizen's Heart

in whom you also are being built together for a dwelling place
of God in the Spirit (Ephesians 2:22).

First Paul says they are fitted together, in verse 21, and now
he states that they are *built together*. Being built together would
indicate that we are built together with other believers, Jews and
Gentiles, men and women of all nations, as one structure whose
foundation is the apostles and prophets, with Christ as the chief
cornerstone. When we think of this building, this holy temple, we're
mindful that someone inhabits it. A *dwelling place* would include
the idea of a permanent home. *In the Spirit* means that God the Holy
Spirit takes up residence in this building, this earthly sanctuary. In
John 14:17, Jesus says about the Spirit, "the Spirit of truth, whom
the world cannot receive, because it neither sees Him nor knows
Him; but you know Him, for He dwells with you and will be in
you." Paul mentions in Romans 8:9, "But you are not in the flesh
but in the Spirit, if indeed the Spirit of God dwells in you. Now if
anyone does not have the Spirit of Christ, he is not His." And again
in 1 Corinthians 3:16, "Do you not know that you are the temple
of God and that the Spirit of God dwells in you?" So what do we
learn about the citizen's heart? It is inhabited by God's Spirit. What
a blessing to have the Holy Spirit dwelling within us! And with that
blessing comes our responsibility to not grieve Him, but to listen to
and obey His still small voice.

Summary

Together, we have learned of *The Citizen's Heritage*, (v 19),
the Household of God, Heaven; *The Citizen's Head*, (v 20), Jesus
Christ the Chief Cornerstone; *The Citizen's House*, (v 21), the body
of Christ; and *The Citizen's Heart*, (v 22), inhabited by God's Spirit.

As wonderful as it is to be a citizen of the United States, it is
far more glorious to be a citizen of the God's Kingdom. Some of the
citizens of God's Kingdom have described their citizenship like this:
"Transformed into another person by His Word and Spirit"; "I have

power to forgive"; "The Holy Spirit changes me"; "I am a follower of Christ"; "I have the hope of heaven, eternal life"; "I am saved from the penalty of sin, saved by His grace"; "I have a relationship with God as I have surrendered all to the will of God." It certainly is a stark contrast when you compare a citizen of the United States with a citizen of God's household. A citizen of God's household has a heritage which is heaven. A citizen of the United States has a heritage in the United States. A citizen of God's household has as their head, Jesus Christ. A citizen of the United States has as their head the President of the United States. A citizen of God's household has a wonderful house filled with holy saints. A citizen of the United States has over 3 million sinners with whom he dwells. A citizen of God's household has a heart that is inhabited by God's Spirit. A citizen of the United States has a heart that is inhabited by the world, the flesh and the devil (unless they have been born again).

One of the things that struck me as I researched testimonies from people who had become citizens of the United States was that almost everyone had one word in common—freedom! My dear friend, true freedom is not being a citizen of the United States; true freedom is knowing the truth, Jesus Christ. And that truth is the only truth that will set you free! May we thank God for the freedom from sin and death that we have because of Christ, and may we thank Him throughout all eternity for our citizenship in heaven!

Questions to Consider
Citizens of the Household of God!
Ephesians 2:19-22

1. Read Ephesians 2:19-22 and answer the following questions. (a) What terms are used to describe Christ? (b) What terms are used to describe His children? (c) Why do you think Christ is described as the chief cornerstone? (d) Memorize Ephesians 2:20.

2. (a) In Ephesians 2:20, Paul says that Jesus Christ is the chief cornerstone. What else is He called, in Isaiah 28:16 and 1 Peter 2:7-8? (b) What has been the response to the chief cornerstone throughout the ages? See Psalm 118:22; Matthew 21:42; Acts 4:11-12; 1 Peter 2:7-8. (c) In what ways do you see Christ, the chief cornerstone, being rejected in our day? (d) In what ways do you see Him being treated as precious in our day? (e) Is He precious to you?

3. (a) What are some of the future privileges of those who are citizens of the household of God, according to Galatians 3:26-29, Philippians 3:20-21; Revelation 20, 21 and 22. (b) Which of these privileges do you look forward to the most?

4. After reading over these verses in chapter 2, what do you think should be our attitude toward those in God's kingdom who differ from us in race, ethnicity, culture or social status?

5. What does it mean to you personally that you are a fellow citizen with the saints and a member of the household of God?

6. Write a prayer of thanksgiving to the Father for calling you to be a daughter in His house.

Chapter 8

God's Purposes Accomplished through a Prisoner, a Table Waiter, and the Chief of Sinners!

Ephesians 3:1-11

I have several precious memories of growing up in a Baptist minister's home. One of those memories is of singing the great hymns of the faith, which are rich in theology. There was one song, *I Surrender All*, which we sang quite often when my Dad would give an altar call at the end of the service. (The other one we sang just as often was *Just As I am*.) The song went like this:

I Surrender All

All to Jesus I surrender, All to Him I freely give;
I will ever love and trust Him, In His presence daily live.
I surrender all, I surrender all.
All to Thee, my blessed Savior, I surrender all.
All to Jesus I surrender, Humbly at His Feet I bow,
Worldly pleasures all forsaken; Take me, Jesus, take me now.
I surrender all, I surrender all.
All to Thee, my blessed Savior, I surrender all.
All to Jesus I surrender, Make me, Savior, wholly Thine;
Let me feel the Holy Spirit, Truly know that Thou art mine.
I surrender all, I surrender all.
All to Thee, my blessed Savior, I surrender all.
All to Jesus I surrender, Lord, I give myself to Thee;
Fill me with Thy love and power, Let Thy blessing fall on me.
I surrender all, I surrender all.
All to Thee, my blessed Savior, I surrender all.
All to Jesus I surrender, Now I feel the sacred flame.
Oh, the joy of full salvation! Glory, glory to His name!
I surrender all, I surrender all.
All to Thee, my blessed Savior, I surrender all.[52]

---

52 Lyrics by Judson W. Van DeVenter, 1896.

This song should really be the heart-cry of every believer in Jesus Christ, as Jesus Himself said, "Whoever desires to come after me, let him deny himself, and take up his cross, and follow Me. For whoever desires to save his life will lose it, but whoever loses his life for My sake and the gospel's will save it. For what will it profit a man if he gains the whole world, and loses his own soul? Or what will a man give in exchange for his soul?" (Mark 8:34-37). Complete surrender of one's life is not taught as it should be in our churches today, yet without a life of surrender to the Lordship of Christ, no one will enter into heaven.

The apostle Paul certainly understood the concept of surrender. He didn't try to save his life but was willing to lose it for Christ's sake and the sake of the gospel. "I surrender all" was his heart-cry, and it should be for all of God's children. Paul's surrender of his life manifested itself in his willingness to be imprisoned for the gospel, having a servant's heart like that of a simple table waiter, and seeing himself as the least of all the saints and the chief of sinners. By his attitude of "I surrender all," he accomplished much for the Kingdom of God and God's purposes. As we begin to study chapter three of Paul's epistle to the Ephesians, we'll see how God's purposes were accomplished through

Paul, the Prisoner, (vv 1-6)

Paul, the Table Waiter, (v 7)

Paul, the Chief of Sinners, (vv 8-11)

Ephesians 3:1-11

For this reason I, Paul, the prisoner of Christ Jesus for you Gentiles— ²if indeed you have heard of the dispensation of the grace of God which was given to me for you, ³how that by revelation He made known to me the mystery (as I have briefly written already, ⁴by which, when you read, you may understand my knowledge in the mystery of Christ), ⁵which in other ages was not made known to the sons of men, as it has now been revealed by the Spirit to His holy apostles and prophets: ⁶that the Gentiles should be fellow heirs, of the same body, and partakers of His promise in Christ through the gospel,

[7]of which I became a minister according to the gift of the grace of God given to me by the effective working of His power. [8]To me, who am less than the least of all the saints, this grace was given, that I should preach among the Gentiles the unsearchable riches of Christ, [9]and to make all see what is the fellowship of the mystery, which from the beginning of the ages has been hidden in God who created all things through Jesus Christ; [10]to the intent that now the manifold wisdom of God might be made known by the church to the principalities and powers in the heavenly places, [11]according to the eternal purpose which He accomplished in Christ Jesus our Lord, (Ephesians 3:1-11).

In our last lesson, we learned what it means to be a true citizen of God's household, and we would have to agree that a true citizen of His household surrenders their all to the Chief Cornerstone, Jesus Christ. With that in mind, let's begin chapter three of Ephesians by first looking at what was accomplished by Paul, the prisoner who indeed surrendered all.

Ephesians 3:1-6
Paul, the Prisoner

For this reason I, Paul, the prisoner of Christ Jesus for you Gentiles— (Ephesians 3:1).

Paul starts out by saying *for this reason*, which is actually the exact thing he says in verse 14. Evidently Paul was beginning his prayer for the church at Ephesus and got sidetracked thinking about the mystery of Christ and the calling of God upon his life. It is not unusual for Paul to do this; we see him do the same thing in Romans 5:13-17 and 11:33-36. I know in my own life, I can think I need to pray for someone and then get sidetracked. Just today, I told someone I would pray for their husband, and as I started to pray for him, I got busy with something else. Later I remembered, "Oh yeah, I need to pray for _____!" Of course, my distractions are not as noble as Paul's!

Notice that Paul calls himself a *prisoner*. (He already called himself an apostle in 1:1.) He was in prison for the sake of the gospel and specifically because he had preached to the Gentiles.[53] (See Acts

---

53 cf. Acts 21:27-30; with 22:21; 26:16-18; Gal. 2:7-10. "Prisoner *of* Christ Jesus," could be translated *belonging to* Jesus Christ or *possessed by* Jesus Christ. cf. Daniel B. Wal-

22:21-30.) At the time that he was writing this epistle he had been imprisoned for about five years. My friend, this has not happened in our country very much, but it could. Are you willing to be in prison for the cause of Christ, because you belong to Him? I find it also convicting that Paul is not whining about his imprisonment, which was not a pleasant experience. Roman imprisonment was usually preceded by flogging. Many times the open wounds were left untreated. Little food or water was provided, and when it was provided it was of poor quality. There were few toilets which made the stench unbearable at times. Female and male prisoners were incarcerated together which led to sexual immorality. Because of the awful conditions many prisoners committed suicide, while others begged for a speedy death. Paul did not consider these things, but instead he saw beyond his circumstances to an eternal perspective. He certainly was living with his Master in heavenly places!

> if indeed you have heard of the dispensation of the grace of God which was given to me for you, (Ephesians 3:2).

Paul says that they had *heard of the dispensation of the grace of God which was given* to him for them. *Dispensation* or stewardship is a word which means one who manages the affairs of others, like taking care of their business or household affairs. It might include preparing meals, bookkeeping, planting and harvesting, etc. Paul looked at his life as one which was called to minister to others. He did not hold his life dear to himself but gave it for others. It should be the same for us. What we have is not ours; it is the Lord's and we should be willing to use what we have for the sake of Christ and the Gospel. And Paul says this was given to him for them, the Gentiles. This was the purpose of what took place on the Damascus road when God saved Paul. One of the reasons God saved Paul was to bring the Gospel to the Gentiles. Consider Acts 9:15: "But the Lord said to him, 'Go, for he is a chosen vessel of Mine to bear My name before Gentiles, kings, and the children of Israel.'" Paul elaborates on this divine calling on his life in verse 3.

lace, *Greek Grammar Beyond the Basics: an Exegetical Syntax of the New Testament* (Grand Rapids: Zondervan, 1996), 81-83. The suggestion of some (i.e.,, Chrysostom, Beza, etc.) to supply the verb "to be," which then would read, "For this reason, I, Paul, *am* a prisoner ..." is unlikely because of the definite article before *prisoner*. Whatever, the fact is clear that although Paul mentions he is a "prisoner of Jesus Christ" four other times (compare with Philemon 1, 9; Eph. 4:1; 2 Tim. 1:8), only here does he add, "for you Gentiles."

how that by revelation He made known to me the mystery (as I
have briefly written already, (Ephesians 3:3).

What Paul is saying is that it was revealed to him on the
Damascus road that he would bring the Gospel message to the
Gentiles. In Acts 26:13-18, we read Paul's words, "At midday, O
king, along the road I saw a light from heaven, brighter than the sun,
shining around me and those who journeyed with me. And when we
all had fallen to the ground, I heard a voice speaking to me and saying
in the Hebrew language, 'Saul, Saul, why are you persecuting Me?
It is hard for you to kick against the goads?' So I said, 'Who are You,
Lord?' And He said, 'I am Jesus, whom you are persecuting. But rise
and stand on your feet; for I have appeared to you for this purpose,
to make you a minister and a witness both of the things which you
have seen and of the things which I will yet reveal to you. I will
deliver you from the Jewish people, as well as from the Gentiles, to
whom I now send you, to open their eyes, in order to turn them from
darkness to light, and from the power of Satan to God, that they may
receive forgiveness of sins and an inheritance among those who are
sanctified by faith in Me.'"

Paul goes on to say that he had *already written briefly* about
this, which would be his mention of this in Ephesians 1:9-10 and
2:11-22. Paul's desire was that the Ephesians, too, would understand
this mystery of Christ, as seen in verse 4.

by which, when you read, you may understand my knowledge
in the mystery of Christ), (Ephesians 3:4).

When Paul says *when you read*, he is not talking in the terms
that we might think of as 21st century believers. The Christians in the
church at Ephesus would not have personal copies of the Scriptures
in their homes, because it was rare and far too expensive for most to
have them. They did not have the privilege that we have of opening
our Bibles at any time to read. They were dependent on hearing
the public reading of the Scriptures. So, when Paul says *when you
read*, he is referring to the public reading of the Scriptures. When
the Scriptures were read aloud to them, Paul hoped they would then
understand the *knowledge* he had pertaining to *the mystery of Christ*,

that is, that the gospel is now offered to the Gentiles, thus bringing Jew and Gentile into one body. This is something that former saints would not have grasped, as Paul goes on to say, in verse 5.

> which in other ages was not made known to the sons of men, as it has now been revealed by the Spirit to His holy apostles and prophets: (Ephesians 3:5).

The Old Testament saints did not have a clue about the truth of God's plan for redemption. Paul says *in other ages* it *was not made known to the sons of men*. It was a mystery, but the New Testament saints have been given the privilege of knowing the mystery of how God's redemptive plan is for both Jew and Gentile. It wasn't revealed then, but it has now been *revealed by the Spirit*, Paul says, and it was revealed to God's *holy apostles and prophets*. This is interesting, because Paul had just written in Ephesians 2:20 that the apostles and prophets were the foundation of the household of God. What is this mystery? Paul states what it is in the next verse.

> that the Gentiles should be fellow heirs, of the same body, and partakers of His promise in Christ through the gospel, (Ephesians 3:6).

This is the secret that is now made known: that *the Gentiles* would now *be fellow heirs*, which means fellow body members.[54] They would be joined together with the Jews. And not only would they be fellow heirs but also *partakers of His promise in Christ*. The term *partaker* means to be a joint possessor of a house. This is a great mystery, as we have already read and studied in chapter 2 of Ephesians. Paul was willing to go to prison for this mystery, this gospel. And not only was he willing to surrender his life to prison, but he also willingly became a table waiter, a minister of the gospel, as we see in verse 7.

---

54 Some suggest Paul mentions *two* mysteries here, i.e.,, the *general* mystery of the Gospel of Jesus Christ and the *particular* mystery of Jews and Gentiles into one body. cf. D. M. Lloyd-Jones, *The Unsearchable Riches of Christ* (Grand Rapids: Baker, 1979), 39-51. However, it seems more likely that one mystery is considered, i.e.,, the revelation that Jew and Gentile believers in the Gospel of Jesus Christ would constitute one body. cf. Markus Barth, *Ephesians 1-3: A New Translation with Introduction and Commentary* (New York: Doubleday Press, 1974), The Anchor Bible, 331.

Ephesians 3:7
Paul, the Table Waiter

of which I became a minister according to the gift of the grace of God given to me by the effective working of His power (Ephesians 3:7).

Christ made this very clear to Paul when He saved him on the Damascus road. While he was relating his salvation experience to King Agrippa in Acts 26:13-18, Paul related Jesus' words to him: "But rise and stand on your feet; for I have appeared to you for this purpose, to make you a minister and a witness both of the things which you have seen and of the things which I will yet reveal to you" (Acts 26:16). The word *minister* means servant, and it indicates one who waits on tables. A servant, a table waiter, is always at the service of those who need him. That's the way it is when you go out to eat. The waiter or waitress is at your beck and call, or should be. Paul was a table waiter; he was a table waiter of the living God, to do whatever His beckoning hand wanted. Paul never got over the fact that God called him to minister to the saints. He mentions this in 1 Timothy 1:12-13: "And I thank Christ Jesus our Lord who has enabled me, because He counted me faithful, putting me into the ministry, although I was formerly a blasphemer, a persecutor, and an insolent man; but I obtained mercy because I did it ignorantly in unbelief."

He was a minister *according to the gift of the grace of God.* God gave Paul this gift of salvation. Didn't he already mention that in Ephesians 2:8-9? "For by grace you have been saved through faith, and that not of yourselves; it is the gift of God, not of works, lest anyone should boast." Our salvation is a gift of God, and God alone! This gift of God—salvation, was given to Paul and to us, to the Jew and to the Gentile, *by the effective working of His power,* which means by the energy of His power. Oh, my friend, it is only the power of God that can transform a wretch into a saint! And Paul understood this power. He understood this undeserved grace, considering himself to be the least of all the saints, the chief of sinners.

Ephesians 3:8-11
Paul, the Chief of Sinners

> To me, who am less than the least of all the saints, this grace was
> given, that I should preach among the Gentiles the unsearchable
> riches of Christ, (Ephesians 3:8).

Paul has the proper view of himself. He could've said I am the chief of all saints, but he says he is *less than the least of all the saints*. This wasn't a pose struck with Paul, as if to commend his own humility; this was his real heart attitude, that he was the least deserving of all believers. And this attitude was the apostle Paul's until the end of his ministry.[55] Albert Barnes helps us here: "The word means here, 'who am incomparably the least of all the saints; or who am not worthy to be reckoned among the saints.' It is expressive of the deep sense which he had of the sinfulness of his past life; of his guilt in persecuting the church and the Savior; and perhaps of his sense of his low attainments in piety…Paul never could forget the guilt of his former life; never forget the time when

---

55 Not only does Paul mention to the Ephesian believers that he was "the least of all saints," but to Timothy Paul admits, "I am (present tense, not past) the chief of sinners" (cf. 1 Tim. 1:15). The Apostle's self-image was one of *lowliness of mind,* where he considered other believers superior to himself. To the Philippian church he admonishes that they consider others "more important (Greek, huperechontas) than yourselves," (vs. 3) which isn't limited to *the things* of others (vs. 4) but to others themselves. Huperechontas means surpassing, superior or better than, commanding a mindset that views others as intrinsically superior. A strong contextual basis can be made for the "others" (Greek, allelous, i.e.,, one another) as fellow believers, which would eliminate a considering of unbelievers as intrinsically superior in our thinking. We are able to consider other believers superior because we evaluate them outwardly and have no access into their thoughts, hearts and motives. But we know the depths of wickedness and compromised motives in our own heart; we know our own vacillating love; too often we realize our own lagging commitment; we realize our own blasphemies and lusts; we know the swelling of our own pride and self-centered temptations, arising from our flesh. Hence, even the aged Apostle Paul could affirm himself to be "the chief of sinners" (cf. 1 Tim. 1:17) as he saw himself as "less than the least of all the saints." cf. Eph. 3:8. Compare with Prov. 30:2; Rom. 12:10; Judg. 6:15; 1 Sam. 9:21. This *self-loathing* is produced by the work of God as promised in the New Covenant: "Then you will remember your evil ways and your deeds that were not good; and you will loathe yourselves in your own sight, for your iniquities and your abominations." cf. Ezek. 36:31. Advance in our Christian maturity leads us to the personal conviction that we are "less than the least of all the saints."

he was engaged in persecuting the church of God."[56] Paul says in 1 Corinthians 15:9, "For I am the least of the apostles, who am not worthy to be called an apostle, because I persecuted the church of God." He also states in 1 Timothy 1:15, "This is a faithful saying and worthy of all acceptance, that Christ Jesus came into the world to save sinners, of whom I am chief."

Paul says, *this grace was given* to me, the least of all the saints, so *that I should preach among the Gentiles the unsearchable riches of Christ.* I, Paul, get to preach *the unsearchable riches of Christ!* And, my friend, they are indeed unsearchable! Paul says in Romans 11:33, "Oh, the depth of the riches both of the wisdom and knowledge of God! How unsearchable are His judgments and His ways past finding out!" And, by the way, he breaks out with these words after a very weighty chapter in Romans 11 on the Gentiles being grafted in with the Jews! So many today are preaching and promoting themselves, but we must preach Christ and Him crucified. It is about Him; it is not about us. This is probably the main reason that God used Paul so greatly. Paul goes on to elaborate in verse 9 about this mystery he proclaims.

> and to make all see what is the fellowship of the mystery, which
> from the beginning of the ages has been hidden in God who
> created all things through Jesus Christ; (Ephesians 3:9).

Paul's mission was *to make all see,* to bring to light, this *mystery,* which once was hidden in times past. And it was *hidden in God who created all things through Jesus Christ.* What was the purpose behind this? Again, it was all for the glory of Christ, as seen in verse 10.

> to the intent that now the manifold wisdom of God might be
> made known by the church to the principalities and powers in
> the heavenly places, (Ephesians 3:10).

What was the purpose of the mystery once hidden now revealed? That *the manifold wisdom of God might be made known by the church to the principalities and powers in the heavenly places.* One man helps us here. "The church, therefore, does not

---

56 Barnes, 57.

exist for itself. It exists for God, for his glory. When the angels in heaven behold the works and the wisdom of God displayed in the church, their knowledge of the God whom they adore is increased and they rejoice and glorify Him."[57] Peter even tells us in 1 Peter 1:12 that the angels are very curious about the gospel; he says, "To them it was revealed that, not to themselves, but to us they were ministering the things which now have been reported to you through those who have preached the gospel to you by the Holy Spirit sent from heaven—things which angels desire to look into." Paul further explains this purpose, and ends this section, by letting his readers know that this was all according to God's purpose.

> according to the eternal purpose which He accomplished in Christ Jesus our Lord, (Ephesians 3:11).

Everything that God has done in time past, time present, and time future is all *according to* His purpose and for His glory. It was His *eternal purpose which He accomplished.* And to think that He, God, the Creator of the earth, the Savior of mankind, used Paul, a prisoner, a table waiter, and the least of all the saints. Of course, Paul had to be a willing sold-out vessel fit for the Master's use. This, too, was all a part of God's master plan.

Summary

God accomplished His purposes through *Paul, the Prisoner,* (vv 1-6); *Paul, the Table Waiter,* (v 7); and *Paul, the Chief of Sinners,* (vv 8-11). What about you, my friend? Are you willing to do whatever the Lord asks you to do? Have you surrendered all to Him? Would you go to prison for the sake of the gospel as Paul did? Are you doing your "table waiting", i.e., washing the dishes, cooking the meals, washing the clothes, running errands, and other tasks, to the glory of God and His purposes? Are you serving in your local church body by using your spiritual gifts? Do you use these "table waiting" times as opportunities for the gospel? Do you consider yourself the least of all the saints, the chief of sinners? Or do you think you deserve some royal treatment and that God is lucky to have you for His daughter?

---

57 William Hendriksen, *New Testament Commentary: Exposition of Ephesians* (Grand Rapids: Baker Book House, 1967), 158.

Oh, my dear sister, Paul accomplished much for the kingdom of God and His purposes because he surrendered all to His Master. Are you willing to surrender all for the sake of the gospel? Are you willing to lose everything for the sake of Christ? Are you willing to go to prison, to be a table waiter, to consider yourself as nothing for the sake of the gospel and God's glory? Amy Carmichael, who was a missionary in India for 55 years without a furlough, once said, "If I covet any place on earth but the dust at the foot of the Cross, then I know nothing of Calvary love."[58]

---

58 Amy Carmichael, *If* (Grand Rapids: Zondervan, 1977), page unknown.

Questions to Consider

God's Purposes Accomplished through a Prisoner, a Table Waiter, and the Chief of Sinners!

Ephesians 3:1-11

1. Read Ephesians 3:1-11 and answer the following questions. (a) What words does Paul use to describe himself in this passage? (b) How does Paul's description of himself compare with the description of those in ministry today? (c) What terms would you use to describe yourself in the spiritual sense? (d) Memorize Ephesians 3:7.

2. (a) Paul mentions in Ephesians 3:1 that he is in prison for the cause of Christ. According to the following passages what is his attitude while he is in prison? Ephesians 6:18-20; Philippians 1:7-21; Colossians 1:24; Colossians 4:3-4; 2 Timothy 1:8-12; 2 Timothy 2:8-10. (b) Also, according to these passages, what does he hope to accomplish while in prison? (c) If you were in prison do you think these would be your attitudes and hopes?

3. (a) What words does Paul use to describe himself in Ephesians 3:8? (b) What other words does he use to describe himself in 1 Corinthians 15:9 and 1 Timothy 1:15? (c) Why do you think Paul was able to think of himself in these terms?

4. (a) Contrast Paul's thoughts of himself in Ephesians 3:8 with those of Herod in Acts 12:21-23. (b) Who did Paul desire to give glory to, according to Ephesians 3:21? (c) Who did Herod desire to give glory to, according to Acts 12:21-23? (d) Do you think your opinion of yourself is more like Paul's or Herod's? (This is a private question.) (e) According to James 4:6-10, what is the remedy for a spirit of pride?

5. Paul mentions in Ephesians 3:7 that he is a minister of the gospel. In what ways have you been a minister of the gospel this past week? (This is a private question.)

6. In what ways can you be a better servant of the Lord? Please write your need in the form of a prayer request.

Chapter 9

Paul's Second Prayer for the Church at Ephesus

Ephesians 3:12-21

There are many times in our lives when God, in His providence, brings monumental changes. We sense that things are getting ready to change; it might be a personal change, a change in the church, a change in our world, or some other change. We know we must walk by faith, and yet the temptation is to want to know what He is doing so we can put all our "ducks in a row." During those times in our lives, we hear that still small voice which says, "Walk by faith, not by sight." At the time I was studying to write this chapter, I was going through just such a monumental time in my own life. I sensed upheaval, I sensed change; I didn't know what God was doing, but I knew He was doing something. So I waited—not always as patiently as I should have—but I waited in faith, knowing that God had a plan that He would unfold in His time.

The blessed thing is that during times like this in our lives, we don't have to worry and fret! We have the assurance, as God's children, that we can come boldly to His throne of grace to find mercy in our time of need. We have the promise that He can do exceedingly abundantly above all that we ask or think! This, my friend, is a blessing beyond imagination. This is where we find ourselves in Paul's epistle to the Ephesians as we draw chapter three to a close. We have come to one of the most encouraging and thought-provoking prayers in the Word of God. We have come to Paul's second prayer for the church at Ephesus. Let's read this prayer together.

Ephesians 3:12-21

in whom we have boldness and access with confidence through faith in Him. [13]Therefore I ask that you do not lose heart at my tribulations for you, which is your glory. [14]For this reason I bow my knees to the Father of our Lord Jesus Christ, [15]from whom the whole family in heaven and earth is named, [16]that He would grant you, according to the riches of His glory, to be strengthened with might through His Spirit in the inner man, [17]that Christ may dwell in your hearts through faith; that you, being rooted and grounded in love, [18]may be able to comprehend with all the saints what is the width and length and depth and height— [19]to know the love of Christ which passes knowledge; that you may be filled with all the fullness of God. [20]Now to Him who is able to do exceedingly abundantly above all that we ask or think, according to the power that works in us, [21]to Him be glory in the church by Christ Jesus to all generations, forever and ever. Amen (Ephesians 3:12-21).

As we look at Paul's second prayer for the church at Ephesus, Paul will help us to see:

The Privilege of Prayer, (vv 12-13)

The Posture of Prayer, (vv 14-15)

Petitions of Prayer, (vv 16-19)

The Praise of Prayer, (vv 20-21)

Now, maybe you think it's odd that we're starting in verse 12, instead of verse 14, since verse 14 is actually where Paul's prayer begins. Paul does begin his actual prayer in verse 14, but he really starts in verse 12 with the theme of prayer, as he considers the wonderful access we have to prayer because of Christ. So let's begin in verse 12 as we consider the privilege we have in prayer.

Ephesians 3:12-13
The Privilege of Prayer

in whom we have boldness and access with confidence through faith in Him (Ephesians 3:12)

The words *in whom* go back to verse 11, where Paul mentions Christ Jesus our Lord. It is only through Him that we have boldness and access.[59] As Paul says in another place, Hebrews 4:14-

---

59 What is the sense of the genitive <u>autou</u>? (English, *in Him*) If this is a *subjective* genitive this would refer to Christ's faithfulness, i.e.,, "we have access and confidence by His faith." cf. Barth, Best, O'Brien, Wallace. If this is an *objective* genitive, as it appears to be, then it refers to the believer's faith, i.e.,, "we have access and confidence by faith

16, "Seeing then that we have a great High Priest who has passed through the heavens, Jesus the Son of God, let us hold fast our confession. For we do not have a High Priest who cannot sympathize with our weaknesses, but was in all points tempted as we are, yet without sin. Let us therefore come boldly to the throne of grace that we may obtain mercy and find grace to help in time of need." My dear sister, this is an amazing truth: we have access to the throne of God in prayer!

When Paul says we have *access* he is saying that we have admission. We are privileged to have access to talk to God. To have *boldness* means we have freedom of speech when we talk to God. This means we can speak to Him as we do to a friend. There is no fear, no shame, nothing to hide. We can come to Him openly and freely. This doesn't mean we can be free to say anything we please, because we still must be reverent when we pray. We are the inferior; He is the superior. We can be free, but we must not be flippant. We may speak boldly, but we may not be bossy! But, we can be candid, without fear of being ridiculed. And we do all this *with confidence through faith in Him*. This means we can trust fully in Him as we come to prayer. Of course, this is only because of our faith in Him. This is the only way we can approach His throne—by faith in Him. No one can approach God's throne without having genuine saving faith. This relationship with Christ is what gives us that access to Him. As John says in John 9:31, "Now we know that God does not hear sinners; but if anyone is a worshiper of God and does His will, He hears him." Paul now moves from writing about the privilege we have in asking God for things in prayer, to asking for something else in verse 13.

> Therefore I ask that you do not lose heart at my tribulations for you, which is your glory (Ephesians 3:13).

When Paul says *I ask*, he could be asking God that the church of Ephesus would not lose heart, or it could be that he is asking the believers of the church of Ephesus themselves not to lose heart. Remember, he had been in prison for about five years at this point, and they probably were losing heart, believing that Paul might not get out. They might have been concerned about his welfare, as well.

placed in Him." cf. Lincoln, Moule, Hoehner.

The fact that he has just mentioned the boldness and access that they have could be a reminder to them to take their needs to the throne of grace. Whether Paul is asking God that they don't lose heart or whether he is telling them to not lose heart, we cannot be sure, but we do know that to *lose heart* means to be discouraged. Paul is saying, "Don't be discouraged at my tribulations, my imprisonment, *which is your glory.*" This is why Paul is in prison—for them! Isn't it amazing that he doesn't complain about his lot in prison, but he sees it as for their glory?! Paul mentions this in 2 Timothy 2:10; he says, "Therefore I endure all things for the sake of the elect, that they also may obtain the salvation which is in Christ Jesus with eternal glory." Paul is reminding them that he is in prison for their behalf, for the cause of the gospel, which is ultimately for their benefit, their glory. And with that in mind, Paul moves to the actual prayer that he prays for his friends, and as he does he lets us know his posture in prayer in verse 14.

Ephesians 3:14-15
The Posture of Prayer

> For this reason I bow my knees to the Father of our Lord Jesus Christ, (Ephesians 3:14-15).

The first question that might come to mind as you read this is, what does Paul mean by saying *for this reason*? Some think he is continuing on from 3:1. That could be true, as we saw in our last lesson. Or he could be saying that because of the fact that we have boldness and access to the throne of grace he is bowing his knees in prayer for them.

When Paul says *I bow my knees*, it means he is bending the knees. This is interesting, because the normal posture of prayer for a Jew would be standing. Bowing the knee was a symbol of submission and adoration. I know in my own life when I have "bowed my knee" in prayer, I seem to have a different attitude than when I am sitting or standing to pray. My husband's mentor would only read God's word on his knees, as he felt reading God's Word should not be done casually. The Psalmist put it well in Psalm 95:6, "Oh come, let us worship and bow down; let us kneel before the LORD our Maker."

This kneeling was *to the Father*, or before the Father, which means it was face to face with the Father. The Father is the one that Jesus told His disciples to address their prayers to, in Luke 11:2: "When you pray, say: our Father in heaven, hallowed be Your name. Your kingdom come. Your will be done on earth as it is in heaven." This Father, Paul says, is not only the Father *of our Lord Jesus Christ*, but also of a whole family, as seen in verse 15.

> from whom the whole family in heaven and earth is named, (Ephesians 3:15).

The same Father who Paul has bowed his knee to, is also the head of the whole family. *The whole family in heaven and earth* would be every saint, those now in heaven and those that are still on earth. One man helps us here, "The Father, then, is Creator and Lord of all family groupings; their existence and significance is dependent on Him."[60]

Paul now begins his petitions for the church at Ephesus in verses 16-19, and what amazing petitions they are! There are five of them. Let's consider the first request, from verse 16.

Ephesians 3:16-19
The Petitions of Prayer

> that He would grant you, according to the riches of His glory, to be strengthened with might through His Spirit in the inner man, (Ephesians 3:16).

Paul's first request for them is that they would be strengthened in the inner man. Now before we get to the meaning of this, notice that Paul says He is asking God to do this *according to the riches of His glory*. This is truly an amazing statement, because God's riches are limitless. For example, I might give you some money out of what I have, but eventually my money will run out. God's riches, however, are endless; they never run out. That's why He is able to do exceedingly abundantly above all that we ask or think. His mercies, His grace, His glory, His answers to our prayers are limitless. Ladies, this is the awesome God to whom we bow our knees!

---

60 Lincoln, *Word Biblical Commentary*, 203.

With that amazing attribute, Paul prays that they would *be strengthened with might through His Spirit in the inner man.*[61] Paul is asking God to give them inner divine power and strength that would enable them to carry out their duties, endure trials, and walk in sanctification, all to the glory of God. Paul speaks of this in 2 Corinthians 4:16, where he says, "Therefore we do not lose heart. Even though our outward man is perishing, yet the inward man is being renewed day by day." This is a true statement for those of us in Christ, as we know our earthly bodies are dying daily, but our inner man is growing stronger daily—all by His mighty power! Paul goes on with yet another request in verse 17.

> that Christ may dwell in your hearts through faith; that you, being rooted and grounded in love, (Ephesians 3:17).

The second request Paul prays is that Christ would dwell in their hearts. Paul is asking that Christ would settle down and be at home in their hearts.[62] Now you might be wondering why Paul prays this prayer for them if they are believers. Paul is not praying that they would be saved, but that they would grow in their nearness to Christ, and have a growing awareness of His Lordship in their lives. Paul wants Christ *to dwell in their hearts* in a fuller way. He wants them to know His constant presence. In his booklet, *My Heart Christ's Home*, Robert Munger pictures the Christian life as a house, through which Jesus goes from room to room:

> "In the library, which is the mind, Jesus finds trash and all sorts of worthless things, which He proceeds to throw out and replace with His Word. In the dining

---

61 Hoehner outlines the prayer: the *request*: "that He may grant you ... to be strengthened ... in the inner person" (3:16); the *result*: so that Christ may dwell in your hearts"(3:17); the *purpose*: "you may be able to comprehend" (3:18); the *result*: "and so to know Christ's love" (3:19a); the *purpose*: "that you might be filled up to all the fullness of God" (3:19b). cf. Hoehner, 476.

62 The Greek term translated "dwell" is katoikeo, which suggests being at home or living comfortably in. This is more intensive than the synonym, oikeo, or the temporary form, paroikeo. The term katoikeo suggests both permanence and comfortable dwelling with. cf. Col. 1:19; 2:9. The sense is, as our inner man is strengthened, becoming strong, we sin less and less, with the Spirit controlling us more and more, such that Christ Himself is comfortable within us! He dwells in our hearts "by faith," which refers to the active sense of faithfulness. The Lord is at home in our heart as we are faithful to His Lordship, living in obedience to His Word and following the leading of the Spirit of God.

room of appetite He finds many sinful desires listed on a worldly menu. In the place of such things as prestige, materialism, and lust He puts humility, meekness, love, and all the other virtues for which believers are to hunger and thirst. He goes through the living room of fellowship, where He finds many worldly companions and activities, through the workshop, where only toys are being made, in the closet, where hidden sins are kept, and so on through the entire house. Only when He had cleaned every room, closet, and corner of sin and foolishness could He settle down and be at home."[63]

This is a good description of what Paul is asking the Father to do.

Paul's third request is that they would be rooted and grounded in love. Paul is praying that their love for God and love for others would be like roots that go deep in the earth. This is a love that cannot be shaken even in the midst of storms! Both words, *rooted* and *grounded*, have the idea of stability. As our foundation is rooted and grounded *in love* and upon the firm cornerstone of Christ, then we not only have a comprehension of His love for us, but we also are able to go through the fiercest of storms knowing that He is able to keep us stable, without shaking and crumbling. With this in mind, Paul goes on to yet another request for the church at Ephesus, that they

> may be able to comprehend with all the saints what is the width and length and depth and height— to know the love of Christ which passes knowledge; (Ephesians 3:18-19a).

Paul's fourth request for this church is that they would be able to comprehend with all saints the love of God. Comprehend means to lay hold of effectively or to grasp something. It was used in the biblical sense to refer to the Israelites capturing a city or an army. The dimensions, *width*, *length*, *depth* and *height* are unusual, as normally only three dimensions are mentioned. No one knows why Paul uses four dimensions, except that he is trying to describe

---

63 MacArthur, 107.

how vast and unimaginable God's love is. "Love goes in every direction and to the greatest distance. It goes wherever it is needed for as long as it is needed. The early church father, Jerome, said that 'the love of Christ reaches up to the holy angels and down to those in hell. Its length covers the men on the upward way and its breadth reaches those drifting away on evil paths.'" [64] As songwriter Frederick Lehman says, "The love of God is greater far than tongue or pen can ever tell. It goes beyond the highest star and reaches to the lowest hell."[65] It is so vast we cannot comprehend it. That's the point.

This love of God is not only vast but it also *passes knowledge*. Now this might seem like a paradox or a contradiction, as Paul prays they would *know the love of Christ*, but then he says that it passes knowledge, that it can't be understood. Just because God's love goes beyond our understanding of it, Paul still prays that we would comprehend it. The love of Christ is something that is so great that we will never fully understand the extent of it. When you think that Christ died for you while you were dead in your sins, when you think that God so loved the world that He gave His only begotten Son, can you understand that kind of love? I can't! As Paul says, "For scarcely for a righteous man will one die; yet perhaps for a good man someone would even dare to die. But God demonstrates His own love toward us, in that while we were still sinners, Christ died for us" (Romans 5:7-8).

> that you may be filled with all the fullness of God (Ephesians 3:19b).

Paul gives yet another request for the Ephesians believers. *His fifth request is that they would be filled with all the fullness of God.* The word *fullness* means total dominance. "A person filled with rage is totally dominated by hatred. A person filled with happiness is totally dominated by joy. To be filled up to all the fullness of God therefore means to be totally dominated by Him with nothing left of self or any part of the old man. By definition, then, to be filled with God is to be emptied of self. It is not to have much of God and little of self, but all of God and none of self."[66]

---

64 Ibid., 110.
65 *The Love of God*, 1917.
66 Ibid., 112.

You might be wondering "How in the world can all these requests really be answered? Am I able to be strengthened in my inner man? How can Christ be at home in my heart? Am I able to be rooted and grounded in love? Can I possibly comprehend the love of God and be filled with all of His fullness?" Paul answers these questions as he comes to the final portion of his prayer. God is able to do above what you think!

Ephesians 3:20-21
The Praise of Prayer

> Now to Him who is able to do exceedingly abundantly above all that we ask or think, according to the power that works in us, (Ephesians 3:20).

God *is able to do exceedingly abundantly above all* that we could ever *ask or think* when it comes to answering our prayers. He is able to do all of these things and more! He is able to answer all of Paul's requests, and all of yours, and all of the saints' requests around the entire world. He is able! And He does this *according to the power that works in us*. What does this mean? This does not mean we can muster up some inner strength to do this; the power *in us* is the Holy Spirit. He is the one working dynamite power in us to do the unimaginable. The Spirit not only helps us in our praying, as seen in Romans 8:26, "Likewise the Spirit also helps in our weaknesses. For we do not know what we should pray for as we ought, but the Spirit Himself makes intercession for us with groanings which cannot be uttered," but He also gives us that inner strength to carry out those things we must do. As Paul says in Galatians 5:22-25, "the fruit of the Spirit is love, joy, peace, longsuffering, kindness, goodness, faithfulness, gentleness, self-control. Against such there is no law. And those who are Christ's have crucified the flesh with its passions and desires. If we live in the Spirit, let us also walk in the Spirit." Paul ends this great prayer with a praise to the only One who is worthy of praise!

> to Him be glory in the church by Christ Jesus to all generations, forever and ever. Amen (Ephesians 3:21).

Paul ends with a desire that God be glorified, not us, not Paul, not even the saints at Ephesus. He says, *to Him be glory*. God alone is to receive the glory. God's glory *in the church* means that we should manifest the glory of God as His bride, the church. As the believers at Ephesus, and as you and I, live out our lives as an answer to these requests, then God through His church *to all generations* receives glory, *forever and ever*. Amen! You might wonder why Paul says *amen* when he's not finished with the letter. It was customary for Paul to use the term amen when praising God for something, as you will see when you answer the Questions to Consider following this chapter. Amen also is used here as it closes Paul's prayer and closes the doctrinal section of Ephesians. Maybe you are saying "Amen!" right now, as well. Don't worry, my friends; the last three chapters of Ephesians will move on to the practical application of all that Paul has taught us in these first three chapters of Ephesians.

Summary

Paul's second prayer for the church at Ephesus is a glorious one. In it, we have seen, first, *The Privilege of Prayer*, (vv 12-13). My dear sister, do you realize what a privilege it is that you and I have been granted access to the Savior of our soul? We can pray with boldness and frankness, and we can come anytime to talk to Him. He is never too busy, and He never puts us on hold or calls us back later. He does not have a recording to listen to, which says, "For prayer requests, press 1. For praises, press 2. For emergencies, call Me back tomorrow." He is available always!

Second, we have seen Paul's *Posture in Prayer*, (vv 14-15). His posture is kneeling. When is the last time you got on your knees to pray? Even if you don't get on your knees to pray, when you pray, is your heart bowed in humble submission?

Third, we have seen Paul's *Petitions of Prayer*, (vv 16-19). There are five of them. I find it amazing that Paul prays for his friends and not for himself, especially considering that he also is going through times of upheaval. Roman imprisonment was not a pleasant experience. Being chained to a Roman soldier 24/7 was no small matter. Waiting to see if you are going to be beheaded is not exactly something any of us would relish waiting for. And yet, the apostle Paul uses this time to pray, and he prays not for himself, but for the church.

Paul's first petition for them is that they would be strengthened in the inner man. How's your inner woman today in the spiritual sense? Are you stronger today spiritually than you were a year ago?

The second petition of Paul's prayer is that Christ would dwell in their hearts. Is Christ at home in your heart? Do you have some hidden secret in a room of your heart of which you need to repent? Can you welcome Christ as a guest in every room of your heart?

Paul's third petition is that they would be rooted and grounded in love. Do you love God and others, no matter what is going on in your life? How does it manifest itself? Is your love strong for God and others even when you are in distressing times?

Paul's fourth petition is that they would be able to comprehend with all saints the love of God. Do you think about the love of God? How has it changed your life this week?

The fifth petition Paul makes is that they would be filled with all the fullness of God. Are you full of yourself or are you full of God?

Lastly, we saw the *Praise of Prayer*, (vv 20-21). Oh, dear sister, our God is able to do exceedingly abundantly above all that we could ever ask and think! Do you believe that? Have you experienced that in your life? He does this in our lives on a consistent basis, not for some momentary pleasure for ourselves, but for His glory, both now and forevermore! Amen!

Questions to Consider

Paul's Second Prayer for the Church at Ephesus
Ephesians 3:12-21

1. (a) Read Ephesians 3:12-21. Do you think Paul literally bowed his knees, or do you think he is using a metaphor? (b) Who else in Scripture bowed their knees when praying? See 1 Kings 8:54; Ezra 9:5; Daniel 6:10; Luke 22:41; Acts 7:60; 9:40; 20:36. (You may need to look before or after these verses to discover who it is.) (c) What do these verses tell you about kneeling when praying? (d) Memorize Ephesians 3:20-21.

2. (a) Read Paul's first prayer for the church at Ephesus in Ephesians 1:15-21 and his second prayer for the church at Ephesus in Ephesians 3:12-21. What things do you notice that are the same in these two prayers? What things are different? (b) Why do you think Paul prays two different prayers for the church at Ephesus?

3. Paul ends chapter three of Ephesians with the word "Amen," and yet he is not finished with the letter. Why do you think this is so? (Reading over these other verses Paul writes in other letters may help in answering this question: Romans 1:25; 9:5; 11:36; 15:33; 16:20; 16:24; 2 Corinthians 1:20; Galatians 1:5; Philippians 4:20; 1 Timothy 1:17; 6:16; 2 Timothy 4:18; Hebrews 13:21.)

4. Paul mentions in Ephesians 3:20 that God is able to do exceeding abundantly above all that we ask or think. Recall a time in your life when this was true and be ready to share with your group.

5. (a) Take some time this week and pray Paul's prayer from Ephesians 3 for someone other than yourself. What blessing(s) did you receive? (b) Which verse from Paul's prayer in Ephesians 3 is the most encouraging to you and why?

6. Take one request from Paul's prayer for the church at Ephesus and write a prayer for yourself.

Chapter 10

The Believer's Conduct in Light of Their Calling

Ephesians 4:1-6

The Lord has been very gracious to me the past several years as I've had the privilege of traveling around the world to speak to women about His Word. It is an awesome responsibility and a great blessing. Not long ago, I returned from a three week speaking marathon and was overjoyed at His mercy. In all honestly, however, I was also disheartened by one particular conversation I overheard at one of the conferences. I listened as a speaker was trying to impress his peers with his accomplishments. I heard things like, "You've never heard of me?" and, "I just spoke at such and such a conference—you've never heard of that conference?" and, "Well, maybe you know so and so; I travel with them from time to time." As I listened, I became very upset in my spirit. Is this the heart of someone who has been called to serve their Lord? Are these the words to be spoken (and even thought of) by someone who has been chosen as God's adopted child? Is this how we are to conduct ourselves as those who have been called by God? I think not. And we will see that the apostle Paul has something a little different to tell us in this lesson. Let's consider what Paul has to say as he writes to the church at Ephesus.

Ephesians 4:1-6

I, therefore, the prisoner of the Lord, beseech you to walk worthy of the calling with which you were called, [2]with all lowliness and gentleness, with longsuffering, bearing with one another in love, [3]endeavoring to keep the unity of the Spirit in the bond of peace. [4]There is one body and one Spirit, just as you were called in one hope of your calling; [5]one Lord, one faith, one baptism; [6]one God and Father of all, who is above all, and through all, and in you all (Ephesians 4:1-6).

We are beginning the practical section of Ephesians as we start studying chapter four of this epistle. Now that Paul has covered the doctrinal portion of the book, now that he has set the foundation of our faith, he begins to write about how we live out that doctrine, how we live out our faith. This is obvious by the use of the imperatives, or commands, that Paul uses in these final three chapters of his epistle.[67] As citizens of God's household who have been adopted into His family we must behave a certain way. For those who are predestined and chosen before the foundation of the world to receive an eternal inheritance, we must act in accordance with our calling.

We now begin the important and vital section on how to conduct ourselves in this life. As we study this portion in chapter four of Ephesians, we will consider the believer's conduct in light of their calling, with:

The Request to Walk Worthy, (v 1);

The Right Way to Walk Worthy, (vv 2-3);

The Reason to Walk Worthy, (vv 4-6).

Let's look at Paul's request for the Ephesians believers to walk worthy in verse 1.

Ephesians 4:1
The Request to Walk Worthy

I, therefore, the prisoner of the Lord, beseech you to walk worthy of the calling with which you were called, (Ephesians 4:1).

Paul beings chapter four in the same way he began chapter

---

67 Harold Hoehner helpfully points out: "This division of doctrine and duty is substantiated statistically in the use of the imperative. The imperative is used sixty-two times in Romans: only thirteen times in chapters 1-11 and forty-one times in chapters 12-16 (though fifteen times with reference to greetings in chap. 16) In Ephesians the imperative is used forty-one times: only once in chapters 1-3 (2:11) and forty times in the last three chapters." (Hoehner, 499).

three, by calling himself *the prisoner of the Lord*. In chapter three he calls himself a prisoner of Jesus Christ, and here in chapter four he calls himself a prisoner of the Lord. It is worth mentioning that in both instances Paul makes clear that he knows God put him there in prison. His imprisonment was not by chance! What a difference this kind of mindset makes as we view our trials, as we see them as being from God! There is a purpose to our trials when we view them from that perspective! Paul says he is a *prisoner of the Lord*, which means in the Lord's service. Oh, that we might have that mindset as we go through life! Whatever our lot is, wherever we are, we are in the Lord's service. We should not stop ministering to the body of Christ just because things are a little tough for us. It always amazes me when Christians vacate church and ministry while they're going through trials. What a blessing they miss out on by not continuing to serve and see the grace of God abundantly at work in their lives.

Paul, however, leaves us an exemplary example. As a prisoner of the Lord, he doesn't beg the Ephesian believers to have sympathy for his sad lot in life. Instead, he begs them to walk worthy of the calling with which they have been called. He thinks of them, not of himself. The word *beseech* means to exhort. It has the idea of begging someone for something, more than simply requesting it. What is Paul exhorting them to do? To *walk worthy of the calling* with which they were called. To *walk* would mean a life style or a way in which one conducts himself. The metaphor of walking speaks of one's daily conduct, or day-by-day living, as it progresses.[68] *Worthy* means to balance the scales; it would pertain to something equal in weight. So then, if we are to walk worthy, it means that our walk should balance or be equal to our calling in Christ. We might say, "Walk your talk!" So, what exactly does Paul mean when he says

---

68 The NIV translates, *live,* which unfortunately fails to suggest progress. To *live* simply suggests existing but to *walk* suggests progress while existing. Martyn Lloyd-Jones comments: "The fact that the Christian life is described as a walk is significant. Walk suggests activity, movement, and progress. We are to walk worthy of our vocation. We do not stay where we were or as we are; we do not say, 'Ah, now I am saved, my sins are forgiven, all is well,' and spend the rest of our lives talking about our conversion, always looking back and remaining in that position. The Christian life is one of progress, of ever going forward; there are always fresh things to be discovered and fresh experiences to be enjoyed." cf. D. M. Lloyd-Jones, *Christian Unity* (Grand Rapids: Baker Book House, 1980), 34.

that we are to walk worthy of the calling with which we have been called? We have already seen Paul set forth in the first three chapters of Ephesians that we have been chosen before the foundation of the world, in order that we might be holy and blameless before Him. God called us—that is true—but He called us to be His sons and daughters, and as His children we must behave in accordance with our calling. We must walk and imitate God, who has called us and saved us. You might be asking, "But, what does that look like? How do I walk worthy?" Paul answers that question in verses 2 and 3, and he mentions five ways that we can walk worthy.

Ephesians 4:2-3
The Right Way to Walk Worthy

> with all lowliness and gentleness, with longsuffering, bearing
> with one another in love, (Ephesians 4:2)

The first way in which we are to walk worthy is with all lowliness. What does it mean to be lowly? The term *lowliness* is a word that means to judge or think with humility of mind. Our English word humility is a synonym, and this is a fundamental virtue of Christians.[69] Humility, or lowliness of mind, is a low estimate of ourselves, a consciousness of our guilt, being aware of our unworthiness, and realizing our weakness or frailty. In Romans 12:16, we see the opposite of this term, when Paul says, "Do not set your mind on high things, but associate with the humble." It is, "that profound humility which stands at the extremist distance from haughtiness, arrogance, and conceit, and which is produced by a right view of ourselves, and of our relation to Christ and to that glory to which we are called."[70] It is the opposite of arrogance and pride. A humble woman is someone who does not promote herself like the individual I mentioned in my introduction. Humility was a virtue that the Greeks did not seek. They thought of it as a weakness. Our world today is no different, as we see people today who promote

---

69 Neither the early Greeks nor the Romans during NT times had a term for *humility*, as the concept was depreciated in their thought. The term tapeinophrosune, as far as we can understand was coined by Christians and perhaps Paul himself, for it is only used by him in the NT. cf. Acts 20:19; Phil. 2:3. No other Christian virtue is as foreign to worldly humanism as this! cf. Matt. 5:3; 11:29-30; 18:3-4; James 4:6 compare with Isa. 2:11; 3:16-26; Jer. 50:31-32; Mal. 4:1; Prov. 11:2; 16:18; 21:4.

70 Eadie, 268.

themselves, their accomplishments, their possessions, their kids, and just about anything that involves them. It's sad to say, but we see this even in the church. I have been in churches that boast of their numbers, how many attend, how many got saved, how many people they witnessed to that week, how much they have done for the Lord, and so on. All this is, of course, done under the guise of spirituality, but it is nothing more than spiritual pride. My friend, we must be so careful, as pride faces us every day and sometimes every waking hour. And before we know it, we are enslaved to pride. Of course, if not kept in check, the next step is destruction, as wise Solomon tells us in Proverbs 16:18-19: "Pride goes before destruction and a haughty spirit before a fall. Better to be of a humble spirit with the lowly, than to divide the spoil with the proud." In fact, it is one of the seven things God hates the most, according to Proverbs 6:16-19.

As a child who has been called by God, we must not just be humble; we must clothe ourselves in humility. Peter tells us in 1 Peter 5:5, "all of you be submissive to one another, and be clothed in humility." The word clothed there means a knot or roll of cloth that was tucked up under any part of one's dress. Peter, more than likely, had the account of John 13 in mind, during which Christ took a towel and girded Himself, readying Himself to wash the disciples' feet. Jesus was at that moment in the position of a servant. He was "clothed in humility." Peter probably never forgot this act of humility from His Lord, especially since Peter himself was the one with all the objections while Jesus humbly went about washing the disciples' feet. We must, as Christians, clothe ourselves in humility. In fact, it was said that the early Christians actually sold themselves as slaves so that they might be able to preach the gospel to those who were in bondage. Now ladies, that's humility! We must ask ourselves, "Instead of promoting myself, am I willing to do the most mundane task for the glory of God?"

The second way Paul says we are to walk is with gentleness. What does it mean to walk with *gentleness*, or meekness, as some translations read? Meekness, or gentleness, means self-control. It was a word that was used of wild animals that were broken and trained, thus becoming tame. Trained animals still have spirit and strength, but they are under the control of someone else. They have strength under control. Meekness is not weakness. A person who is meek or gentle can become righteously angry but doesn't become sinfully angry. It is interesting to consider that a humble person is a meek person. Jesus said this about Himself, in Matthew 11:29: "Take My yoke upon you and learn from Me, for I am gentle and lowly in heart, and you will find rest for your souls." Also, meekness is an attribute that we as women should possess, as Peter points out in 1 Peter 3:4, where he calls us to demonstrate the "incorruptible beauty of a gentle and quiet spirit." Now ladies, this does not mean you are to be a mouse in regards to your relationships, but you are to be a woman who has strength under control. This characteristic of a Christian is a sign that they are genuine in their faith, according to Galatians 5:22-23: "But the fruit of the Spirit is love, joy, peace, longsuffering, kindness, goodness, faithfulness, gentleness, self-control. Against such there is no law."

The third way Paul says we are to walk as God's chosen people is to be longsuffering. Again, someone who is humble and meek will also be longsuffering. What does it mean to be longsuffering? The word has the idea of being patient. This person endures difficult people and difficult circumstances and does not give in to sinful responses.

> When H. M. Stanley went to Africa in 1871 to find and report on David Livingstone, he spent several months in the missionary's company, carefully observing the man and his work. Livingstone never spoke to Stanley about spiritual matters, but Livingstone's loving and patient compassion for the African people was beyond Stanley's comprehension. He could not understand how the missionary could have such love for and patience with the backward, pagan people among whom he had so long ministered. Livingstone literally spent himself in untiring service for those whom he had no reason to love except for Christ's sake. Stanley wrote in his journal, "When I saw that unwearied patience, that unflagging zeal, and those enlightened sons of Africa, I became a Christian at his side, though he never spoke to me one word."[71]

---

71 MacArthur, 127.

The fourth way Paul says we are to conduct ourselves as God's daughters is by bearing with one another in love. What does it mean to bear with each other in love? *Bearing* means to hold up, to put up with one another. We must be willing to put up with others who are not like us. People have different ideas about how to do things, and we should be okay with that. They might dress differently than we do, use their time differently than we do, decorate their house and cook differently than we do, and a myriad of other things. But we must not let those "quirks" irritate us and cause us to not be Christlike. I once heard someone say, "To dwell above with saints we love, that will be grace and glory. To live below with the saints we know, now that's another story." I think, as a married woman, this might be the quality that is most tested in me. When God brings two people together in marriage, He must desire that we work on this virtue. In regards to my own marriage, I don't know of two people who are more different than my husband and me. And yet, God has used the differences in my husband and me to sanctify me and grow me up in this area of forbearance. For example, I am a neat freak; my husband is not. He loves golf; I do not. I love to be outside; he does not. He loves crowds and big parties; I do not. I love Mexican food; he does not. I like quiet; he likes noise. I sleep soundly almost every night; he is up often during the night and rarely sleeps an entire night. I could spend the rest of this lesson sharing our differences with you, but it is what we have in common that is important. Thankfully, my husband and I both love the Lord, the church, God's Word, and our kids and our grandkids, which are really the most important things. There is a fifth way Paul says we are to walk worthy, and he mentions it in verse 3.

> endeavoring to keep the unity of the Spirit in the bond of peace (Ephesians 4:3).

Unity is the fifth way in which Paul begs the Ephesians, and us, to walk. Endeavoring means to make every effort. Paul says we are to make every effort to have unity. What does it mean *to keep the unity of the Spirit in the bond of peace*? It means we guard or hold fast the unity we have as followers of the Lord Jesus Christ. Notice, we are not commanded to create this unity but to preserve it. In answer to Christ's prayer in John 17:20-23, God the Father has placed believers into a vital unity with one another.[72] And we must make every effort to live in that peace with each other. If we will practice the first four virtues he mentions—humility, gentleness, longsuffering and forbearance—then we will, more than likely, be unified as Christians. "Humility gives birth to gentleness, gentleness gives birth to patience, patience gives birth to forbearing love, and all four of those characteristics preserve the unity of the Spirit in the bond of peace. These virtues and the supernatural unity to which they testify are probably the most powerful testimony the church can have, because they are in such contrast to the attitudes and the disunity of the world."[73]

Endeavoring to preserve unity is an imperative virtue that we must possess as Christians, as Jesus prays for it four times in the High Priestly Prayer in John 17. Now, there are times when it is not possible, as Paul says in Romans 12:18: "If it is possible, as much as depends on you, live peaceably with all men." I have seen this fail more than once, but it should always be our goal to make every effort—until we have exhausted every effort—to be at peace and to be unified. Of course, it goes without saying that we cannot sacrifice truth for unity; truth must always prevail. Paul now gives the reasons why we are to walk worthy in verses 4-6, and there are seven of them.

Ephesians 4:4-6
The Reason to Walk Worthy

> There is one body and one Spirit, just as you were called in one hope of your calling; (Ephesians 4:4).

Paul uses the word *one* seven times in this passage, to emphasize the importance of the theme of unity. We are to conduct ourselves in this way because we are one; we are to be united. This is why Paul puts the word one before each of the seven concepts of

---

72 The Achilles heal of the modern *ecumenical movement* is found in Ephesians 4:1-6, which confirms a vital unity of all believers regardless of outward ecclesiastical divisions. Outward unity at the expense of ignoring doctrinal essentials is foreign to Scriptural teaching, which has given rise to just criticism of the World Council of Churches, the Charismatic movements and the recent so called *Evangelical and Catholic Accord* and the *Promise Keepers* movement.

73 MacArthur, 128-129.

unity. Also, on a note of interest, the number seven is the number of perfection in the Bible, so it goes without saying that Paul through the Holy Spirit is stressing unity.

The first reason for our unity is that there is <u>one body</u>. There are not several bodies; there is one body. All who are called by God are in one body. Obviously, this speaks of the church throughout the world and throughout the ages.[74] The metaphor of a body is a favorite of the apostle Paul, and it speaks of the essential unity of all believers in one living organism, though there are many distinct parts and functions.[75] Paul also puts it this way in Galatians 3:28: "There is neither Jew nor Greek, there is neither slave nor free, there is neither male nor female; for you are all one in Christ Jesus." When you think about this amazing truth, there should be no cause for division among those who are going to live together in harmony forever!

The second reason for our unity is that there is <u>one Spirit</u>. There is only one Holy Spirit, and He is the only one who is in us. He is the one who seals us; He is the one who is the earnest of our inheritance; He is the one we are to be filled with; He is the one we grieve or quench; but He is the only one. This is certainly imperative in our day, as there are many spirits out there, but they are not holy. Some time ago, we had a young man visit our church, and after one of the services he came and told my husband that the Lord had given him a revelation during the church service that we had two people in our congregation with back and arthritic issues. My husband looked him square in the face and said, "You know that is not true and that you are trying to impress me and others." He also called him out on his sinful life, knowing that this young man's life was engrossed in

---

74 There is a purposeful abruptness to each of these seven unites, as the expected particle *for* (Greek, <u>gar</u>) is omitted. Normally we would expect it, i.e., "keep the unity of the Spirit... *for* there is one body, *for* there is one Spirit, *for* there is one hope," etc. The sense is emphatic without the particle, i.e.,, "keep the unity of the Spirit: there is one body; there is one Spirit; there is one hope," etc. cf. Abbott, 107-8.

75 The Apostle Paul uses <u>soma</u> 68 times in his epistles, mostly in the literal sense. Those passages that contribute to the *metaphor* of the church body (either universal of local) include: Rom. 12:4-5; 1 Cor. 10:16-17; 12:12-29; Eph. 1:23; 2:16; 3:6; 4:4; 4:12-16; Col. 1:18; 2:17-19; 3:15. Some debate exists of <u>soma</u> in Ephesians 5:23 and 30, which will be considered in the exposition of those passages.

sin. Ladies, this is not what Paul is talking about. There is one Spirit and He is holy! And because He is holy, the work He does is holy in nature, and it promotes holiness and unity.

The third reason for our unity is that there is <u>one hope of our calling</u>. *One hope* refers to our future hope in heaven. Today, the hope of heaven and the reality of hell are not popular topics. Some people will even tell you that we are annihilated when we die, or that we are reincarnated, or that there is no hell. I am confident that when these people die, they will find that not to be true! There is one hope, my dear friend, and it is heaven, and those who are called by God will be there! In this life, as believers, we might hope for the earthly, temporal joys of a raise, a child, a new car, or a husband. This can cause strife, jealousy and even anger within us. But as Christians we can have unity as we pursue the one hope we all have in common, the hope of heaven. Paul continues on in verse 5 with three more reasons for unity.

> one Lord, one faith, one baptism; (Ephesians 4:5).

The fourth reason for our unity is that there is <u>one Lord</u>. Deuteronomy 6:4 says "Hear, O Israel: The LORD our God, the LORD is one!" This was quoted by the Jews often, and we would do well to remind ourselves of it as well. Since those who are called by God have one Master, the Lord Jesus Christ, it motivates us to be unified, knowing that we will all one day give an account to that one Lord for the things we have done in our body, whether good or bad. The New Testament gives specific emphasis to the issue of the Lordship of Jesus Christ, who is our sovereign Master and to whom we pledge the allegiance of commitment. This concept of Jesus' Lordship is essentially twofold: ownership and sovereignty. He owns us as His possession, and this means that He is our sovereign Master. There is no other! (See Acts 4:12; Galatians 1:8; and Romans 10:12.) As believers, we should guard the unity which is produced by the Spirit of God, because we share in a common allegiance to the Lord Jesus Christ, in contrast to the other lords of this world, like self, Satan, idols or false gods.[76]

---

76 The debate of *Lordship salvation* among dispensational evangelicals would be non-sense to the early church. New Testament Christianity knows nothing about an optional commitment to the Lordship of Christ. This foundation to unity Paul assumes would be

The fifth reason for our unity is that there is <u>one faith</u>. Some think the phrase *one faith* is referring to our faith, or our salvation. This is certainly true; Jesus made it clear in John 14:6, "I am the way, the truth, and the life. No one comes to the Father except through Me." There are not many ways to heaven, but one: faith in Christ alone. Today, we have many things or persons or gods we could potentially put our faith in. But there is truly only one faith, and that faith is in the Lord Jesus Christ. Others think that the term *faith*, here, is referring to doctrine. In other words, there is one interpretation of truth. This is also true; there is only one truth. And we can see how one faith in that sense promotes unity, as various doctrinal positions have the potential to divide us. I know of people who are divided over eschatology, soteriology, pneumology, etc. Some are Calvinists, while others are Arminians. Some hold to dispensational theology; some hold to covenant theology. But there can only be one right interpretation of God's Word. As we study to show ourselves approved unto God, rightly dividing the Word of truth, then we will endeavor to come to agreement on the truth of God's Word, thus promoting unity.

There is a sixth reason for our unity and that is that there is <u>one baptism</u>. This is in reference to a believer's *baptism*, and not the baptism of the Holy Spirit, because Paul has already mentioned that there is one Spirit. In Paul's day, water baptism was performed immediately upon one's profession of faith in the Lord Jesus Christ, as identification that one had become a part of the family of faith. Baptism is a sign of unity, as the act of baptism itself is something that all of God's children have in common. Our baptism is a sign of our unity with Christ and with each other. There is one more important reason for unity and this is the seventh one Paul mentions in verse 6.

> one God and Father of all, who is above all, and through all, and in you all (Ephesians 4:6).

The seventh reason for our unity is that there is <u>one God</u>. Paul

---

an axiom to all the believers at Ephesus.

says in 1 Corinthians 8:6, "yet for us there is one God, the Father, of whom are all things, and we for Him; and one Lord Jesus Christ, through whom are all things, and through whom we live." Albert Barnes helps us here. "People who worship many gods cannot hope to be united. Their affections are directed to different objects, and there is no harmony or sympathy of feeling. But where there is one supreme object of attachment there may be expected to be unity. The children of a family that are devoted to a parent will be united among themselves; and the fact that all Christians have the same great object of worship should constitute a strong bond of union among themselves—a chain always kept bright."[77]

Paul ends by saying this *God* is the *Father of all*, and He is *above all, and through all, and in you all*. This is similar to what Paul said in Ephesians 1:21-23: "far above all principality and power and might and dominion, and every name that is named, not only in this age but also in that which is to come. And He put all things under His feet, and gave Him to be head over all things to the church, which is His body, the fullness of Him who fills all in all." He is *above all* things as sovereign ruler; He is *through all* things as He accomplishes His purposes through all His creation; and He is *in you all*, as He indwells all of His children whom He has called.

Summary

The Request to Walk Worthy, (v 1): Paul exhorts the church to walk worthy of their calling. Are you walking worthy of your calling? Would others look at your life and have no question as to the fact that you are imitating the Lord Jesus Christ? Are you the same at home as you are at church or at ladies' Bible study?

The Right Way to Walk Worthy, (vv 2-3): Paul gives us five ways to walk worthy—humility, gentleness, longsuffering, bearing with others, and pursuing unity with one another. Are these virtues present in your life today? Do you think you are something special? Do you offer to do mundane tasks like clean the church, work in the nursery, cook a meal for someone, babysit for a weary mom, or do you think those tasks are beneath you? Are you gentle in your tone

---

77 Barnes, 75.

of voice and even in your thoughts? Are you forbearing with others, and are you longsuffering in difficult circumstances?

The Reason to Walk Worthy, (vv 4-6): Paul gives us seven reasons why we must walk worthy, and they all have to do with unity. There is one body, one Spirit, one hope, one Lord, one faith, one baptism, one God and Father. Do you believe in and do you adhere to these doctrines? How has it aided in your unity with the brethren? Do you have an open mind to truth or are you so set in your theological viewpoints that you think that those who do not believe exactly like you do are crazy?

I exhort you, dear sister, to walk worthy of the one who has called you! As you do, you promote unity in the body of Jesus Christ and please our God and Father, our Master who is in heavenly places!

Questions to Consider

The Believer's Conduct in Light of Their Calling
Ephesians 4:1-6

1. (a) According to Ephesians 4:1-6, what are the virtues God's children should possess? (b) Why do you think Paul emphasizes the word "one" (actually seven times) in these verses? (c) Memorize Ephesians 4:1.

2. (a) In Ephesians 4:1-6, Paul lists several ways in which we can walk worthy of our calling. According to the following verses, what are some other ways we can conduct our Christian walk in a manner worthy of our calling? Romans 12:1-2; Romans 13:13; Colossians 1:10; Colossians 2:6-7; 1 Thessalonians 4:1-7. (b) What other ways do you think believers can walk worthy of their calling?

3. (a) Numbers 12:3 records for us that Moses was the meekest man on the earth (at that time). From the facts you already know about Moses (or from facts you can look up), why do you think this is true?

4. (a) Who in Scripture comes to your mind as someone who was longsuffering (besides the Lord) and what do you learn from his or her life? (b) Who do you know that is living today who is an example of being longsuffering, and what do you learn from his or her example?

5. Would you say your life is being conducted in the manner that Paul speaks of in Ephesians 4:2-3? Is there something that you need to change in order to be conformed to Christ's image? The following questions might be helpful in deciding what you need to change: Are you quick to get angry? If so, then you need to work on patience. Are you proud or boastful? If so, then you need to work on humility. Are you bossy and rough with your words? If so, then you need to work on being gentile. Are you intolerant of other's shortcomings? If so, then you need to work on bearing with others in love. (These are all private questions to answer.)

6. After considering question 6, write a prayer request to be shared with your group.

Chapter 11

The Structure and Purpose of the Body of Christ

Ephesians 4:7-16

The human body is made up of a head, neck, torso, two arms and two legs. The body also has 100 trillion cells, 206 bones, 600 muscles and 22 internal organs. Every square inch of the human body is covered in about 19 million skin cells, and every hour about 1 billion cells in our bodies must be replaced. Within our bodies there is a circulatory system, a respiratory system, an immune system, a skeletal system, a urinary system, an excretory system, a muscular system, an endocrine system, a digestive system, a nervous system and a reproductive system. The skeletal system has 206 bones that protect the organs and help give the body shape. The nervous system is like an information system that controls everything a person does, like walking, breathing, thinking and more. The muscular system helps with movement and posture. The immune system helps to protect the body from pathogens, like viruses, bacteria, or any other foreign thing that may try to hurt the body. The cardiovascular system includes the heart, blood vessels and blood. It delivers nutrients to the cells and removes waste. The digestive system breaks down food and absorbs nutrients so that the body has energy. The urinary system consists of the kidneys, bladder and urethra, which all work together to get rid of waste and excess fluid. The respiratory system helps the body to breathe. It's made up of the trachea, lungs and diaphragm. The endocrine system keeps the body growing, developing and working the way it's supposed to. Its glands are found throughout the body and regulate our hormones. And the brain is like the "boss" of the entire body. It controls movement, sleep, hunger, thirst and virtually every other vital activity necessary to survive. It is connected to all the main organs in the body. No part of the human body works in isolation; each part does it job, day and night, supported and aided by all the other parts.

You might be wondering if this is a lesson on the human body, and the answer is "no." But it is a lesson on the spiritual body. You see, our physical body is much like our spiritual body. There is a head, Christ, and there is a body, which is made up of all those Christ has redeemed. Each one of us has a part in Christ's body, and if we don't do our part then the whole body doesn't function properly. What is the structure and purpose of the body of Christ? Well, Paul gives us a glimpse of this as we look into our text for this lesson.

Ephesians 4:7-16

> But to each one of us grace was given according to the measure of Christ's gift. [8]Therefore He says: "When He ascended on high, he led captivity captive, and gave gifts to men." [9](Now this, "He ascended"—what does it mean but that He also first descended into the lower parts of the earth? [10]He who descended is also the One who ascended far above all the heavens, that He might fill all things.) [11]And He Himself gave some to be apostles, some prophets, some evangelists, and some pastors and teachers, [12]for the equipping of the saints for the work of ministry, for the edifying of the body of Christ, [13]till we all come to the unity of the faith and of the knowledge of the Son of God, to a perfect man, to the measure of the stature of the fullness of Christ; [14]that we should no longer be children, tossed to and fro and carried about with every wind of doctrine, by the trickery of men, in the cunning craftiness of deceitful plotting, [15]but, speaking the truth in love, may grow up in all things into Him who is the head—Christ—[16]from whom the whole body, joined and knit together by what every joint supplies, according to the effective working by which every part does its share, causes growth of the body for the edifying of itself in love (Ephesians 4:7-16).

In our last lesson we learned about the believer's conduct in light of their calling. In this lesson, as we consider the structure and purpose of the church, our outline will include:

Words from Paul (vv 8-10)

Gifts from God (vv 7, 11)

Motivational Reasons to Serve (vv 12-16)

In our last lesson, we learned that Paul said there is one body (Ephesians 4:4). That one body, however, is made up of many individuals, and Paul tells us that we each have a role in that body, in verse 7.

Ephesians 4:7, 11
Marvelous Gifts from God

> But to each one of us grace was given according to the measure of Christ's gift (Ephesians 4:7).

Paul has been talking about the overall theme of unity in the body of Christ. But in our unity there is diversity of people and gifts. Just as the human body is made up of many parts which have different functions, so the spiritual body is made up of many individuals with different functions that make the body work together properly. *Each one of us*, each individual member of God's church, has been given at least one spiritual gift. The word *us* includes Paul, as well. I, for one, am glad that God gifted Paul the way He did, or we wouldn't have all of his letters to study! We not only have been given a gift, but also we have been given *grace ... according to the measure of Christ's gift*. What does Paul mean by this? Paul is saying that God gives *grace* to each of His children as it pertains to the spiritual *gift* or gifts He gives them. In other words, He equips us and enables us to use the gift He has given us to carry out His purposes. I have seen this in my own life. People ask, "How do you do all you do?" I don't! And that's the point. God does it in me. That's the way it is for each of us. We don't all have the same gifts, nor do we have the same measure of grace for the gift. But God chooses the gifts He gives us and the measure of grace He gives us to carry out the work He has called us to do.

Now, you might be wondering when these gifts were given. Paul answers that question in verse 8, and here we have some rather mysterious words.

Ephesians 4:8-10
Mysterious Words from Paul

Therefore He says: "When He ascended on high, He led
captivity captive, and gave gifts to men" (Ephesians 4:8).

Now the question might come to mind, "Where is this quote
taken from?" The quote is from Psalm 68:18, which states, "You
have ascended on high, you have led captivity captive; you have
received gifts among men, even from the rebellious, that the LORD
God might dwell there." Psalm 68 was written by David after some
celebrated victory, where he evidently subdued some enemies of
God. Some think it is the battle that is recorded in 2 Samuel 12:26-
31, which was David's last battle, and this could be true. When a
king like David would win a battle he would bring home spoils and
prisoners to parade before the people. This would be referred to as
recaptured captives. Let's look at 2 Samuel 12:26-31 for reference:

> "Now Joab fought against Rabbah of the people
> of Ammon, and took the royal city. And Joab sent
> messengers to David, and said, 'I have fought against
> Rabbah, and I have taken the city's water supply.
> Now therefore, gather the rest of the people together
> and encamp against the city and take it, lest I take
> the city and it be called after my name.' So David
> gathered all the people together and went to Rabbah,
> fought against it, and took it. Then he took their
> king's crown from his head. Its weight was a talent of
> gold, with precious stones. And it was set on David's
> head. Also he brought out the spoil of the city in
> great abundance. And he brought out the people who
> were in it, and put them to work with saws and iron
> picks and iron axes, and made them cross over to the
> brick works. So he did to all the cities of the people
> of Ammon. Then David and all the people returned
> to Jerusalem."

Also consider 1 Samuel 30:26, for a similar example: "Now when
David came to Ziklag, he sent some of the spoil to the elders of

Judah, to his friends, saying, 'Here is a present for you from the spoil of the enemies of the LORD.'"

Others, like Pastor John MacArthur, put the quote of Psalm 68 in a different historical context: "Psalm 68 is a victory hymn composed by David to celebrate God's conquest of the Jebusite city of Jerusalem and the triumphant assent of God up to Mt. Zion (cf. 2 Sam. 6:7; 1 Chr. 13). After such a triumph the king would bring home the spoils and the prisoners. Here Paul depicts Christ returning from the battle on earth back into the glory of the heavenly city with the trophies of His great victory at Calvary."[78] Either of these contexts makes sense; just as King David returned from battle with gifts to give to others, and prisoners whom he had taken captive, so Christ also, when returning from battle on earth (His death and ascension) back to the glory of heaven, brought His gifts and captive prisoners. The captive prisoners would be the principalities, powers, and authorities whom He defeated by His death and are now subject to Him. Christ stripped them of their power. In this way, *He led captivity captive.* But Paul also says, when Christ *ascended on high*, He *gave gifts to men.* After His ascension to heaven, the Holy Spirit came and gave gifts to the church. We see the fulfilling of this in Acts 2. Now, before Paul mentions what gifts these are, he explains a bit further with a parenthesis in verses 9 and 10.

(Now this, "He ascended"—what does it mean but that He

---

78 John MacArthur, *The MacArthur Study Bible* (Nashville: Word, 1997), 1808. Commentators have questioned the apostle's use of Psalm 68:18, where it reads that God ascended the mount, "receiving gifts to men." but Paul says He "gave gifts unto men." In the OT world both the *receiving* of tribute from their enemies and *distributing* it to the victor's own army, was considered one traditional act. War spoils were gathered and then shared. "Finally, it is quite possible that instead of trying to quote Ps. 68:18 specifically, Paul is summarizing Ps. 68 with words that resemble verse 18. It is similar, perhaps, to the way a news reporter summarizes a thirty-minute speech in just two or three sentences...Some could accuse the reporter of inaccuracy because it is not identical. However, the reporter's purpose is not direct citation on any one sentence but a summary of the whole speech...Regardless of the interpretation one prefers, it must be acknowledged that Ps 68:18 has been changed by Paul to make it applicable to the present Ephesians context." (Hoehner, 528) "A more recent attempt to solve this problem is made by Gary Smith. By use of an analogy from Num 8:6-19 where the Levites were taken "captive" by God and given as a gift to Israel for tabernacle service. Smith sees the leaders in the church as taken captive by God given to the church for ministry." Ibid., 527.

also first descended into the lower parts of the earth? He who descended is also the One who ascended far above all the heavens, that He might fill all things.) (Ephesians 4:9-10).

If Christ *ascended* into heaven, which He did, He had to have *descended* to earth first. But before He came down to earth He was in heaven, right? Christ came from heaven to earth, and then after His death and resurrection, He went back from earth to heaven. Paul gives this vast measurement between heaven and earth by the words *lower parts of the earth* and *far above all the heavens*. This descending into the lower parts of the earth would be the three days He spent in the grave, as Matthew 12:40 states, "For as Jonah was three days and three nights in the belly of the great fish, so will the Son of Man be three days and three nights in the heart of the earth."

Paul says Christ did this so *that He might fill all things*, which means that He fills the entire universe with His power and presence and blessing. In Jeremiah 23:24, we read, "'Can anyone hide himself in secret places, so I shall not see him?'" says the LORD; 'Do I not fill heaven and earth?' says the LORD." He rules and reigns over the whole universe, even though mankind does not recognize that, for the most part. And though He fills all things with Himself, He has a body, the church of Jesus Christ.

We leave these mysterious words of Paul's to look at some marvelous gifts from the Lord. Paul sets forth these marvelous gifts that were given to the beginning of the church, the foundation of the church. These were the gifted ministers of the New Testament church, as seen in verse 11.

Ephesians 4:11
Marvelous Gifts from God

And He Himself gave some to be apostles, some prophets, some evangelists, and some pastors and teachers, (Ephesians 4:11).

These gifts were not the only gifts given to the church, but these were the foundation of the church, as we saw when we were studying Ephesians 2:20: "having been built on the foundation of the apostles and prophets, Jesus Christ Himself being the chief cornerstone." These are leaders in the church. *He Himself gave some*—not everyone has the gifts of apostle, prophet, evangelist, pastor and teacher. The words *He Himself gave* indicate that all gifts are from Him. We think we are gifted in some way, but, ladies, *He* gives us gifts. Now there are other listings of spiritual gifts in the Scriptures, but here, specifically, Paul mentions the gifts that have to do with those who minister the Word and equip the saints.

The first gift Paul mentions is that of *apostle*. An apostle was one who was sent on a mission. They also would have to have personally seen the risen Christ, according to Acts 1:22 and 1 Corinthians 9:1. This would have been the twelve disciples of Christ and others, like Paul. The second gift Paul mentions was that of a *prophet*. Acts 13:1 mentions some who held this role: "Now in the church that was at Antioch there were certain prophets and teachers: Barnabas, Simeon who was called Niger, Lucius of Cyrene, Manaen who had been brought up with Herod the tetrarch, and Saul." A prophet would be someone who heralded the truth. It also could have the meaning of prophecy in the sense of foretelling the future. The apostles and prophets were what the church was founded upon, as we have already seen.

The third gift Paul mentions is that of *evangelist*. An evangelist is one who shares the gospel where it has not been proclaimed and to those who have not believed. Acts 21:8 talks about Philip the evangelist. Paul tells Timothy to do the work of an evangelist, in 2 Timothy 4:5.

The fourth gift is that of pastor-teacher, or it could be the gifts of *pastor* and *teacher*; some divide these as two separate gifts. A pastor would be a shepherd, one who shepherds people, tending to their needs spiritually. A teacher is one who understands and communicates biblical truth in a clear manner. I am not convinced it is one gift, as I know some teachers who are not gifted as good shepherds. And some are quite good at shepherding people's souls but are not good teachers.[79]

79 My husband in his notes on this question comments on the grammar: "The Granville Sharp rule (i.e., definite article + noun + kai + noun, as in Eph. 4:11) does not always

Ephesians 4:12-16
Motivational Reasons to Serve

for the equipping of the saints for the work of ministry, for the edifying of the body of Christ, (Ephesians 4:12).

Paul goes on to give five motivational reasons for the use of spiritual gifts, in verses 12-16. *The first motivational reason to use our gifts is for the equipping of the saints.* Paul says believers are given these gifts so that they might equip the saints, so that the saints might go and do the work of the ministry, so that the body of Christ would be edified. If your leaders are not motivating you by their teaching and preaching, and by their example, to go out and get busy for the kingdom, then you need to find a new church or examine your heart as to why this is not the case. The word *equipping* means to be made complete. It is actually a medical term for the setting of bones which have been broken or the mending of a net. Leaders of the church should be using their gifts to equip their flock, *the saints*, to do the work of ministry. This would include helping them put off sin in their lives, which might be hindering them from what they should be doing for Christ, teaching them to use their gifts for the kingdom, and teaching them doctrine and practical principles from God's Word. When the shepherds of the church are doing their work faithfully, then that will motivate their people to faithfully do *the work of the ministry* that God has called them to do. Every member of the body of Christ should be involved in serving each other and ministering to one another.

Many times, we get this idea that it is the job of the pastor and his wife to do all of the work in the church, but that is not biblical. We all should be ministering our gifts and serving the body. As each member does their part, Paul says the result is *the edifying of the body*

---

apply to *plural* constructions, so to use this to dogmatically suggest grammatical rule for the one gift view is weak. cf. Wallace, 284. "Others think that the reason for one article is to designate these two gifts as functioning primarily in a local setting as distinguished from those gifts listed earlier which functioned more in an itinerate ministry... Wallace suggests that the first is the subset of the second and thus "all pastors are to be teachers, though not all teachers are to be pastors." Hence, while there is a distinction between the two, the distinction is not total" cf. Hoehner, 54; Wallace, *Semantic Range of the Article-Noun-kai-Noun Plural Construction,* 83; idem, *Greek Grammar*, 284.

of Christ, which means the church is built up. The word *edifying* has the meaning of a building, of some type of construction. As we go and evangelize, the church is built up numerically as we preach and teach the Word, the church is built up spiritually and matures. When we fail to use our gifts for the body we become handicapped, just as a physical body will not function if all the parts are not working and it, too, becomes handicapped. "Christ gave foundational gifts to the church for the immediate purpose of preparing all the saints for the goal of service and in turn this service is for the final goal of building up the entire body of Christ."[80] Paul continues on with another reason to serve in verse 13.

> till we all come to the unity of the faith and of the knowledge of the Son of God, to a perfect man, to the measure of the stature of the fullness of Christ; (Ephesians 4:13).

The second motivational reason to serve is for the unity of the saints. Paul begins Ephesians 4 with the seven "ones" that we saw in our last lesson, and his whole theme was the importance of unity, (i.e.,, there is one Lord, one baptism, etc.). As members of the body use their gifts, it results in the building up of the body, which results in spiritual *unity* and growth *in the knowledge of the Son of God*. The goal, Paul says, is to be mature or *perfect*, to attain to *the measure of the stature of the fullness of Christ*, to be like Christ. Paul makes this clear in Colossians 1:28, "Him we preach, warning every man and teaching every man in all wisdom, that we may present every man perfect in Christ Jesus." Paul gives us yet another reason to serve, in verse 14.

> that we should no longer be children, tossed to and fro and carried about with every wind of doctrine, by the trickery of men, in the cunning craftiness of deceitful plotting, (Ephesians 4:14).

The third motivational factor for using our gifts is for the maturing of the saints. The term *children* is a contrast to the mature man of verse 13. If the body is not being built up by godly men who are using their gifts to equip the members of the local body, then the result is children that are immature and susceptible to false teaching.

---

80 Hoehner, 551.

Children, we know, are foolish at times, easily influenced, and immature in their thinking. Paul describes them as being *tossed to and fro and carried about with every wind of doctrine*, which means they are whirled around, blown here and there by every new and novel thing that comes their way. I have met some Christians who are like that, and it is very concerning, because they buy into every new and novel idea that comes to the Christian world. They certainly are what Paul describes, in that they are led astray *by the trickery of men*. *Trickery* comes from the Greek word from which we get our English word dice. The term actually means dishonest trickery. We know Eve was tricked by Satan, which led to her sinning, along with her husband. Christians who are not mature are gullible, like Eve, and readily listen to those who are *cunning* and *deceitful*. If we are not being taught sound doctrine, then we will be like gullible children who believe everything and we will never grow up. This evidently was a concern of Paul's for the church at Ephesus, because in Acts 20 he tells the elders at Ephesus, "For I know this, that after my departure savage wolves will come in among you, not sparing the flock. Also from among yourselves men will rise up, speaking perverse things, to draw away the disciples after themselves. Therefore watch, and remember that for three years I did not cease to warn everyone night and day with tears. So now, brethren, I commend you to God and to the word of His grace, which is able to build you up and give you an inheritance among all those who are sanctified" (Acts 20:29-32). Paul says, "Beware! This will happen, so make sure you are walking with God and in His Word, which will build you up. Otherwise, the results will be disastrous." There is a fourth reason for each of us to be using our gifts.

> but, speaking the truth in love, may grow up in all things into Him who is the head—Christ— (Ephesians 4:15).

The fourth reason we use our gifts is for the growth of the saints. Instead of getting caught up in heresy, we speak the truth in love. The words *speaking the truth* mean to tell the truth in doctrine as well as in your daily living. We are to speak the truth—the gospel—and are to live the truth—the gospel. And it is to be done *in love*. We don't cram religion down people's throats; we don't share holy things with dogs or cast our pearls before swine. It only makes sense that, as we learn the truth, speak the truth, and live the truth, we will *grow up in all things into Him*. Then we will be more like Christ, as He Himself is truth. Those who are immature and deceptive, which is the opposite of truth, are the ones tossed to and fro and who never grow up to be like Jesus. In my own life, I am encouraged to love and do good deeds when fellow brothers and sisters use their spiritual gifts to exhort and encourage me. It presses me to move on and grow in my own faith. Paul now gives the fifth reason to be using our gifts in verse 16, and with this we draw our lesson to a close.

> from whom the whole body, joined and knit together by what every joint supplies, according to the effective working by which every part does its share, causes growth of the body for the edifying of itself in love (Ephesians 4:16).

The fifth motivation for using our gifts is for the working together of the saints. One man helps us understand this verse; he says, "Just as the human body when held together by every supporting joint grows strong, so also the church when it receives the active support of every member, each co-operating according to his ability, will be built up in love."[81] Each part of the physical body has to be working properly and together in order for the body to function. So it is in the spiritual realm. We must all work together and each do our part; whether we have a small job or a big job, we must do our part or else the body of Christ will not function or work. Another man says, "The precision with which these medical terms are employed make us wonder whether Paul checked the details with Luke."[82] Paul gives us a beautiful picture here! As the spiritual body is working together, no one is overworked, all are doing their part, even the tiniest member is working so that the whole body grows together and is edified in love. Now, I don't know about you, but I long to be a part of a church like that! Ladies, we must realize that we are not to be sitting on the sidelines as Christians. God saved us to serve Him, and it is imperative that we use our spiritual gifts and our talents for His glory, for His kingdom, and for the good of the body of Christ.

---

81 Hendriksen, 205.

82 Homer A. Kent, *The Expositor's Bible Commentary; Ephesians through Philemon* (Grand Rapids: Zondervan, 1978), 60.

Summary

We have considered *Mysterious Words from Paul* (vv 8-10); *Marvelous Gifts from God* (vv 7, 11); and *Motivational Reasons to Serve* (vv 12-16). Those reasons include: the equipping of the saints, the unity of the saints, the maturing of the saints, the growth of the saints, and the working together of the saints.

Can you say that you know what your gifts are? Have you thanked God for giving them to you and for the grace He gives you to serve Him? Has the use of your gifts benefited the body of Christ by helping its members to grow? Have others matured in Christ by the use of your gifts? Have others been equipped by the example and use of your gifts? By using your gifts, have you encouraged unity in the body? Are others being motivated to work together as they watch you use your gifts? As Kevin DeYoung writes, "In more than a decade of pastoral ministry I've never met a Christian who was healthier, more mature, and more active in ministry in being apart from the church. But I have found the opposite to be invariably true. The weakest Christians are those least connected to the body. And the less involved you are, the more disconnected those following you will be. The man who attempts Christianity without the church shoots himself in the foot, shoots his children in the leg, and shoots his grandchildren in the heart."[83] May God help us to know what our gifts are and to use our gifts for our Master in Heavenly Places!

---

83 Kevin DeYoung, *The Hole in Our Holiness* (Wheaton: Crossway, 2012), 132.

Questions to Consider

The Structure and Purpose of the Body of Christ
Ephesians 4:7-16

1. (a) Read Ephesians 4:7-16 and write down the gifts that God gave to the leaders of the church. (b) According to the text, what are the reasons that God gave them these gifts? (c) Memorize Ephesians 4:7.

2. (a) Paul mentions in this passage that God gave gifts to men; in particular, this passage draws our attention to the gifts He's given to the leaders of the church (see verse 11). What are the other spiritual gifts that are mentioned in Romans 12:6-8; 1 Corinthians 12:1-30; and 1 Peter 4:9-11? (b) Do you know what your spiritual gifts are, and are you using them for the edification of the body? (c) If not, why not? (d) If you are using your gifts, are you sharpening them so that you might serve God with excellence?

3. (a) According to the following passages, what should be our response to doctrine that is not sound, or to those who are teaching doctrine that is not sound? Romans 16:17-18; Galatians 1:6-8; Colossians 2:4-9; 1 Timothy 4:6-8; Hebrews 13:9; 1 John 4:1-2. (b) What might happen if we listen to false doctrine, according to Ephesians 4:14? (c) Are you in a church that teaches truth? (d) Do you listen to teachers that teach sound doctrine? (e) Do you read books that teach the truth?

4. What do you think Paul means in Ephesians 4:8-10?

5. (a) Would you say that you are growing up as a child of God (see verse 15), or are you still walking around in your "spiritual diapers," as one man has put it? (b) What things do you need to change so that you might grow and mature in your walk with Christ?

6. Write a prayer request for the leaders of your church, especially focusing on their service to the body of Christ, according to Ephesians 4:12-15.

Chapter 12

Off with the Old Man; On with the New Man!

Ephesians 4:17-24

Several weeks ago I was having lunch with a couple of my Christian friends. The topic of our world came up and how ungodly it has become. A recent article in our local newspaper described the growing surge in atheism and how in our city atheists are actually gathering together for services. I'm not sure what they call these services or who or what they worship, but they gather nonetheless. One thing led to another in our conversation, and the topic of same sex marriage also came up, since the Supreme Court declared same-sex marriage legal in all 50 states. One woman present thought we should embrace these couples in our churches and said that new studies show that these individuals are born with those desires. Well, I wasn't going to let that go. So I graciously spoke up and said, "We are all born with the propensities for sexual sins, because we are born depraved. But Christ comes in and changes all that."

I went on to say that I would evangelize a lost homosexual, but someone who was claiming to know Christ and living a life of homosexuality was an oxymoron. And I said further, "Either we uphold the standard of God and His Word and what He says regarding homosexuality, or we don't, and God says it is sin. God's Word is the standard for all truth, and either He is a liar or He is the truth, and He is the truth!" I won't bore you with the rest of the conversation, only to say that it got tense and it was definitely one of those I-can't-believe-this-conversation-is-happening moments. I went away persecuted for the cost of Christ and sobered and frightened at the thinking of a few of my friends. What does the Bible say? Is there no difference between the old man and the new man? Is there no hope for those who are enslaved in sin, whether it is homosexuality or some other sin? What does God say? Let's see what He says through the apostle Paul as He writes to the saints at Ephesus.

Ephesians 4:17-24

This I say, therefore, and testify in the Lord, that you should no longer walk as the rest of the Gentiles walk, in the futility of their mind, [18]having their understanding darkened, being alienated from the life of God, because of the ignorance that is in them, because of the hardening of their heart; [19]who, being past feeling, have given themselves over to lewdness, to work all uncleanness with greediness. [20]But you have not so learned Christ, [21]if indeed you have heard Him and have been taught by Him, as the truth is in Jesus: [22]that you put off, concerning your former conduct, the old man which grows corrupt according to the deceitful lusts, [23]and be renewed in the spirit of your mind, [24]and that you put on the new man which was created according to God, in true righteousness and holiness (Ephesians 4:17-24).

In our last lesson, we considered the structure and purpose of the church. In this lesson, we'll consider what it means to be out with the old man and in with the new man! We'll see *The Characteristics of the Old Man*, (vv 17-19), and there will be five of them. We'll also see *The Characteristics of the New Man*, (vv 20-24), and there will be five of them, as well. Let's begin by looking at some of the characteristics of the old man.

Ephesians 4:17-19
The Characteristics of the Old Man

This I say, therefore, and testify in the Lord, that you should no longer walk as the rest of the Gentiles walk, in the futility of their mind, (Ephesians 4:17).

You will see that Paul, once again, uses the word *therefore*. Paul says this because of all that he's just finished teaching us. Because we have been redeemed, because our foundation as believers is Christ and the apostles, because we are citizens of the household of God, because we have been given spiritual gifts for the maturity of the body of Christ, we are to walk like a Christian and not like a lost Gentile. Now Paul is not picking on the Gentiles, and actually the word *Gentile* is not in the original manuscripts. But it is a term that represents ungodly lost men and women. Remember, Paul is addressing believers in Ephesus who are surrounded by pagan idols and the grand temple of Artemis. Artemis, or Diana, was a goddess of sex, and every perversion of sexual activity was known to take place at her temple. So the believers in Ephesus were much like us today, surrounded by a sexually perverted culture. Because of this, Paul testifies in the Lord that we should no longer walk as the rest of the Gentiles walk. The phrase *testify in the Lord* is an important one that Paul uses, because anything he exhorts them to do will have its foundation in what the Lord says. We might use the phrase "thus sayeth the Lord" for this kind of statement. Often people give advice based on their opinions or experiences, but only the counsel of the Lord and what He says will stand. We can always be assured that we are speaking the truth when we have the Word of God as the foundation for what we say. God's Word must always be the standard for how we make decisions and how we evaluate truth. This was my point with my friend at our lunch conversation. I can speak with boldness and assurance regarding homosexuality because God has been very clear on that issue.

Paul admonishes them that they *should no longer walk as the rest of the Gentiles walk.* How do they walk? *In the futility of their mind. This is be the first characteristic of the old man: they walk in the futility of their mind.* What does that mean? To say that unbelievers walk in the futility of their mind suggests an emptiness of their thinking.[84] The term for futility (Greek, mataiotes) speaks of something that fails to produce its desired result or, being empty, amounts to nothing. Christianity is a cognitive religion, a thinking religion, which radically changes the futile thinking of man! This is why the first step toward God is repentance, a change of mind toward self, toward sin, toward God, toward Christ, toward one's behavior, etc. The unsaved have a mind that is depraved, empty, and delusional. Their minds are so full of mental folly that they have completely lost all rational thinking. I read the news almost

---

84   Robert Thomas writes: "In these eight verses eleven Greek terms pertaining to the mind are mentioned, which is a heavy concentration of mental faculty terms: *mind* (Gk. naos), vs. 17; *understanding* (Gk. dianoia), *ignorance* (Gk. agnoian), *heart* (Gk. kardias), vs. 18; *being past feeling* (Gk. apalgakotes), vs. 19; *learned* (Gk. emathete), vs. 20; *you heard* (Gk. ekousate), *were taught* (Gk. edidachthete), *truth* (Gk. aletheia), vs. 21; *mind* (Gk. naos), vs. 23; and *truth* (Gk. aletheia), vs. 24. The Christian life is one of thinking a certain way, reflecting in a definite direction and personal conviction." cf. Robert L. Thomas, *The Self-Concept of a Christian Disciple: Ephesians 4:17-24* (Copyright 1988, by Robert L. Thomas), 2-3.

daily and I see how true this is: women are killing their children; husbands are killing their wives, wives are killing their husbands; family members are raping other family members, dismembering them, raping dead corpses—even children! I think what is wrong is that these people have lost their minds! Ladies, this is the state of the old man. One man gives this helpful description: "Men with thinking, willing minds, rational creatures, walking and walking on and on throughout life, following the dictates of a mind that leads them at every step and at the end to nothing, to monumental, tragic failure!"[85] Pastor John MacArthur summarizes the point: "The life of an unbeliever is bound up in thinking and acting in an arena of ultimate trivia. He consumes himself in the pursuit of goals that are purely selfish, in the accumulation of that which is temporary, and in looking for satisfaction in that which is intrinsically deceptive and disappointing."[86] If that isn't disturbing enough, Paul goes on to give two more characteristics of the old man in verse 18.

> having their understanding darkened, being alienated from the life of God, because of the ignorance that is in them, because of the hardening of their heart; (Ephesians 4:18).

The second characteristic of the old man is that their understanding is darkened. This means their reasoning process is dark. They can't see light. Jesus describes it as sitting in darkness in Matthew 4:16: "The people who sat in darkness have seen a great light, and upon those who sat in the region and shadow of death light has dawned." In fact, in John's gospel, Jesus speaks of the unregenerate man as loving darkness, in John 3:19: "And this is the condemnation, that the light has come into the world, and men loved darkness rather than light, because their deeds were evil."

Third, the old man's life is alienated from the life of God. This means they are separated from God in the sense that they do not know Him; they have no personal relationship with Him. Paul says they are *alienated from the life of God* because of two reasons. First of all, it is *because of the ignorance that is in them*. This *ignorance* is not in the sense that they do not know better, because Paul says in

85 Lenski, 554.
86 MacArthur, *The MacArthur New Testament Commentary: Ephesians*, 168.

Romans 1:20 that mankind is without excuse. Rather, this ignorance of God is because they have rejected Him, which results in not knowing Him. Paul mentions this same truth during his sermon on Mars Hill in Acts 17:30: "Truly, these times of ignorance God overlooked, but now commands all men everywhere to repent." Peter also mentions this ignorance in 1 Peter 1:14: "as obedient children, not conforming yourselves to the former lusts, as in your ignorance." As man rejects God in his thinking and in his decision-making, he becomes more alienated from God and ignorant of what His will is.

They are not only alienated from God because of the ignorance that is in them, but also *because of the hardening of their heart*. This describes their callous hearts. The word *hardening*, or callous, describes a thickening of the outer skin. We can all identify with that, as we have all certainly had calluses on our feet or hands. Calluses, or hardening, result in being insensitive, as one loses their ability to sense feeling. This truly is a great description of the old man as they become desensitized to anything spiritual. God describes the hard heart in Ezekiel 11:19 when He is explaining the work He will do in the New Covenant: "Then I will give them one heart, and I will put a new spirit within them, and take the stony heart out of their flesh, and give them a heart of flesh." It is such a joy to know that the new man has a different heart, isn't it? Jesus also mentions the calloused condition of the lost man in John 12:40, when He quotes from Isaiah: "He has blinded their eyes and hardened their hearts, lest they should see with their eyes, lest they should understand with their hearts and turn, so that I should heal them." Paul isn't finished yet with his description of the old man; he has still more to say in verse 19.

> who, being past feeling, have given themselves over to lewdness, to work all uncleanness with greediness (Ephesians 4:19).

The fourth description of the old man is that they are <u>*given over to lewdness.*</u> *Lewdness* is a word that is used in the Old Testament to describe anything that is ritually unclean, such as dead bodies, certain animals, and menstrual blood. It is also a word that describes any type of moral uncleanness, especially relating to sexual sins. And the reason they are given over to this is because they have lost all feeling; Paul describes them as *being past feeling*. This means they have ceased to feel pain. Just as one might not feel pain physically because of nerve damage, a lost man doesn't feel pain spiritually because he is insensitive to the voice of God. He doesn't feel shame or embarrassment. These are people who know no restraint and act as if they are without boundaries. Josephus talks about this when describing a Roman soldier who exposed his genitals during Passover in order to insult the Jews. At the time that I was writing this lesson, a big news item in our country was a group of people in San Francisco who wanted to shed their clothes and walk around nude. The city was actually having to vote on a law to ban public nudity because of this group of demonstrators who demanded their right to walk around nude. They have no shame, no embarrassment! And Paul describes the old man as being given over to lewdness, which means a complete surrender to evil.

Paul's fifth description of the lost man is that <u>they work all uncleanness</u>. The word *work* means a practice, which could refer to making a living off of *uncleanness*, which is a moral and physical impurity. This is perhaps why Paul uses the words *with greediness*. In other words, lost man is so obsessed with sin and the money he can make off of it that it obsesses him. I read just recently that human trafficking is the third largest source of profit for international organized crime, with revenue amounting to billions of dollars every year. The pornography industry now makes about 13 billion dollars each year. It's a business for greedy people. This phrase could also mean that in their sinning they are greedy in the sense that their lust is never satisfied, and so they become more perverted; they have to seek new perversions because the old is boring. This is someone who always wants more, whether it is money or sex. This person will take whatever he or she wants and use others to their advantage. Again, we see this same thing in our world today. Having sexual relations with one's own spouse isn't enough, so one commits adultery. Or one looks at porn, but that doesn't suffice, so they start looking at child porn or bestiality. This is working all uncleanness with greediness. This is the life of the old man, my friend, and it is a disgusting one. It is not the life of the new man, as Paul goes on to say in verse 20.

Ephesians 4:20-24
The Characteristics of the New Man

But you have not so learned Christ, (Ephesians 4:20).

Paul says you haven't *learned* Christ this way. *This is the first characteristic of the new man—we have learned Christ*. To have *learned Christ* means to have submitted to who He is and to His Lordship. This is now how we act once we have come to Christ. Jesus illustrates this in Matthew 11:28-30, where He says, "Come to Me, all you who labor and are heavy laden, and I will give you rest. Take My yoke upon you and learn from Me, for I am gentle and lowly in heart, and you will find rest for your souls. For My yoke is easy and My burden is light." This is really a call to salvation; Jesus is saying learn of me, follow me. Paul goes on to say more in verse 21.

if indeed you have heard Him and have been taught by Him, as the truth is in Jesus: (Ephesians 4:21).

The word *if* means since. You are not like that old man I just wrote about, Paul says, since you have *heard* Christ and you *have been taught by Him*. The hearing Paul speaks of here means the hearing of the gospel. As Paul says in Romans 10:17, "So then faith comes by hearing, and hearing by the word of God." They not only heard Him, but they have also been taught by Him through His words. My friend, throughout our Christian life we are hearing and being taught by Him as we read and study the Word of God and as we listen to it being preached. And all this hearing and teaching is in *truth*. Jesus is truth and so what He teaches us is truth; it is not a lie. *The second characteristic of the new man is that we have heard and been taught by Jesus*. Because we have learned Christ, heard Christ, been taught by Christ, then we have a responsibility to put off the old man, as Paul mentions in verse 22.

that you put off, concerning your former conduct, the old man which grows corrupt according to the deceitful lusts, (Ephesians 4:22).

This is the third characteristic of the new man in Christ, that is, we have put off the old man. The words *put off* mean to take something off as you would take off filthy clothes. And the Greek tense indicates that this is done once and for all. This could also refer to what they did in the New Testament times when they were baptized, that is, they would take off their old clothing and put on a white garment in which to be baptized. I remember this was the custom in the church in which I grew up. This makes sense, because baptism is a symbol of putting off the old life and being raised to new life, and the white robe is a symbol of purity. This *old man*, Paul says, *grows corrupt according to the deceitful lusts.* This describes the old man with its corruption and decay. Now, the question might come to your mind, "What is the old man?" The old man is that which was dead in trespasses and sins, as Paul already mentioned in Ephesians 2:1-2. Now these Ephesian saints (and us, hopefully!) have been saved by grace through faith and are no longer dead. But we still have remnants of the old man that need to be put off. We need to wage war, as Paul will write about in chapter six of his epistle, when he gives instructions regarding the believer's armor that must be worn in order to fight the darts of the wicked one. When we put off something we must put on something, right? That's what Paul tells us to do in verses 23-24.

and be renewed in the spirit of your mind, (Ephesians 4:23).

This is the fourth characteristic of the new man: we have renewed our minds. The believer's mind is renewed as they read, study, listen to and obey the Word of God. My friend, this is why I am such an advocate of Scripture memorization. It will renew your mind like nothing else I know. Memorization of Scripture, along with application of it, will transform your mind. And as your mind is transformed, so are your actions. Paul says Romans 12:1-2, "I beseech you therefore, brethren, by the mercies of God, that you present your bodies a living sacrifice, holy, acceptable to God, which is your reasonable service. And do not be conformed to this world, but be transformed by the renewing of your mind, that you may prove what is that good and acceptable and perfect will of God." As you memorize and obey the Word of God, it will change how you think about God, other people, your circumstances, your sin, everything. You will start thinking like Him and, hopefully acting like Him as well, which is Paul's next point in verse 24.

> and that you put on the new man which was created according to God, in true righteousness and holiness (Ephesians 4:24).

The fifth characteristic of those who are redeemed is that <u>we have put on the new man</u>, which resembles our Maker. Why do we do that? Because, Paul says, that new man has been *created according to God, in true righteousness and holiness*. This is the opposite of corrupt and deceitful lusts. The new man should resemble the One whose image he or she bears. This would include *righteousness*, which is doing what is right, living right, acting right, and thinking right. But it also includes *holiness*, which is being and doing that which is pure and clean. Paul uses the word *true* to describe these, as he has already said in verse 20 that the truth is in Jesus. Truth is not in the unredeemed man, the old man. That man is false, dark, and wicked. The new man is true, light, and holy.

Summary

Indeed, this is the glorious work that happens at our conversion! These three statements are used by the apostle Paul to summarize what believers have learned from Christ: *to put off the old man* (like a garment; Romans 12:12-14; Colossians 3:8; James 1:21) *concerning our former conduct* (v 22), *to be renewed in the spirit of our mind* (v 23) and *to put on the new man of righteousness and holiness* (v 24). It is interesting that, in this passage, in the Greek, Paul is not technically exhorting the Ephesians to do these things, but he is reminding them of what they have already done. These infinitives, or statements, are not in the imperative mood, as commands, but rather are statements about the Ephesians' commitment to the Lord at the time of their salvation.

Characteristics of the Old Man, (vv 17-19), are:
1. They walk in the futility of their mind.
2. Their understanding is darkened.
3. They are alienated from the life of God

4. They are given over to lewdness.
5. They work all uncleanness.

The Characteristics of the New Man, (vv 20-24), are:
1. We have learned Christ.
2. We have heard and been taught by Christ.
3. We have put off the old man.
4. We have renewed our minds.
5. We have put on the new man.

So what about you, my friend? Which category do you find your life in right now, the new man or the old man? Are you calloused to the voice of God? Are you committing acts of immorality and desiring more and more? (Maybe not in acts but, perhaps, in your mind?) Do you have a hard heart or are you submitting to Christ and His Lordship? Are you continuing to be taught by Him through careful study of His Word? Are you renewing your mind through His Word? Are you given over to uncleanness or to holiness? Are you submitting to Christ or are you submitting to evil? I pray you find yourself in the life of the new man.

Another question to consider is this: Are you of the same notion as my friend was, that somehow you can be engrossed in sin and still enter into heaven? Perhaps we should remind ourselves of the exhortation we find in Hebrews 12:14: "Pursue peace with all people, and holiness, without which no one will see the Lord."

Questions to Consider

Off with the Old Man; On with the New Man!
Ephesians 4:17-24

1. (a) What are some of the ways we used to walk, according to what Paul says in Ephesians 4:17-24? (b) Also, what do 1 Corinthians 6:9-11; Galatians 5:19-21; Ephesians 2:1-3; Colossians 3:5-9; and 1 Peter 4:1-3 say about the old man? (c) What does the walk of the new man look like, according to Romans 13:12-14; Ephesians 4:17-24; and Colossians 3:10-4:1? (d) What are some other passages that come to your mind regarding the characteristics of the old man and the characteristics of the new man? (e) Memorize Ephesians 4:23.

2. (a) Compare Romans 1:18-32 and Ephesians 4:17-24. What things does Paul write in these passages that are similar regarding mankind in their unredeemed state? (b) Why do you think Scripture is replete with descriptions of man in his lost condition?

3. (a) Paul mentions in Ephesians 4:19 that one of the deeds of an unredeemed man is "all uncleanness with greediness." What is the danger of greediness, according to Ecclesiastes 5:9-20; Luke 12:15; and 1 Timothy 6:6-10? (b) What should we be pursuing instead, according to 1 Timothy 6:11-12? (c) How do you see this sin manifested in our world today? (d) How do you personally fight the sin of greed in your own life?

4. How would you use Ephesians 4:17-24 to help someone who claims they know Christ but whose life is characterized by the old man?

5. (a) What are some practical ways that you have found to be helpful in putting off the old woman and putting on the new woman? (b) How do you practically renew your mind, as Paul says in Ephesians 4:23?

6. Is there any area in your life where you are struggling to put off sin? Please write your need in the form of a prayer request to share.

Chapter 13

The Need for God's Children to Put off Socially Acceptable Sins!

Ephesians 4:25-29

As our world becomes more and more wicked, God's children are faced with the question of how to handle the sins that the world calls "acceptable." It is commonplace in the government, as well as in the workplace, to lie and get away with it. Many people call these "white lies" or "minor deceptions" and excuse such behavior by saying that "Everybody does it; it's acceptable!"

Our world is also becoming comfortable with stealing from the government by lying on income taxes, and employees are comfortable with stealing from their employers by lying about their hours or taking merchandise or supplies they haven't paid for. And again, we hear, "Everyone is doing it," in an effort to make it seem right.

Being loose with our speech is also becoming the norm in our world and deemed as socially acceptable. Hardly a day goes by that we don't overhear someone else's foul language, whether in the workplace, the marketplace, or the media. And worse, even in the church, some ministers think foul language, or "shock preaching," makes them relevant to the culture they're trying to reach. "Why not?" they cry, "Everyone does it, and it's socially acceptable. Are you still in the dark ages?

Are we as believers in Jesus Christ behind the times? Do we need to get with the world and its program? Should we acknowledge these socially acceptable sins as the new normal and simply go with the flow? In order to answer these questions, let's not turn to the world for the answers. Instead, let's turn to the One who died to save us from these socially acceptable sins and see what He has to say about it.

Ephesians 4:25-29

Therefore, putting away lying, Let each one of you speak truth with his neighbor, for we are members of one another. [26]Be angry, and do not sin: do not let the sun go down on your wrath, [27]nor give place to the devil. [28]Let him who stole steal no longer, but rather let him labor, working with his hands what is good, that he may have something to give him who has need. [29]Let no corrupt word proceed out of your mouth, but what is good for necessary edification, that it may impart grace to the hearers (Ephesians 4:25-29).

In our previous lesson, we looked at Ephesians 4:17-24 and discovered the Characteristics of the Old Man, (vv 17-19), and the Characteristics of the New Man, (vv 20-24). The Apostle Paul has commanded the Ephesian believers to stop walking as those who know not God, because those who know God have decisively put off their former manner of life and have decisively put on a new manner of life, just as they have been taught by Christ. Believers are to be continually renewing their minds and, in so doing, bringing their thoughts captive toward the ethical distinctives of their new life.

Here Paul moves from the general to the particulars: instead of lying, we are to speak the truth; instead of stealing, we are to work so as to give; instead of communicating with corrupt speech, we are to use edifying speech; instead of allowing resentment and anger to dominate our lives, we are to be forgiving and gentle. These are sins that are not socially acceptable for the new man, but the virtues are totally acceptable. In this lesson, we'll consider the first three sins that Paul says are not acceptable for the new man and the first three virtues Paul says we ought to put on instead:

Put off Lying and Put on Speaking the Truth, (v 25)
Put off Stealing and Put on Working with our Hands, (v 28)
Put off Corrupt Speech and Put on Edifying Speech, (v 29)

Let's begin by considering the first sin that is not socially acceptable for a child of God as well as the first virtue that is totally acceptable for God's child, as we consider verse 25.

Ephesians 4:25
Put off Lying and Put on Speaking the Truth

Therefore, putting away lying, Let each one of you speak truth with his neighbor, for we are members of one another (Ephesians 4:25).

Paul begins this section of Scripture with the word *therefore*, which means because of. Because of the fact that we are created after God in true holiness and righteousness, we are to act like God, whose likeness we are to bear, and not like the old man. If we truly want to behave like the One whose image we bear, who is righteous and holy, then these sins will have no place in our lives. Paul says *putting away*, which means putting off something, and the tense in the Greek indicates that we are to do it once and for all. Putting off has the idea, as we saw in our last lesson, of ridding ourselves of a filthy garment.

The first socially acceptable sin that we are to put off is lying. This is unacceptable for a child of God. It is interesting that Paul starts with lying, because as he mentioned in the previous verse, lying is the opposite of God, who is true. God is truth and He tells the truth, so He expects the same of His children. Lying is from the devil, as Jesus says in John 8:44. It does not have anything to do with God; Titus 1:2 states that He is a God who cannot lie. The Bible says that we come out of the womb speaking lies. Consider Psalm 58:3: "The wicked are estranged from the womb; they go astray as soon as they are born, speaking lies." What is lying? It is any type of falsehood or deceit. And the prohibition against it is one of the 10 commandments that God gave to Moses, in Exodus 20:16; it states, "You shall not bear false witness against your neighbor."

Statistics tell us that men lie 6 times a day, and women lie half as much. I don't know where these statistics come from, but I would have to say the average person probably lies much more than that in a day. That same poll said that the number one lie men tell is saying, "Nothing's wrong, I'm fine." And the number one women lie women tell is also saying, "Nothing's wrong; I'm fine." Now, this is not all we lie about. We lie to ourselves about the way we look. We lie to ourselves about our marriages, making them better or worse than they really are, in our minds and also in our communication with others. We also lie to others in order to make ourselves look good or someone else look bad. We lie about how much money we make, how much we spend, and where we shop. We lie on our income taxes; we lie by embellishing stories; we lie by making promises we don't keep; we lie by betraying confidences, and we lie by speaking flattery. John MacArthur says, "Our society today is so dependent on lying that if it suddenly turned to telling the truth our way of life would collapse. If world leaders began speaking only the truth, World War III would certainly ensue. So many lies are piled on other lies, and so many organizations, businesses, economies, social orders, governments, and treaties are built on those lies that the world system would disintegrate if lying suddenly ceased. Resentment and animosity would know no bounds and the confusion would be unimaginable."[87]

Instead of using our mouth to lie, we must use our mouth to speak truth. This is the first totally acceptable virtue of the new man—*speaking the truth*. Paul says each one of us is to speak the truth, which simply means that we say what is true. Because we bear the image of God who is true, we as His children are to speak and live what is true. Speaking the truth doesn't mean we go around telling everybody everything we know or feel. We should be discreet with our speech, but we should be truth-tellers. For example, often someone will ask us, "How are you today?" And our pat answer is, "I'm fine." Is that always true? No! Many times I say, "I'm okay," or "I'm partly cloudy," or "It's been a rough day," or "I'm trusting in the Lord even though it's rough right now."

Paul goes on to say the believer is to *speak the truth with his neighbor*, which isn't necessarily our next door neighbor, even

---

87 MacArthur, *The MacArthur New Testament Commentary: Ephesians*, 183. Lying is forbidden by God (cf. Lev. 19:11; Col. 3:9) and hated by God (cf. Prov. 6:16-19; Prov. 12:22); it is also hated by saints (Ps. 40:4; 119:29, 163; Prov. 13:5; 30:8; Isa. 63:8). Lying is practiced by unbelievers (Ps. 58:3; 52:3; 62:4; 4:2), resulting in punishment and ultimately being cast into the lake of fire (Ps. 5:6; 120:3-4; Prov. 19:5; Jer. 50:36; Rev. 21:8, 27; 22:15. The Bible records many examples of lying: the devil (cf. Gen. 3:4; John 8:44), Cain (cf. Gen. 4:9), Jacob (cf. Gen. 27:19), Samson (cf. Judg. 16:10), Saul (cf. 1 Sam. 15:13), David (cf. 1 Sam. 21:2), Peter (Matt. 26:72), etc.

though it would be a good idea to speak the truth to them. The word *neighbor* could mean anyone, but in this context it seems to be referring to fellow believers, because Paul goes on to say that we are members one of another, speaking of the body of Christ. We have the account in Luke 10 of the lawyer asking Jesus who was his neighbor, and Jesus told the story of the Good Samaritan, indicating that even a total stranger is our neighbor. It is a good idea to speak the truth to everyone, whether it's a fellow believer, a neighbor, or even an enemy.

We speak the truth because *we are members of one another*. Paul has so clearly set this forth in Ephesians 2 and 3 when speaking of God's children as members of a household, a temple, and a body. We belong to each other; therefore, we do not lie to one another. When we lie to one another it hurts the whole body. Chrysostom once said, "If the eye sees a serpent does it lie to the foot? Or if the nose smells a deadly drug will it lie to the mouth? Or if the tongue tastes something bitter will it lie to the stomach?"[88] That's the point Paul is making; each member belongs to one body.

Ephesians 4:26-27

> Be angry, and do not sin: do not let the sun go down on your wrath, nor give place to the devil (Ephesians 4:26-27).

Now you might have looked at verses 26 and 27 and thought that anger was another sin that was to be put off. Even though it is true that we should put away sinful anger, and many passages teach us that anger is a sin worthy of damnation, it doesn't seem to be what Paul is saying here. Also, it would be the only sin in this text that doesn't have a virtue that we are to put on in place of the sin we are to put off. It also would be the only sin Paul mentions that doesn't have the body of Christ as a motivation for putting it off. For example, we put off lying because we are members of each other. We put off stealing, and work instead, so that we can give to others. We put off foul speech and put on edifying speech to minister grace to others who are listening. So, bear with me as I endeavor to explain these two verses in their context.

---

88 Chrysostom.

Most commentators explain that these verses mean we are to be angry, but we are not to sin in our anger. If that is true here, then it would only be righteous anger that is allowable, according to the Word. But then, that would make the next phrase confusing; when Paul says we are not to let the sun go down on our wrath or give place to the devil. Nor would that phrase make sense, because what difference would it make if I am angry but it is righteous anger?

Others will hold that when we do get angry we should not go to bed angry. In other words, we need to work things out before bedtime or we give place to the devil. That, too, certainly has truth to it, as the Bible teaches that we are to take care of offenses quickly, according to Matthew 5:25. But then, why would Paul say to be angry? Is he saying that I can be angry all day, which is sinning, but yet just make sure I get rid of my anger before I go to bed? That is nonsense!

Neither of these interpretations seems to fit with what Paul is saying. We have to keep in mind that Paul was a Jew and he is thinking as a Jewish scholar. Another way of seeing these two verses is to consider that Paul is saying we are to be angry with sin. Notice he is commanding them to *be angry*. We are not to ever cool down our wrath when it comes to our sin, but we are to be continually vigilant to fight against it—to *not sin*. It is very possible that Paul has in mind that story of Israel's battle with the Amorites, recorded in Joshua 10:1-15, when God caused the sun not to go down until the battle was won. We are to not let the sun go down on our battle with sin; we fight until the battle is won. The whole of this paragraph is governed by this command to always be angry with sin, to continue to fight against it, by remembering (renewing our minds) that we have decisively put away lying, stealing, corrupt speech, resentment and malice. When believers become mentally lazy and discontinue their vigilant hatred of their sin, they cease fighting against it, and in so doing, they *give place to the devil*, which means to give him room. This is what Paul will deal with again when we get to chapter six and the metaphor of the believer's armor that we must put on in order to wage war against sin (Ephesians 6:10-18). With this understanding of our need to wage war against our sin, let's consider the second sin that Paul mentions that is not acceptable for the new woman!

Ephesians 4:28
Put off Stealing and Put on Working
with Your Hands

> Let him who stole steal no longer, but rather let him labor, working with his hands what is good, that he may have something to give him who has need (Ephesians 4:28).

The second sin we are to put off is *stealing*. Paul says *let him who stole steal no longer*. Stealing is taking something that belongs to someone else with no intention of returning it. The Ephesian believers, having already made a definitive decision to turn from sin, are to no longer steal. Instead, they are to vigilantly resist the temptations of the flesh to compromise in the area of stealing. This would include any type of cheating, embezzlement, theft, or compromise, in not rendering someone their due, such as wages or taxes.[89] And, like all these commands to put off these particular sins, these sins were too often continuing in the saints at Ephesus. The command to stop these sins is in the present tense, indicating that the action was still going on and it needed to stop. Unfortunately, the believers at Ephesus were too often still lying and stealing; they needed Paul's admonishment to cast off these practices of the old life.

Exodus 20:15 says, "You shall not steal." This is one of the ten commandments God gave to Moses. Statistics tell us that more than 13 billion dollars' worth of goods are stolen from retailers alone every year. That's about 35 million dollars a day. Now, that is just in retail stores. This does not include people's personal belongings that are stolen, like things from their homes, their cars or even having their children stolen from them. (Statistics indicate that about 60,000 children are kidnapped every year.) They also tell us that there are

---

89 Stealing is hated and forbidden by God (cf. Exod. 20:15; Jer. 7:9-10; Mark 10:19; Rom. 13:9). Unbelievers practice it (cf. Ps. 119:61; Amos 3:10; Hos. 6:9; Job 24:14) and even associate with those who lie (cf. Isa. 1:23) and make excuses for it (cf. Jer. 7:9-10). It is such a crime against God that He excludes those who practice it from heaven (cf. 1 Cor. 6:10).

27 million shoplifters in America. But stealing material things is not the only form of stealing. In our world today, thieves can rob you of your identity. We call this identity theft. Other ways we steal are stealing people's time or stealing their virginity. Borrowing money and not paying it back is stealing; borrowing anything that you don't return is stealing. Lying to your employer about how many hours you've worked is stealing from him or her (of course, it's also lying). These are just some of the ways that we steal.

Now, when does a thief stop being a thief to get what he wants? When he starts working! And this is Paul's point. We put off stealing and instead, we put on working. Paul says *let him labor, working with his hands*. This second virtue that the new man or woman is to put on is *working with our hands*. This means that instead of stealing, we pursue employment. God made us to work, and I think it is such a shame in our culture to see so many people who do not want to work and who are content to live off the government. Paul is clear in another place that this is not acceptable for God's children. Consider 2 Thessalonians 3:10-12: "For even when we were with you, we commanded you this: If anyone will not work, neither shall he eat. For we hear that there are some who walk among you in a disorderly manner, not working at all, but are busybodies. Now those who are such we command and exhort through our Lord Jesus Christ that they work in quietness and eat their own bread." Now I want to get a little personal with you as women, because many of us are privileged to stay home and to take care of our homes and families as God commands us. But I fear many of us are stealing from our families and even from our Lord when we waste idle hours in front of the television or on the computer or cell phone, when we could be working with our hands to clean our homes, cook meals, provide a meal for someone else, plant a garden or some other thing we could be doing. Idle hands are certainly the devil's workshop, and we, as women, would do well do examine ourselves to see what we are doing with our hands. I have seen moms who are so engrossed in their phones out in public that they have no idea that their child needs their attention. This is a sad indictment of some mothers.

Now, most of us will agree that working is a good idea. As we work diligently, it enables us to make a living, buy a house, save up for retirement and enjoy a good life. But Paul has something to say about why we should put off stealing and work instead, and it's not so we can take luxurious vacations and enjoy the here and now. Paul says one of the motives of working is so that we may have something to give to him who has need. Just as our telling the truth is for the benefit of others, so also is our working with our hands; it is for the benefit of others. This doesn't mean we can't enjoy what God has given us, but if we are oppressing the poor and the widows and not giving to help others, then we have the wrong idea about money. (Consider Acts 2:41-47 and Acts 4:32-37.) Paul now moves to the third socially acceptable sin that is not acceptable for a member of God's household: corrupt speech.

Ephesians 4:29
Put off Corrupting Speech and Put on Edifying Speech

> Let no corrupt word proceed out of your mouth, but what is good for necessary edification, that it may impart grace to the hearers (Ephesians 4:29).

The third socially acceptable sin we are to put off is *corrupt speech*. *Corrupt* means rotten, bad, decaying, depraved, evil, or contaminating. It was used of food, like fruits and vegetables, which had become spoiled. I am amazed at some of the things that I hear Christian people talk about: ungodly slang, foolish jesting, dirty jokes, sexual innuendos, sarcasm, and hurtful joking. My friend, these words should not be a part of a believer's speech. James tells us that our tongues are unruly and full of evil, but ladies, we must learn to tame our tongues; especially when we stop and consider that Jesus says we will give account for every idle word we speak (Matthew 12:36). We should taste every word before we let it come out of our mouth.

Instead of using our mouths for rotten speech we are to use our mouths for *good* speech, speech that is edifying. *Edifying* speech is the third virtue that is totally acceptable for the follower of Christ, and, may I add, very welcomed for the new creature in Christ. The words that come out of our mouths should be words that build up and encourage. Now this doesn't mean we never confront people or exhort people, as that is not what Paul is speaking about here. But it does mean that we put off foul language and put on gracious and kind and encouraging speech.

Note again, Paul says we do this for others, *that it may impart grace to the hearers*. I don't know about you, but I would much rather hear a fellow believer say something like, "What a beautiful day today, God is so good to give us this great weather," than to hear them say, "My (negative adjective) husband; do you know he did not kiss me good-bye today?! He is such a jerk!" Now, which one do you think is more edifying to listen to? Our words should be gracious and not graceless. In Luke 4:22, it is recorded for us that some in the synagogue, upon listening to Jesus speak, mentioned that His words were gracious. And yet even though Christ was gracious when He spoke, He was always truthful and did not shy away from exhortation or confrontation.

Summary

Paul has shown us three sins that are not acceptable for the new man that we must put off: *Lying*, (v 25); *Stealing*, (v 28); and *Corrupt Speech*, (v 29). He's also shown us three virtues that are acceptable for the new man that we must put on. What are they? *Speaking the Truth*, (v 25); *Working with Our Hands*, (v 28); and *Edifying Speech*, (v 29). It is also worth mentioning again that each of these is for the purpose of benefiting someone else, because we are members of each other, we are a body. Too often, we think our sins do not affect others, but, ladies, they do!

What about you? Have you become like many today who are comfortable with socially accepted sins? Do you lie and justify it, by saying it was just a white lie or that it's not a big deal because everyone is doing it? Are you stealing? Maybe you're not actually taking material things from others, but perhaps you are stealing time from your employer, time from the Lord, time from others. Have you examined your speech lately? What kinds of words come out of your mouth? Have you become coarse in your talking in order to fit in with your peers? If we were to play a recording of the words you have spoken this past week, would we find corrupt speech coming out of your mouth or good and edifying speech?

Are you angry about your sin? Are you waging war against sin? Or do you excuse it as justifiable because it is the acceptable thing to do? Let's determine with the help of the Holy Spirit to put off the socially acceptable sins of lying, stealing, and corrupt speech, and put on the acceptable virtues of truth-telling, working with our hands, and edifying speech!

Questions to Consider
The Need for God's Children to Put off Socially Acceptable Sins!
Ephesians 4:25-29

1. (a) Read Ephesians 4:25-29 and make a list of the sins that Paul says believers are to put off. (b) What are believers to put on instead of these sins? (c) List the reasons, according to the text, that we are to put off what is wrong and put on what is right. (d) Memorize Ephesians 4:29.

2. (a) One of the sins that Paul says we are to put off is lying. According to the following passages, why should we put off lying? Proverbs 6:16-19; Proverbs 12:19; John 8:44; Colossians 3:9-10; Revelation 21:8; and Revelation 22:15. (b) What are some of the ways we, as Christians, lie today? (c) Since the Bible states that we come out of the womb speaking lies (Psalm 58:3), how then are you teaching your children and grandchildren to put off this terrible sin?

3. (a) Read Acts 4:32-5:11, and list the sins from Ephesians 4:25-30 that Ananias and his wife Sapphira committed. (b) What was the result of their sinning?

4. (a) What does Exodus 22:1-4 say about the punishment for stealing? (b) What happens to a person who continually steals, according to 1 Corinthians 6:9-10? (c) What are some ways people steal from others, besides actually taking their material possessions?

5. What do you think Paul means when he says, "Be angry, and do not sin" (Ephesians 4:26a)?

6. Do any of these sins have a dominating hold on your life? (This is a private question). If so, please put them off today and do not delay, as these are sins of the old woman and not the new woman.

7. After studying this lesson, please write out a prayer to God based on the need in your life.

Chapter 14

Are You Grieving the Spirit or Walking in the Spirit?

Ephesians 4:30-32

Recently, I was browsing through the books I have on my office bookshelf. I pulled one off the shelf that is one of my favorites, *Prayers of the Martyrs*. I don't look at it often, as I find it to be a sobering reminder of my brothers and sisters in Christ who have gone before me and have died unthinkable deaths. Yet, it struck me that all these martyrs had died without bitterness or anger; they died with forgiveness in their hearts toward their persecutors! Some were set on fire; some were beheaded, executed by drowning, tortured to death; stoned to death; shot to death, crushed to death; dismembered—and some were killed by wild beasts.

Some of the prayers these martyrs offered up as they were dying are recorded for us: "May God have mercy on you! May God Bless you! Lord, you know that I am innocent. I forgive my enemies with all my heart. Hail, Christ our King!" "I beg you, Lord God our Father, forgive them, for they are unaware of what they are doing." "O God Most High, do not consider the actions of my persecutors as sin. God have pity upon them!" This last one was found in the clothing of a dead child. "O Lord, remember not only the men and women of good will, but also those of ill will. But, do not remember all of the suffering they have inflicted upon us: Instead, remember the fruits we have borne because of this suffering—our fellowship, our loyalty to one another, our humility, our courage, our generosity, the greatness of heart that has grown from this trouble. When our persecutors come to be judged by you, let all of these fruits that we have borne be their forgiveness."[90]

These saints are now in heaven, but their prayers have been left for our benefit, and serve as a reminder to each of us that

---

90 Excerpts from Duane W. H. Arnold, *Prayers of the Martyrs* (Grand Rapids: Zondervan, 1991), page numbers unknown.

forgiveness should be the norm for all who profess the name of Christ, even when we might be facing death because of persecution. As we close chapter 4 of Ephesians, let us remind ourselves of our calling as believers.

Ephesians 4:30-32

And do not grieve the Holy Spirit of God, by whom you were sealed for the day of redemption. [31]Let all bitterness, wrath, anger, clamor, and evil speaking be put away from you, with all malice. [32]And be kind to one another, tenderhearted, forgiving one another, just as God in Christ forgave you (Ephesians 4:30-32).

In our last lesson we saw three sins that are not acceptable for the new man, and three acceptable virtues which believers must put on. We also learned that each one of these virtues is intended for the benefit of someone else, as we are members of one another. Our outline for this lesson will include:

The Command to Not Grieve the Spirit, (v 30)

The Sins that Grieve the Spirit, (v 31)

The Signs of Walking in the Spirit, (v 32)

Ephesians 4:30
The Command to Not Grieve the Spirit

And do not grieve the Holy Spirit of God, by whom you were sealed for the day of redemption (Ephesians 4:30).

Why does Paul say *and do not grieve*? Some think that the word *and* seems to indicate that the corrupt speech Paul mentions in the previous verse, verse 29, grieves the Holy Spirit. But when I think through this, it doesn't make sense, because all sin grieves the Holy Spirit. So why are the words *and do not grieve the Holy Spirit of God* placed here? When we think of the context of what Paul is saying, that is, that we are the household of God (2:19), a holy temple (2:21), and a dwelling place of God (2:22), then it becomes clear why Paul says we are not to grieve the Spirit. We are the temple of

God, and the temple is indwelt by the Holy Spirit, as Paul says in 1 Corinthians 3:16: "Do you not know that you are the temple of God and that the Spirit of God dwells in you?" Every time we sin we drag the Holy Spirit into it and that, my sister, is grieving to Him. John MacArthur says, "Whenever you sin, it's as if you've ascended to the throne room of God, walked to the foot of His throne, and sinned right there. Whatever you do, you do in the presence of God."[91] My friend, this should give us pause to think before we commit any sin!

Now what does it mean to *grieve the Holy Spirit*? This word, *grieve*, is not used anywhere else in the New Testament, but it means to afflict with sorrow, to make sad, to cause grief. This makes sense when we think of the Holy Spirit being a part of the Godhead. He is a person and He and the Father and the Son are one. So when we grieve one member of the Godhead, we also grieve the others. When we think of grieving someone in the human realm, this also gives meaning to what Paul is saying. When a child disobeys, we grieve; when a friend betrays us, we grieve; when a spouse is unfaithful, we grieve. In fact, when anyone we love sins, we grieve. I think of that passage in Genesis 26:34-35 which says, "When Esau was forty years old, he took as wives Judith the daughter of Beeri the Hittite, and Basemath the daughter of Elon the Hittite. And they were a grief of mind to Isaac and Rebekah." Esau's foolish decision to take these two wives—pagan, Canaanite women—was a grief to his parents. And so it is when we sin; we make the Holy Spirit grieve; we make Him sad.

Paul also states in 1 Thessalonians 5:19 that we are not to quench the Spirit, which is different from grieving Him. To quench

---

91 John MacArthur, Jr., *God: Coming Face to Face with His Majesty* (Wheaton: Victor Books, 1993), 71. The warning about grieving the Spirit of God (vs. 30) could refer to each of these specific applications as we suggest, i.e.,, believers would grieve the Spirit of God by lying and not telling the truth; by stealing and not giving; by communicating with rotten speech and not by edifying words, etc. For indeed, whenever believers relax their vigilant fight against sin, slip back into old behavior, they grieve the Spirit of God. Yet, a good case could be made that the context suggests the grieving of the Spirit of God takes place when we don't build each other up by gracious words but use corrupt communication to tear each other down. In other words, Paul would be adding a basic warning that applies to anything we put off and put on, but he adds it here for special emphasis on the particular struggle to graciously communicate in order to build up others.

means to extinguish or to go out. The Holy Spirit is often referred to as a fire, and the idea here is that we are not to put Him out like we would pour cold water on a burning fire. This would seem to indicate that one has stopped fanning the flame of devotion and become indifferent to the Spirit's leading and conviction in their life. I have met Christians like this, who seem to have no passion, no fire. Neither quenching, nor grieving, the Spirit is something that we as believers want to be guilty of. Our lives should be marked by walking in the Spirit and burning with zeal for our God. Notice also that Paul says it is the Holy Spirit of God whom we grieve. He is Holy and He expects those whom He inhabits to be holy, as Paul has already written in Ephesians 1:4: "Just as He chose us in Him before the foundation of the world, that we should be holy and without blame before Him in love."

Paul reminds us, here in Ephesians 4:30, that we *were sealed* with the Holy Spirit. When we were in Ephesians 1:13, we saw that we are sealed with the Holy Spirit of promise. We learned that sealing has a couple of meanings. First of all, it was used in reference to an official mark that was put on a letter or some important document. In fact, all possessions that were important were marked with a seal. The seal was made with hot wax and then pressed with some type of ring. Esther 8:8 refers to this idea, "You yourselves write a decree for the Jews, as you please, in the king's name, and seal it with the king's signet ring; for whatever is written in the king's name and sealed with the king's signet ring no one can revoke." We can conclude that this type of seal was used for the purpose of securing important documents. Second, a seal was used for marking animals. We call this practice branding in our day. This sealing was used as a mark of ownership. When we put these two ideas together—keeping in mind that we have been sealed with the Holy Spirit—we can conclude that this sealing is, first, for the purpose of making us secure in Christ and, second, intended to be a sign of ownership. The believer is secure, praise God, but we also are owned by someone other than ourselves—our wonderful Master.

We are sealed with the Holy Spirit of Promise by the authority of God and nothing can take that away; He owns us; we are His. So why does Paul say we are sealed *for the day of redemption*? The *day of redemption* is the time in the future when we will go to glory and our bodies and spirits will be fully redeemed. This is the time when we will grieve the Holy Spirit no more! As Paul puts it in Philippians 3:20-21, "our citizenship is in heaven, from which we also eagerly wait for the Savior, the Lord Jesus Christ, who will transform our lowly body that it may be conformed to His glorious body, according to the working by which He is able even to subdue all things to Himself."

It is encouraging that Paul says we are sealed until the day of redemption, because it is proof that even our sinning will not cause us to lose our salvation. We are sealed unto the day of redemption! I remember once having a discussion with a gal who believed that every time she sinned she had to get saved and baptized all over again. I remember asking her, what if she sinned and then was suddenly killed, would she go to hell? She said, "Yes." I remember thinking to myself, "What an awful way to live life!" We belong to God, just as a child belongs to his parents, and no matter what evil that child does, he is still their child. We cannot cease to be God's child. This does not, however, give us license to sin, because our sin grieves the Holy Spirit. In light of sin that grieves the Holy Spirit, let's move on from the command to not grieve the Spirit to the sins that do grieve the Spirit in verse 31.

Ephesians 4:31
The Sins that Grieve the Spirit

Let all bitterness, wrath, anger, clamor, and evil speaking be put away from you, with all malice (Ephesians 4:31).

Now, obviously these are not the only sins that grieve the Spirit of God, but they certainly are grievous enough for Paul to mention six of them. *The first sin he mentions is bitterness.* What is bitterness? Bitterness, in the New Testament, is described as a "gall of bitterness" (Acts 8:23, KJV). In that passage, we read that Peter perceived that Simon the sorcerer had a heart of great wickedness and was "in the gall of bitterness, and in the bond of iniquity." It refers to someone who has a bitter frame of mind. Bitterness is a poison, a sharp arrow, venomous. When we allow bitterness to grow in our hearts it poisons our relationships not only with others, but also with God, and we become deeper in bondage to it. One who has a "root of bitterness," mentioned in Hebrews 12:15, is a wicked person with a sin that leads ultimately to denial of the faith.

The second sin that Paul mentions that grieves the Spirit is wrath. Wrath is indignation, an abiding and settled habit of mind, like a roaring furnace. It describes a fierce passion (as if breathing hard). The Greeks would liken it to a fire in straw, which would flare up briefly and then be gone. *The third sin Paul mentions is anger,* and it describes someone who is quick-tempered, who exhibits violent passion or a deep smoldering bitterness. One man describes anger like this: "growing, inner anger, like sap in a tree on a hot day which swells the trunk and branches until they are in danger of bursting." We have all had that inner feeling of anger inside, if we're truthful with ourselves, and some of us more than others. I had a real problem with anger before my new life in Christ. If you don't believe me, just ask my husband!

What is the difference between wrath and anger? Anger often lies below the surface and gives rise to eruptions of wrath. Wrath is that anger boiling over, which results in sudden outbursts of anger. Whoever said, "Sticks and stones may break my bones, but words can never hurt me," must have never been the recipient of anger and wrath. My daughter-in-law shared with me that she read that murder is now the number one cause of death among pregnant women. This usually is caused by the anger or wrath of a husband or a boyfriend. We are living in a society that seems to be exploding with angry men, women and children.

The fourth sin Paul mentions that should be put away from God's children is clamor. Clamor is described as an outcry, grief, disorder, a brawl. This was a term that was used to describe people shouting back and forth at each other. This is what happens when we give way to bitterness, wrath, and anger, as we start clamoring or yelling or screaming. Just recall the last time you were clamoring with someone, and I am sure you can identify the bitter or angry heart which allowed you to spew forth that clamor.

The fifth sin that grieves the Spirit is evil speaking. This would be anything that comes out of one's mouth that is defaming. It might be slander, gossip, corrupt communication, or blasphemy against God. Paul adds that it is to *be put away from you*, which means to make a clean sweep, to pick it up and carry it away. This progression of ideas makes sense, as when we are arguing, or clamoring, we spew forth evil speaking out of our mouths, which we usually end up regretting.

The sixth sin that grieves the Spirit of God is malice. Malice is a wicked desire with respect to others, that determines to do them harm. This progression also makes sense, as when bitterness goes unchecked and unrepented of, we become angry and wrathful, which leads to screaming and yelling with all sorts of evil speaking, which if unchecked, can lead to a desire to harm and hurt others. You might be thinking, "I have been this person at times; I am guilty of grieving the Spirit. What should I do?" Thankfully, Paul doesn't end with this ugly description of our sin but ends with what we are to do instead. As we close, we will move from the sins that grieve the Spirit to the signs that one is walking in the Spirit. Again, these are not the only indicators that one is walking in the Spirit, but they are certainly worthy of great consideration.

Ephesians 4:32
The Signs of Walking in the Spirit

And be kind to one another, tenderhearted, forgiving one another, just as God in Christ forgave you (Ephesians 4:32).

In this verse, Paul gives three indicators of those who are walking in the Spirit. The first sign that we are walking in the Spirit is *being kind to one another*. Instead of being malicious we are to show kindness. Kindness is the opposite of malice. What does it mean to be kind? It means to be gracious, sweet, and to have a generous disposition. There have been times in the past when my husband has graciously reminded me of my need to be kind, by reminding me that my name, Susan, means "tender lily."

Second, we are to *be tenderhearted*. This means we are to be compassionate, or sympathetic. It comes from a Greek word which speaks of one's intestines; it refers to a deep feeling that is expressed by being empathetic toward others. We should hurt with those who are hurting, along with seeking ways to relieve their misery, if at all possible.

Then, Paul says we are to *be forgiving one another*. Forgiveness means to pardon freely. And Paul says we forgive just as God in Christ forgave us. In Colossians 3:13, Paul teaches us that we are to be "bearing with one another, and forgiving one another, if anyone has a complaint against another; even as Christ forgave you, so you also must do." We are to forgive *just as God in Christ forgave you*, which means that we are to forgive even as, according to, just as, in proportion to, and in the same degree as He has forgiven us. And how did Christ forgive us? Was it a partial forgiveness? Did He say, "Well, I will forgive you for that sin, but I can *never* forgive you for that one—that one is unforgivable!"? No, He forgave us fully and completely. We must forgive others completely because our Lord has forgiven us completely. The apostle Peter evidently struggled with this concept, as we have recorded in Matthew 18:21-22 these words: "Then Peter came to Him and said, 'Lord, how often shall my brother sin against me, and I forgive him? Up to seven times'? Jesus said to him, 'I do not say to you, up to seven times, but up to seventy times seven.'" Jesus tells Peter that he must not forgive seven times but 490 times! It is doubtful that we have ever had to forgive someone that many times for the same offense! And yet the Lord has forgiven us 490 times, plus more, for the same offenses that we repeat over and over again!

There are other biblical examples we can follow as well. Let's look at Joseph in Genesis 50:19-20, when his brothers sought his forgiveness for selling him into slavery. He said, "Do not be afraid, for am I in the place of God? But as for you, you meant evil against me; but God meant it for good, in order to bring it about as it is this day, to save many people alive." Genesis 50:21 says that he comforted them and spoke kindly to them. Consider also Stephen, in Acts 7:60, while he was being stoned to death. There the Scriptures record for us, "Then he knelt down and cried out with a loud voice, 'Lord, do not charge them with this sin.' And when he had said this, he fell asleep." An unforgiving Christian is a contradiction of terms because we are the ones who have been forgiven.

May I offer you three practical steps to help you with an unforgiving attitude? 1. First, confess it to the Lord, and ask Him to help you mend the relationship. 2. Go to the person, ask for their forgiveness, and seek reconciliation with them. 3. Give the person something you highly value, such as your time, perhaps financial help, or some special gift. This is a practical approach to dealing with an unforgiving spirit, as Jesus said that where your treasure is, there will your heart be also (Matthew 6:21). You simply cannot ignore an unforgiving heart, as bitterness and resentment will set in and will rob you of your joy. And by the way, an attitude of avoidance is not forgiveness.

Now, before we go on I do want to say that there is a biblical principle in Leviticus 19:17 that is often overlooked when we're struggling with bitterness. Often, we use bitterness as an opportunity to gossip or slander the person we're bitter toward, but we need to do what is right before God, especially where sin is involved. We need to go to the person who has sinned against us and confront the sin issue. Leviticus 19:17, "You shall not hate your brother in your heart. You shall surely rebuke your neighbor, and not bear sin because of him." Jesus also tells us, in Matthew 18:15-20, that we are to go to our brother if they have sinned and we are to confront them. He gives us steps on how this is to be done. When we do what God has set before us to do, it takes away the bitterness and hatred in our heart that might be festering. Now, I know that is not Paul's point here in Ephesians, but I thought it was worthy of mentioning before we draw our lesson to a close. As we put into practice the admonitions of Ephesians 4:32, we stop grieving the Spirit and instead make Him happy or glad!

Summary

The Command to Not Grieve the Spirit, (v 30). My dear sister, are you breaking one of God's commands by grieving the Spirit of God who dwells in you?

The Sins that Grieve the Spirit, (v 31): bitterness, wrath, anger, clamor, evil speaking, and malice. Have you made the Spirit sad by holding onto bitterness in your heart toward someone? Do you find yourself throwing fits of rage, speaking evil words, while screaming and yelling at your kids or your husband? Have you wanted to murder someone, even if it was only in your thoughts? These are evil things that make the Spirit of God sorrowful.

The Signs of Walking in the Spirit, (v 32): kindness, tenderhearted compassion, forgiveness. Instead of these awful, grievous sins, why not determine today to be kind with your words instead of evil with your words? Why not offer compassion to others instead of getting angry and wrathful toward them? Instead of wanting to harm someone, why not forgive them? Interestingly enough, as I was browsing through the book, *Prayers of the Martyrs*, I noticed that it had been given to me on my birthday, more than 17 years before, by a woman who eventually slandered my reputation and tried to destroy me. I thought as I held the book in my hand, "How ironic, that it was she who gave this book to me." And then I thought, "Oh, the mercy and goodness of my Lord, that I have no bitterness or resentment toward her, no anger, no malice, no ill will." God has granted me the ability to forgive her and to do so long ago. How is that possible? It is possible only by the Holy Spirit of God who dwells within me and helps me put off all those ugly, dreadful sins and helps me put on tender compassion and forgiveness. These things are possible as we live our days with our Master in Heavenly Places!

Questions to Consider

Are You Grieving the Spirit or Walking in the Spirit?
Ephesians 4:30-32

(a) Read Ephesians 4:30-32 and make note of the sins that are to be put off and the characteristics that are to be put on. (b) What else do you notice that is unique about these three verses? (c) Memorize Ephesians 4:32.

1. (a) Paul states in Ephesians 4:30 that we are not to grieve the Holy Spirit. In 1 Thessalonians 5:19, he states that we are not to quench the Spirit. Do you think there is a difference between these two ideas? If so, what do you think is the difference? (b) How do we as believers grieve the Holy Spirit?

2. (a) Paul reminds us of our biblical responsibility to forgive each other, in Ephesians 4:32. Besides the Lord, who in Scripture comes to your mind as an example of how to forgive? Write down the person or persons, what happened to them that caused them to need to forgive, and what you learn from their example for your own life. (b) According to Matthew 6:14-15; Matthew 18:21-35; and James 2:13, what happens to one who refuses to forgive?

3. (a) What do the following verses say about being kind? Nehemiah 9:17; Proverbs 31:26; Luke 6:35; 1 Corinthians 13:4; Galatians 5:22. (b) How would you define the words "kind" and "kindness"? (c) If you are brave, ask your husband or a close friend if they think your words are kind.

4. Is there anyone that you are bitter toward? Are you harboring a grudge? Would you say you are a forgiving person? (These are private questions.)

5. After carefully considering question 6, please write a prayer request for yourself.

Chapter 15

Imitators of God or Partakers of Sin?
Ephesians 5:1-7

A few years ago some of our grandchildren were spending the night with my husband and me. One of my grandsons, who was two at the time, was watching a little Christmas show, as it was that time of year. During a break in the show, a commercial came on that was advertising moisturizer, and in the commercial a woman was digging deep into a jar and slathering moisturizer on her face. The program resumed, and I looked over at my two year old grandson to see him standing on the couch reenacting the whole commercial almost exactly as he'd seen it. I got to laughing so hard that I was crying! (Of course, it was one of those moments where you had to be there to get the full effect.) Imitating—that is what my grandson, Ethan, was doing.

Around the same time, I was grieved to hear of some professing Christians who were committing sexual sins and thinking nothing of it. Some of them were even accusing people of not being understanding and forgiving, though they had no intention of giving up their sin. Others were claiming that God forgives their sins, so why should they *not* continue in fornication?!

I think that both of these events were timely in light of our study of this passage. In these verses, Paul is saying that we are either imitators of God or we are partakers of sin. Let's consider his sobering words.

Ephesians 5:1-7

Therefore be imitators of God as dear children. [2]And walk in love, as Christ also has loved us and given Himself for us, an offering and a sacrifice to God for a sweet-smelling aroma. [3]But fornication and all uncleanness or covetousness, let it not even be named among you, as is fitting for saints; [4]neither filthiness, nor foolish talking, nor coarse jesting, which are not fitting, but rather giving of thanks. [5]For this you know, that no fornicator, unclean person, nor covetous man, who is an idolater, has any inheritance in the kingdom of Christ and God. [6]Let no one deceive you with empty words, for because of these things the wrath of God comes upon the sons of disobedience. [7]Therefore do not be partakers with them (Ephesians 5:1-7).

As we finished studying chapter 4 of Ephesians in our previous lesson, we learned about grieving the Spirit of God. As we begin studying Ephesians 5 in this lesson, we'll see:

The Call to Imitate God as Dear Children, (vv 1-2, 4b)

The Call to Not Involve Ourselves in Sin, (vv 3-4a)

The Call to Isolate Ourselves from Those Who Practice these Things, (vv 5-7).

Ephesians 5:1-2
The Call to Imitate God as Dear Children

Therefore be imitators of God as dear children (Ephesians 5:1).

Paul's thoughts here in Ephesians 5 are a continuation of his thoughts in Ephesians 4; there is no division of thought here between the two chapters. Remember, Paul is writing a *letter* to his Ephesian friends. The chapters and verses were not included in Paul's original writing but were inserted at a later time. Paul begins this section by saying *therefore be imitators of God*. In other words, just as God is kind, tenderhearted and forgiving, as mentioned in verse 32 of Ephesians 4, so we should be kind, tenderhearted and forgiving, as His children. This is the nature of God and this should be the nature of His children. Consider Luke 6:35-36: "But love your enemies, do good, and lend, hoping for nothing in return; and your reward will be great, and you will be sons of the Most High. For He is kind to the unthankful and evil. Therefore be merciful, just as your Father also is merciful."

Now, what does it mean to *be imitators of God*? The word *imitate* means to emulate, impersonate, mimic. To imitate someone would mean that we copy the specific characteristics and actions of someone else. This is what my grandson was doing. It's like the phrase that was popularized a number of years ago, "What Would Jesus Do?" to the point that people wore bracelets with the letters WWJD on them. And as we ask ourselves, "What would Jesus do?" we, hopefully, follow that question up with doing what Jesus would do; we mimic Him. Now, my friend, we will only be able to know what Jesus would do when we know the nature and character of God as revealed through His Word. If you are not in the habit of saturating your mind with His Word through reading, study, and memorization of His Word, then you will not know what He is like, and you will not know how to mimic or imitate Him. Ethan had to carefully watch that commercial in order to know how to reenact it. So we must carefully study the Word in order to know how to reenact the character of God. It's not by chance that Paul follows this phrase with the words *as dear children.* Dear children of God should imitate their parent—God. One of the most essential ways we imitate God is by love, which is Paul's next point in verse 2.

> And walk in love, as Christ also has loved us and given Himself for us, an offering and a sacrifice to God for a sweet-smelling aroma (Ephesians 5:2).

It's interesting to me that Paul mentions we are to *walk in love* right after his admonition to forgive, because forgiveness seems to be at the core of love. Isn't that what Christ did when He died for us? He forgave us our sins! What love! Again, the template for our love is God the Father and Christ His Son. Hymnist F. M. Lehman writes:

> *The Love of God is greater far*
> *than tongue or pen can ever tell,*
> *It goes beyond the highest star*
> *and reaches to the lowest hell;*
> *The guilty pair, bowed down with care,*
> *God gave His Son to win:*
> *His erring child He reconciled*
> *and pardoned from his sin.*
> *O love of God, how rich and pure!*
> *How measureless and strong!*
> *It shall forevermore endure—*
> *the saints' and angels' song.*

When years of time shall pass away
and earthly thrones and kingdoms fall,
When men, who here refuse to pray,
on rocks and hills and mountains call,
God's love so sure shall still endure,
all measureless and strong:
Redeeming grace to Adam's race—
the saints' and angels' song.
O love of God, how rich and pure!
How measureless and strong!
It shall forevermore endure—
the saints' and angels' song.

Could we with ink the ocean fill
and were the skies of parchment made,
Were ev'ry stalk on earth a quill,
and ev'ry man a scribe by trade,
To write the love of God above
would drain the ocean dry,
Nor would the scroll contain the whole,
tho stretched from sky to sky.
O love of God, how rich and pure!
How measureless and strong!
It shall forevermore endure—
the saints' and angels' song.[92]

Paul has already written to the Ephesians that they are to walk worthy of their calling, in 4:1, and now he says one of the ways they do that is to walk in love. What does it mean to walk in love? Well, Paul goes on to tell us what it means. We walk in love just *as Christ ... has loved us and given Himself for us*, as *an offering and a sacrifice*. The word *offering* means to bring, in the same way that an offering would be offered in the Old Testament. When one would offer a sin offering or a peace offering or some other offering, they would bring a lamb or a dove or some animal to offer as a sacrifice. The word *sacrifice* means a slaughter sacrifice. So it was with Christ. He brought Himself to offer as a sacrifice; He willingly handed Himself over to death, to a slaughter sacrifice. Isaiah puts it well in

92 *The Love of God*, 1917.

Isaiah 53:7: "He was oppressed and He was afflicted, yet He opened not His mouth; he was led as a lamb to the slaughter, and as a sheep before its shearers is silent, so He opened not His mouth." And Paul says we are to walk like this. We too, must lay down our lives, just as Christ said in John 15:12-13, "This is My commandment, that you love one another as I have loved you. Greater love has no one than this, than to lay down one's life for his friends." Paul, in Romans 12:1, says, "I beseech you therefore, brethren, by the mercies of God, that you present your bodies a living sacrifice, holy, acceptable to God, which is your reasonable service." Offering ourselves as a sacrifice is what we are to do. That is normal Christianity! My dear sisters, we are to willingly offer ourselves, we are to hand ourselves over to be sacrifices for others. We are to willingly do whatever is needed, whatever is asked, and we are to do it with a joyful heart. Paul will mention this again when we get to Ephesians 5:25, where he admonishes husbands to "love your wives, just as Christ also loved the church and gave Himself for her." This is a tall order for husbands (and it makes me thank the Lord often that He made me a woman!).

Paul goes on to say this offering and sacrifice of Christ to God was *a sweet-smelling aroma*. Leviticus 4:31 speaks of the sweet aroma of an animal sacrifice: "He shall remove all its fat, as fat is removed from the sacrifice of the peace offering; and the priest shall burn it on the altar for a sweet aroma to the LORD. So the priest shall make atonement for him, and it shall be forgiven him." The words *sweet-smelling aroma* would indicate that the Lord's offering of Himself was pleasing to His Father. It is the same for us; Paul mentions this idea in Philippians 4:18: "Indeed I have all and abound. I am full, having received from Epaphroditus the things sent from you, a sweet-smelling aroma, an acceptable sacrifice, well pleasing to God." The things we do that are a sacrifice and an offering are sweet-smelling to God, as well as others. Paul again mentions this in 2 Corinthians 2:15-16, "For we are to God the fragrance of Christ among those who are being saved and among those who are perishing. To the one we are the aroma of death leading to death, and to the other the aroma of life leading to life. And who is sufficient for these things?" Paul moves on from our responsibility to imitate God to our responsibility to not partake in certain sins.

Ephesians 5:3-4a
The Call to Not Involve Ourselves in Sin

> But fornication and all uncleanness or covetousness, let
> it not even be named among you, as is fitting for saints;
> (Ephesians 5:3).

In contrast to walking in love, some walk in sin. Paul has already written to the Ephesians regarding sins that should no longer be a part of their life, and now he lists some more. Paul's list here deals basically with sexual sins. *The first of these sins is fornication.* The Greek word for *fornication* is <u>porneia</u>, from which we get our English word pornography. However, in the New Testament, the word is broadened to include any kind of illicit sex. This would include every kind of immoral sexual act: adultery, fornication, incest, homosexuality, bestiality. As we think about sexual sins, ladies, we must admit that we are faced with this temptation in a way that no other generation has been faced, due to the availability of pornography on the internet, television and magazines. I know of numerous families that have been ruined by this terrible sin, much of which was started on the computer. Sexual sin is not just a problem in our day, but it was in Paul's day, as well. One man says, "Illicit sexual activity was an enormous problem for new Gentile Christians to overcome in the early church. Adulterous relationships, men sleeping with their slave girls, incest, prostitution, 'sacred' sexual encounters in the local temples, and homosexuality were all a part of everyday life."[93]

The second sin Paul mentions is *uncleanness*. We learned about this in chapter 4, verse 19, so we don't need to elaborate much here. *Uncleanness* means any moral or physical impurity. This might be passions, ideas or fantasies. In Ephesians 4:19, Paul called it uncleanness with greediness. This is what he seems to indicate here, as the third sin he says needs to be put off is *covetousness*. Sexual sins are nothing more than *covetousness*, wanting something that is not ours to have. This is one of the Ten Commandments that God gave to Moses in Exodus 20:17: "You shall not covet your neighbor's house; you shall not covet your neighbor's wife, nor his male servant, nor his female servant, nor his ox, nor his donkey,

---

93   Arnold, 320.

nor anything that is your neighbor's." Sexual sins are nothing more than greed, desiring and taking something that is not ours to have, coveting someone else's body for our own pleasure.

Paul says these sins are not even *to be named* once among those who are God's *saints*; they are not *fitting*. In fact, he will say in verse 12 that it is shameful to even talk about such things. As believers, we should not be talking as believers about sexual sins. Now, Paul doesn't mean we're never to mention them, because he just did. He means that we are not to have anything to do with them; we do not participate in them at all. We flee from them, as Joseph did when he was tempted by Potiphar's wife to have sex with her (Genesis 39:12). We do not have anything to do with these sins, or even hint at them or flirt with them. One man says, "What does it mean that there must not be even a hint of immorality among the saints (v. 3)? It must mean something. In our sex-saturated culture, I would be surprised if there were not at least a few hints of immorality in our texts and tweets and inside jokes. And what about our clothes, our music, our flirting, and the way we talk about people who are in the room?"[94] "We have to take a hard look at the things we choose to put in front of our eyes. If there was a couple engaged in sexual activity on the couch in front of you, would you pull up a seat to watch? No, that would be perverse, voyeuristic. So why is it different when people record it first and then you watch? What if a good-looking guy or girl, barely dressed, came up to you on the beach and said, 'Why don't you sit on your towel right here and stare at me for a while?' Would you do it? No, that would be creepy. Why is it acceptable, then, when the same images are blown up the size of a three-story building? If we're honest, we often seek exposure to sexual immorality and temptations to impurity and call it 'innocent' relaxation."[95] "Try turning off the television and staying away from the movies for a month and see what new things you see when you come back. I fear many of us have become numb to the poison we are drinking. When it comes to sexual immorality, sin looks normal, righteousness looks very strange, and we look a lot like everybody else."[96] And if the sins Paul has already listed aren't bad enough, he goes on to list more sins for us to shun in verse 4.

---

94 DeYoung, 20-21.
95 Ibid. 118-119.
96 Ibid., 120.

neither filthiness, nor foolish talking, nor coarse jesting, which
are not fitting, (Ephesians 5:4a).

The fourth sin on the list is *filthiness*. What is that? *Filthiness*
is obscene or indecent language, dirty talk, and disgraceful speech.
I would give you an example, but if I did I would be doing what
Paul says not to do![97] You can, however, go out in the world and
more than likely hear within five minutes an example of what Paul
is saying. I don't know about you, but I am appalled at some of the
things people say today!

Fifth on the list of sins to flee from is foolish talking. The
phrase *foolish talking* is not mentioned anywhere else in Scripture. It
means stupid, foolish or idle talk. It would also entail sexual talk or
dirty jokes. Along with this, sixth on the list, *we are to rid ourselves
of coarse jesting. Course jesting* means sarcastic ridicule. This is
when someone will say anything to get a laugh even if they have
to cut people down and embarrass them. This would also would
connote filthy or sexual talk. This type of talking is not fitting or
appropriate for God's children. And let me say a word to you moms:
Please do not allow your children to participate in these things. I
hear young children saying things that are not appropriate, that are
not fitting, and their moms just ignore it! Instead of using our mouths
for that kind of speech, we are rather to give thanks.

Ephesians 5:4b
The Call to Imitate God as Dear Children

but rather giving of thanks (Ephesians 5:4b).

This is yet another way we imitate God. Paul states in
Hebrews 13:15, "Therefore, by Him let us continually offer the
sacrifice of praise to God, that is, the fruit of our lips, giving thanks
to His name." Now, perhaps you think it's odd that Paul injects right
here that we are to be using our mouths for the *giving of thanks*. If

97 This may likely indicate jesting that has gone too far, thus becoming sarcastic ridicule
that cuts people down and embarrasses others who are present. It is humor in bad
taste. Believers should build up and not destroy, even in humor. However, since in the
context the preceding words were concerned with sexual sins, filthiness (Greek, eutra-
pelia) could even have reference to dirty jokes or humor with suggestive overtones.
(Hoehner, 656).

we are using our mouths for thanksgiving to God and others, we are doing the opposite of the sins that Paul has just mentioned. Instead of being selfish with sexual perversions and sexual talk, we are to be selfless by praising God. Instead of being selfish, we are to be thankful. Can you imagine how our lives would change and be challenged if every time we gathered with the saints we obeyed this verse alone? Instead of foolish talk, we praise God for His goodness; instead of coarse jesting, we encourage a sister who's going through a struggle. "When was the last time we took a verse like, 'Let there be no filthiness nor foolish talk nor crude joking, which are out of place, but instead let there be thanksgiving' (Ephesians 5:3) and even began to try to apply this to our conversation, our motives, our YouTube clips, our television and commercial intake?"[98] Perhaps one of the most motivating verses in Scripture in regards to our speech is Matthew 12:36-37, where Jesus says, "But I say to you that for every idle word men may speak, they will give account of it in the day of judgment. For by your words you will be justified, and by your words you will be condemned."

Just in case you might be thinking, as some well-meaning professing Christians do today, that these things are okay and becoming of a dear child of God, Paul wants to remind you that it is not okay. In fact, not only are these sins not okay, they are worthy of damnation. And we see now the call to isolate ourselves from those who practice these things, in verse 5-7.

Ephesians 5:5-7
The Call to Isolate Ourselves from Those Who Practice These Things

> For this you know, that no fornicator, unclean person, nor covetous man, who is an idolater, has any inheritance in the kingdom of Christ and God (Ephesians 5:5).

Paul says *this you know*—you know with certainty—that people who are involved in the sins mentioned here will not inherit the kingdom of God. When well-meaning people tell me that they are doing these things, I am like, "Are you kidding me?! Are you completely ignorant of what God says?!" What do these people

---

98 DeYoung, 20.

do with passages like this one in Ephesians and Galatians 5:19-21? "Now the works of the flesh are evident, which are: adultery, fornication, uncleanness, lewdness, idolatry, sorcery, hatred, contentions, jealousies, outbursts of wrath, selfish ambitions, dissensions, heresies, envy, murders, drunkenness, revelries, and the like; of which I tell you beforehand, just as I also told you in time past, that those who practice such things will not inherit the kingdom of God." And what about 1 Corinthians 6:9-10? "Do you not know that the unrighteous will not inherit the kingdom of God? Do not be deceived. Neither fornicators, nor idolaters, nor adulterers, nor homosexuals, nor sodomites, nor thieves, nor covetous, nor drunkards, nor revilers, nor extortioners will inherit the kingdom of God." Paul goes on to say,

> Let no one deceive you with empty words, for because of these things the wrath of God comes upon the sons of disobedience (Ephesians 5:6).

My friend, we are living in an age when everyone does what is right in their own eyes, and well-meaning friends, "Christians" included, will tell you to go ahead and fornicate, commit adultery, be a homosexual, go see that movie with sex scenes and vulgarity, do what is right by your own standards. But Paul says *let no one deceive you with empty words*. These types of words are empty, not truthful. Don't believe it, Paul says. God doesn't change His character to suit our sexual perversions. And Paul goes on to say *because of these things the wrath of God comes upon the sons of disobedience*. Paul says the same thing in Colossians 3:5-6: "Therefore put to death your members which are on the earth: fornication, uncleanness, passion, evil desire, and covetousness, which is idolatry. Because of these things the wrath of God is coming upon the sons of disobedience." Since they have no inheritance in the kingdom of God, then the wrath that is coming upon them would be the torment of eternal hell. My friend, this is a high price to pay for temporal pleasure. I think of that wonderful chapter on faith in Hebrews 11 and the example of Moses in Hebrews 11:24-25, which says, "By faith Moses, when he became of age, refused to be called the son of Pharaoh's daughter, choosing rather to suffer affliction with the people of God than to enjoy the passing pleasures of sin." Paul ends his call to flee by saying,

Therefore do not be partakers with them (Ephesians 5:7).

Paul says *do not be partakers with them*, do not co-participate with them. Paul says in 1 Corinthians 5:11, "But now I have written to you not to keep company with anyone named a brother, who is sexually immoral, or covetous, or an idolater, or a reviler, or a drunkard, or an extortioner—not even to eat with such a person." I would caution you about being good friends with someone who claims to be a believer and yet whose ideas are contrary to what Paul is saying. You might be saying to yourself, "I would not do these things! Fornicate—no way! Use my mouth for obscenities—not on your life!" But, we'll listen to it and watch it in the theater, on TV and the internet. We will let others speak in these ways without correcting them, and so we become partakers with them.

Summary

The Call to Imitate God as Dear Children, (vv 1-2, 4b): We imitate God by being kind, tenderhearted, forgiving, loving to the point of offering ourselves up as a sacrifice, and being thankful. *The Call to Not Involve Ourselves in Sin,* (vv 3-4a): We are not to involve ourselves in sexual sins of fornication, uncleanness, covetousness, filthiness, foolish talking, or course jesting. *The Call to Isolate Ourselves from Those who Practice These Things,* (vv 5-7): We are not to be deceived by well-meaning friends and take part in these things. We must remember that these sins are worthy of hell and prohibit one from entering the kingdom of God.

Are you an imitator of God? Are you studying with carefulness the Word of God so that you know how you are to behave, like my grandson who studied the commercial to know how to fully reenact it? Or have you become a partaker with those who say it's fine to watch smut and tell dirty jokes? Are you partaking of sexual sins by watching them on television, in the theater or on the internet? Do you remain silent when people tell dirty jokes? Do you love Christ enough to stand up for Him and confront sexual perversion? Oh, my sister, do not be deceived by these things! God's Word is very clear; there is no middle road. There are only two ways: One road is walked by those who imitate God, by being kind, tenderhearted, forgiving, loving, sacrificial, and thankful. The other is walked by those who partake of fornication, uncleanness, greediness, filthy and foolish talk, and coarse jesting—and these have no inheritance with the Master in Heavenly Places!

Questions to Consider

Imitators of God or Partakers of Sin?
Ephesians 5:1-7

1. (a) Read Ephesians 5:1-7 and make a list of the sins Paul says believers should have no part in, as well as their definitions (you will need to look these up). (b) According to these verses, what should characterize our lives instead of these sins? (c) Memorize Ephesians 5:1-2.

2. (a) What does Paul say that we should not be deceived about, in Ephesians 5:5-6? (b) According to Matthew 24:3-5, 24; 1 Corinthians 6:9-10; Galatians 6:7-8; Colossians 2:8-9; 2 Thessalonians 2:1-4 and 1 John 1:8, what other things is it possible to be deceived about? (c) Why do you think the Scriptures have warnings about being deceived? (d) Has there been a time in your life in which you were deceived about something, only later to find out that you were dead wrong? What did you learn?

3. (a) According to Ephesians 5:2, Christ loved us so much that He gave Himself as an offering. Read Isaiah 53 and write down any observations you see regarding Christ's offering of Himself. (b) Since we are to walk in love as He did, how would this offering up of ourselves be fleshed out in our daily lives?

4. How can we protect our youth from violating Ephesians 5:3-4 in our culture, where sexual innuendos and pictures flash before our eyes and ears on a regular basis?

5. (a) In looking over your speech today or this past week, can you honestly say that you have refrained from all foolish talking and coarse jesting? (b) Have you partaken in the sexual sins of others by viewing them on television or in the theater or on the internet? (c) What does God say about this from our text?

6. (a) How do you handle conversations with others that are laced with foolish and filthy talk or coarse jesting? (b) What do you do when something is being viewed (media) that has sexual overtones or sexual content? (c) How have you obeyed what Paul says by not partaking of these things?

7. How has God the Spirit spoken to you through this lesson? What is your prayer request for your personal life? Please write it down to share.

Chapter 16

How to Walk as Children of Light!

Ephesians 5:8-14

Remember the days when Christians used to blush over conversations about sex? Sermons on the Song of Solomon left us avoiding eye contact with our pastors and safe sex talks in public school meant guaranteed giggling after class. I guess we're all grown up now. The generation of kids who once kissed dating goodbye and held fast to the promise that True Love Waits is no longer hanging its moral hat on the hook of sexual purity. According to the National Association of Evangelicals, 80 percent of unmarried evangelical Christians between ages 18-29 admit to having had premarital sex, a shocking figure when measured against the number of pledges made in youth ministries and wristbands worn endorsing abstinence around the country throughout the late '80s and early '90s. For a generation fed a steady diet of "just wait until you're married for sex," why are so many of us losing our virginity before we say "I do"? What is causing the growing chasm between our Christian belief and sexual purity?[99]

Not long ago, I came across the article I just quoted above. It goes on to list the reasons why so many "Christians" are fornicating. If this isn't shocking enough, I also read recently of other statistics that are equally concerning: 1 in every four Christians commits adultery, and 1 in every 10 ministers commits adultery. This, of course, destroys their ministry and taints the purity and reputation of the church.[100] Now, ladies, maybe you think I am old fashioned

99 Chanel Graham, "Why Unmarried Christians are Having Sex," *Urban Faith* (July 24, 2012), http://www.urbanfaith.com/2012/07/why-unmarried-christians-are-having-sex. html/ (accessed July 2012)

100 Rob Morton, "The 1990 Kinsey Report States that around ...," *Sermon Central* (June 2001), http://www.sermoncentral.com/illustrations/sermon-illustration-rob-morton-sta-tistics-marriagefaithfulness-adultery-3020.asp (accessed December 2015)

and need to keep in touch with the culture we live in, but I am horrified and deeply saddened by these statistics. And, quite frankly, the statistics don't surprise me, because we certainly are a nation that is close to looking like Sodom and Gomorrah. Is this the type of behavior that is acceptable for God's children, children of light? Is this how we are to walk in order to please God? I think you will find yourself questioning the validity of these supposed "Christians" I just read about, when you consider the words Paul pens for us in Ephesians 5:8-14. Let's read them together.

Ephesians 5:8-14

> For you were once darkness, but now you are light in the Lord. Walk as children of light [9](for the fruit of the Spirit is in all goodness, righteousness, and truth), [10]finding out what is acceptable to the Lord. [11]And have no fellowship with the unfruitful works of darkness, but rather expose them. [12]For it is shameful even to speak of those things which are done by them in secret. [13]But all things that are exposed are made manifest by the light, for whatever makes manifest is light. [14]Therefore He says: "Awake, you who sleep, arise from the dead, and Christ will give you light." (Ephesians 5:8-14).

In this lesson, we'll consider how children of light should be walking, and as we do our outline will form an acrostic: WALK. We'll learn to: *Walk in the Light*, (vv 8-9); *Aim to Please the Lord*, (v 10); *Lay Open the Darkness*, (vv 11-13); and *Keep on Staying Awake*, (v 14). It certainly appears that those I read about in the introduction of this book, who are claiming to be children of light, have forgotten how they are to walk! In our last lesson, Paul started this theme of sexual sins. We must remember that these sins are worthy of hell and prohibit one from entering the kingdom of God. In the passage we'll study here, Paul is continuing on with the theme of the importance of withdrawing ourselves from sexual sins, as well as from those who practice them. He begins by reminding us, who are children of light that we should walk in the light.

Ephesians 5:8-9
Walk in the Light

> For you were once darkness, but now you are light in the Lord. Walk as children of light (Ephesians 5:8).

The word *for* is there because of what Paul has just said. As we saw in our last lesson, when we were considering verse 7, we are not to partake with those who are involved in sexual sins. We are not to partner with them. Why? Because this is how we used to live, as Paul has already written numerous times in this epistle. We were once dead in our trespasses and sins, as Paul said in 2:1; we used to be in darkness, as he mentioned in 4:18; but we are to put off our former manner of life which was corrupt and involved in deceitful lusts, as Paul also told us in 4:22. As I was studying this I wondered why anyone would want to go back to the darkness after being exposed to the light. This was Peter's thought, as well, after Jesus gave His discourse on being the Bread of Life and many disciples went away and walked no more with Him. John records for us, in John 6:68-69, that Jesus turned to His twelve disciples and asked if they too will leave Him, to which Peter replied, "Lord, to whom shall we go? You have the words of eternal life. Also we have come to believe and know that You are the Christ, the Son of the living God." I admit, at times the Christian life can get difficult and sometimes quite discouraging, but, really, where would we go? As the songwriter says, "Lord, to give up I'd be a fool; you are my all in all."[101]

Notice that Paul does not say you were in darkness, but *you were once darkness.*[102] You were the embodiment of darkness, *but now you are light in the Lord.* And again, he doesn't say you are in the light, but you are light. You were once the picture of darkness; you are now the picture of light. Darkness and light are complete opposites and they cannot coexist. Paul says because of this fact, you should then *walk as children of light.* Children of light walk differently than those in darkness. How do they walk? Pastor MacArthur writes, "In Scripture the figurative use of light has two aspects, the intellectual and the moral. Intellectually it represents truth, whereas morally it represents holiness. To live in light therefore means to live in truth and holiness. The figure of darkness has the same two aspects. Intellectually it represents ignorance and

---

101 Words by David Phelps.
102 The KJV translation *sometimes* (Greek, pote), i.e., *you were sometimes darkness*, is somewhat misleading, as if formerly we were sometimes darkness and sometimes not. Rather, the term is normally translated *then*, i.e., for ye were *then* darkness.

falsehood, whereas morally it connotes evil."[103] Paul goes on to explain this specifically in verse 9.

(for the fruit of the Spirit is in all goodness, righteousness, and truth), (Ephesians 5:9).

Children of light don't want to live in darkness. They produce *fruit* that is from *the Spirit* who lives within them.[104] Now, obviously, this is not the only way we are to walk, but those Paul mentions here are a tall order indeed for all of God's children! Literally, the Greek text here reads like this: all goodness, all righteousness and all truth. It's not just some or enough to get by. Instead, children of light desire to be consumed with living like their Father.[105] It is similar to what Jesus says in Matthew 5:6, "Blessed are those who hunger and thirst for righteousness, for they shall be filled." Jesus says here that true kingdom citizens hunger for all the righteousness there is, not just some of it!

The first virtue Paul mentions is all goodness. Goodness is moral excellence with a generous spirit. If we are walking in goodness, then we will not be committing sexual sins. We cannot be good while committing adultery or fornication or looking at

103 John F. MacArthur, *The MacArthur New Testament Commentary: Ephesians*, 206. Pastor MacArthur further comments: "Can a Christian walk in darkness? No. Saying someone is in the light is like saying he is saved. If you are going to say a Christian can be in darkness, you will have to say that a person can be saved and unsaved at the same time. A believer cannot walk in darkness because he is one with God, Christ, and the Spirit. God is light, and in Him is no darkness .... When you sin, you do so in the light." cf. *Confession of Sin: 1 John 1:1-2:2* (Panorama City: Word of Grace Communications, 1986), p 33.

104 The NKJV wrongly inserts *fruit of the Spirit*. "The reading photos [English, *light*] is strongly supported by early and diversified witnesses, representing both the Alexandrian and the Western text-types." cf. Bruce M. Metzger, *A Textual Commentary on the Greek New Testament* (New York: United Bible Society, 1975), 607-608. Hence the NASV rightly translates this: "For the fruit of the Light consists in all goodness and righteousness and truth."

105 A central doctrine of the Bible is the *moral holiness of God,* which is illustrated by the figure of *light.* cf. Isaiah 6:1-8; Rev. 4:6-11; Exod. 15:1-21; Rev. 15:1-4; 1 Chron. 16:10; Psalm 47:8; 60:6; 108:7; 89:35; 145:17; Job 15:15; 25:5; Isa. 57:15; Hos. 11:9; Hab. 1:12-13; Luke 1:49; Heb. 1:8, etc. Following this special emphasis, are the many passages where God is demanding *holiness from man:* Lev. 19:2; 11:44; 20:26; 21:8; Exod. 3:5; John 5:15; Matt. 5:6, 48; 1 Cor. 15:34; 2 Cor. 7:1; Eph. 1:4; 1 Thess. 3:13; 4:3-7; Titus 2:12; Heb. 12:1, 14; 1 Pet. 1:15-16; 2:1-12; 2 Pet. 3:11, 14; 1 Jn. 2:1, 29, etc.

pornography! That's absurd! It is interesting that in Titus 2 older women are instructed to teach young women several qualities, and two of those qualities are to be good and to be chaste. *The second way Paul says we walk as God's children is in all righteousness. Righteousness* is the rule of doing what is right. Again, one who is practicing righteousness and doing what is right will not be using their body to participate in sexual sin. We will never regret doing what is right, but we will always regret doing what is wrong. *The third evidence that we are walking in the light is that we are known by truth,* and once again it is all truth. The word *truth* means being genuine and honest, having integrity. This is a person in whom is no pretense, no hypocrisy. Paul has already said we are to speak the truth in 4:15, so it makes sense that we are also to live the truth. This also makes sense in the context of sexual sins because, more often than not, when one is involved in sexual sin there is a whole lot of deception and lying that takes place. I heard just the other day of a man who called a certain store and asked the owner to lie for him if his wife called and asked if he purchased an item for another woman! The owner did not comply, but this combination of sexual sin and deception is commonplace in our day. (This may be why Paul doesn't give the full list of spiritual fruit here, as he does in Galatians, as these three virtues in Ephesians 5 seem to relate to the sexual sins Paul is specifically addressing here.) People often ask, "How do I know if I am a believer?" or "How can I discern if someone else is a believer?" Scripture is replete with help on how we can know this, but right here Paul says people who are in the light bear fruit, and it is these three great fruits: the fruits of all goodness, all righteousness and all truth. Paul moves on to another way that children of light should walk and this is the A on our acrostic. We aim to please the Lord.

Ephesians 5:10
Aim to Please the Lord

finding out what is acceptable to the Lord (Ephesians 5:10).

One who is walking in the light will make a point of *finding out what is acceptable to the Lord*. What does this mean? *Finding out* means to discern, to put to the test. They will discern what is *acceptable*, what is well-pleasing, *to the Lord*. Those living in darkness cannot do this, as Paul says in Romans 8:8: "So then, those who are in the flesh cannot please God." Our desire should be as Paul says to the church at Thessalonica in 1 Thessalonians 4:1, "Finally then, brethren, we urge and exhort in the Lord Jesus that you should abound more and more, just as you received from us how you ought to walk and to please God." We endeavor to do what Paul prays for the church at Philippi, when he says, "And this I pray, that your love may abound still more and more in knowledge and all discernment, that you may approve the things that are excellent, that you may be sincere and without offense till the day of Christ" (Philippians 1:9-10). We don't just get by in the Christian life; we determine to find out and do what is acceptable to the Lord, and we approve things that are excellent. A genuine child of the light does not try to see how much darkness he can get by with, or how much sin he or she can commit and still enter into heaven; but instead, seeks to find out what is acceptable to the Lord.

In the context of what Paul is saying, we could ask ourselves questions like: Is this activity good? Is it righteous? Is this in keeping with the truth? Does it please the Lord? And it's not just our actions, we can ask ourselves these questions in our words and thoughts as well. Is what I'm saying pleasing to the Lord? Is what I'm thinking acceptable to the Lord? Children of Light desire to please the Lord, so they turn to the Light and not the darkness, just as a plant turns toward the light to grow and not toward the darkness. Paul moves on to yet another way children of light should walk, and that is to lay open or expose the darkness.

Ephesians 5:11-13
Lay Open the Darkness

And have no fellowship with the unfruitful works of darkness, but rather expose them (Ephesians 5:11).

As we practice the three fruits of the Spirit that Paul mentions in this passage, seeking to do what is right before God, then we obviously will not have *fellowship with the unfruitful works of darkness*. The more light we have, the more holy we are, and the more we will hate evil. Jesus put it well in John 3:20-21: "For everyone practicing evil hates the light and does not come to the light, lest his deeds should be exposed. But he who does the truth comes to the light, that his deeds may be clearly seen, that they have been done in God." Now the question might come to your mind, "Is it the sins we are to have nothing to do with, or are we to avoid those those who practice these things?" And the answer to that question is, "Both!" Paul has just said in verse 7 that we are not to be partakers with those people who are involved in sexual talk and sexual sin, and, obviously, those who are God's children don't practice these actual sins, so both are true. This does not mean we don't try to befriend them and win them to Christ, but it does mean that we do not partner with them. Paul states in 1 Corinthians 5:9-13, "I wrote to you in my epistle not to keep company with sexually immoral people. Yet I certainly did not mean with the sexually immoral people of this world, or with the covetous, or extortioners, or idolaters, since then you would need to go out of the world. But now I have written to you not to keep company with anyone named a brother, who is sexually immoral, or covetous, or an idolater, or a reviler, or a drunkard, or an extortioner—not even to eat with such a person. For what have I to do with judging those also who are outside? Do you not judge those who are inside? But those who are outside God judges. Therefore 'put away from yourselves the evil person.'" Also, in 1 Timothy 5:22, Paul tells Timothy, "Do not lay hands on anyone hastily, nor share in other people's sins; keep yourself pure." Even here, both are true; keep yourselves pure and don't share in others' sins.

Now, perhaps you are thinking, "Oh, that's not that hard. I'm pure and I certainly don't like being around people who are sinning sexually. Why, it's disgusting, especially if they claim to belong to Christ!" You might not think that is hard, but the next statement I know for sure as a pastor's wife, that many Christians balk at this: *but rather expose them. Expose* means to admonish, rebuke, lay open, but also to convince them that what they are doing is wrong. Some of us would rather gossip about others' sin or talk to our husbands or friends about it. But the loving thing to do is to warn those who are sinning of the danger they are in. And we do this by doing three things: do, speak and live. First of all, we do what Matthew 18:15-17 tells us to do, we go to the one who is sinning, and we do it in a spirit of meekness as Paul mentions in Galatians 6:1. Second, we speak by using Scripture to impress God's Word upon their mind. Hebrews 4:12-13 tells us how important God's Word is in this process: "For the word of God is living and powerful, and sharper than any two-edged sword, piercing even to the division of soul and spirit, and of joints and marrow, and is a discerner of the thoughts and intents of the heart. And there is no creature hidden from His sight, but all things are naked and open to the eyes of Him to whom we must give account." Third, we expose them and their sin by living out the attributes of goodness, righteousness and truth. As we are salt and light in this world, as Jesus says we should be, in Matthew 5:13-16, then we expose men's deeds by our lives. By living in holiness, they and their evil deeds are exposed. Paul goes on to say,

> For it is shameful even to speak of those things which are done by them in secret (Ephesians 5:12).

How do we expose the unfruitful works of darkness and those who do them if *it is shameful even to speak of those things* they do? Obviously, Paul is not saying we don't ever mention the sins they are committing, like fornicating or committing adultery, because God's Word mentions those words. In fact, in Matthew 18:17 it says when we are involved in the process of church discipline we name the sinner as well as the sin or sins that they are committing. This does not mean that we give the details of their sins. We may name the sin of adultery for example, but we do not go into the details of the act. We do not expose details like where the person was when they did this, or how many times they did this; we do not share details that are not necessary, the details of what they have done in secret or private. Sexual sins are most often done in private, not out in the open, though our culture is getting disgustingly brazen about these things. Paul continues on with our responsibility to expose the deeds of darkness by saying,

> But all things that are exposed are made manifest by the light, for whatever makes manifest is light (Ephesians 5:13).

Paul says *all things that are exposed are made manifest by the light*. Those that are involved in unfruitful works of darkness, when their deeds are exposed, are exposed by those who are walking in the light or by God's truth, which is light. Just like in the physical realm, when we turn on the light and we can see what was once dark, so it is the spiritual realm, when we turn on the light of truth; we expose or lay open the deeds of sin. Jesus says in Mark 4:22, "For there is nothing hidden which will not be revealed, nor has anything been kept secret but that it should come to light." Paul ends with another way children of light should walk and that is to keep on staying awake.

Ephesians 5:14
Keep on Staying Awake

> Therefore He says: "Awake, you who sleep, arise from the dead, and Christ will give you light" (Ephesians 5:14).

It is supposed that this quote is taken from Isaiah 60:1-2, which says, "Arise, shine; for your light has come! And the glory of the LORD is risen upon you. For behold, the darkness shall cover the earth, and deep darkness the people; but the LORD will arise over you, and His glory will be seen upon you." Before we get into the meaning of what Paul is saying here, it is interesting to note that this verse in Ephesians was a hymn that was sung by the early church during Easter. Now what is Paul saying here? He might be saying that those who are in darkness, those whose deeds need to be exposed, need to awake out of sleep and arise from the dead. They are dead in their trespasses and sins, as we have already seen in Ephesians, and they arise from the dead and Christ will shine on them. As John writes in John 8:12, "Then Jesus spoke to them again, saying, 'I am the light of the world. He who follows Me shall not walk in darkness, but have the light of life.'" But since Paul is writing to believers—the saints at Ephesus—then that explanation doesn't make much sense. Paul is exhorting believers to awake from their lethargic spiritual sleep, to stop participating in evil deeds and fellowshiping with those who do. Paul says wake up out of your slumber! Paul tells us in 1 Corinthians 15:33-34, "Do not be deceived: 'Evil company corrupts good habits.' Awake to righteousness, and do not sin; for some do not have the knowledge of God. I speak this to your shame." Of course, we know that the church at Corinth was involved in all types of sins, so this was an appropriate admonishment for them. We, too, are a people who are thinking wrongly today regarding sexual sins. In these days of post-modern culture, sexual sins have become the norm.

If we are not careful and applying ourselves to the means of grace as we should, we can soon begin thinking and acting like the world, and participating in their sexual sins. It's just like the article referenced at the beginning of this chapter. How did we get to the point where statistics that tell us that 80 percent of unmarried professing evangelical Christians between ages 18-29 are having premarital sex? Christians are shrinking their souls, and they are looking like the world. It's a wake-up call indeed for all of God's children of light! This is not how God's children walk; His children keep themselves awake and alert to sinful temptations.

Summary

Do you want to know how to walk as a child of light? First, you must *Walk in the Light*, (vv 8-9), by realizing that you were once darkness, but that is not who you are anymore. You are light. You must also put on all goodness, all righteousness and all truth. Are these fruits evident in your life today?

Second, you must *Aim to Please the Lord*, (v 10). Are you making it your effort every moment of every day to walk in a way that pleases the Lord? Are you pleasing the Lord by the things you view, the things you read, and even the people you spend your time with? Do you ask yourself if the things you do, say, and think are pleasing to the Lord?

Third, you must *Lay Open the Darkness*, (vv 11-13). You do this by living out a holy life before others and by verbally admonishing them for their sin. Are you living your life in such a way that those who are involved in darkness are put to shame by your good works? Are you willing to risk your reputation by confronting those who are involved in evil deeds?

And last, we walk as children of light as we *Keep on Staying Awake*, (v 14). Have you become sluggish in your spiritual battle? Paul is going to tell us in chapter 6 of the importance of battling with the right armor on. Have you laid your weapons down and given up? Have you bought into the cultural lie which says, "Everyone is doing it, so why not join in?" Will you be one of the statistics, or are you now one of the statistics of Christians who are involved in sexual sin? Are you willing to confront other believers who are involved in sin and carry it out to the end, practicing what Scripture tells you to do?

My dear sister, walk in the light, make it your aim to please the Lord, expose deeds of darkness, and awake out of your slumber. As you do, you can be assured of one day being with your Master in Heavenly Places!

Questions to Consider
How to Walk as Children of Light!
Ephesians 5:8-14

1. (a) Read Ephesians 5:1-17 and make note of the three ways Paul says we are to walk. (b) What do you think these each mean? (c) According to Romans 6:4; Romans 13:13; 2 Corinthians 5:7; Galatians 5:16; Colossians 4:5; 2 John 6; and 3 John 3, what are some other ways we, as God's children, should be walking? (d) Are you walking in these ways? (e) Memorize Ephesians 5:11-12.

2. (a) Paul mentions in Ephesians 5:9 that the fruit of the Spirit involves three elements: goodness, righteousness and truth. Skim the Sermon on the Mount in Matthew 5-7, making note of how these three virtues should be carried out for those who are children of light. (You may want to make three columns on the back of your paper for this assignment.)

3. (a) Compare Ephesians 5:9 with what Paul says in Galatians 5:22-23. Why do you think these two lists are different? (b) Is your life characterized by the three virtues Paul mentions in Ephesians 5:9?

4. (a) We have a moral responsibility, according to Ephesians 5:11, to reprove or expose deeds of darkness. This would include those individuals who are involved in these sins, as well. According to Matthew 18:15-17; Galatians 6:1; Hebrews 3:12-13; James 5:19-20; and Jude 22-23, how are we to do this? (b) Why are we to do this? (c) Do you leave exposing sin to others, so as not to strain relationships with family or friends? (d) Do you ignore sin or tolerate it?

5. What do you think the criteria should be for approving or finding out what is acceptable in the Lord (Ephesians 5:10)?

6. After considering these words from Paul, what is your prayer request for yourself that would encourage you to walk more faithfully as a child of the light? Please write it down to share.

Chapter 17

The Wise Man in Contrast with the Foolish Man

Ephesians 5:15-20

Growing up in a minister's home gave me the opportunity to learn dozens of children's songs, many of which I still have in my mind after all these years. As I was studying the passage for this lesson, one particular song kept going through my head. If my memory serves me right, the lyrics go something like this:

"The wise man built his house upon the rock …
and the rains came tumbling down.
The rains came down and the floods came up …
and the house on the rock stood firm.
The foolish man built his house upon the sand …
and the rains came tumbling down.
The rains came down and the floods came up …
and the house on the sand went splat.
So build your house on the Lord Jesus Christ …
and the blessings will come down.
The blessings come down as the prayers go up …
so build your house on the Lord."[106]

In many ways, this is what Paul is trying to say through the words he writes in Ephesians 5:15-20, as he contrasts the foolish man with the wise man. Let's read together what he has to say.

Ephesians 5:15-20

See then that you walk circumspectly, not as fools but as wise, [16]redeeming the time, because the days are evil. [17]Therefore do not be unwise, but understand what the will of the Lord is. [18]And do not be drunk with wine, in which is dissipation; but be filled with the Spirit, [19]speaking to one another in psalms and hymns and spiritual songs, singing and making melody in your heart to the Lord, [20]giving thanks always for all things to

---

106   Author unknown.

God the Father in the name of our Lord Jesus Christ (Ephesians 5:15-20).

In our passage of study in this lesson, Paul is continuing with his admonitions for those who are children of light, but as he does he contrasts the foolish man with the wise man. We will see five contrasts in our study:

Wise Man Redeems the Time—
  A Foolish Man Wastes It, (v 16)
Wise Man Understands the Will of the Lord—
  A Foolish Man Doesn't, (v 17)
Wise Man is Filled with the Spirit—
  A Foolish Man Gets Drunk with Wine, (v 18)
A Wise Man Makes Melody in His Heart to God—
  A Foolish Man Doesn't, (v 19
Wise Man Gives Thanks to God—
  A Foolish Man is Ungrateful, (v 20)

Ephesians 5:15

See then that you walk circumspectly, not as fools but as wise, (Ephesians 5:15).

Paul says *see then that you walk.* In other words, observe how you walk, pay careful attention to how you walk. I wonder how many of us actually slow down long enough during our day to observe how we are walking. Does our daily life reflect someone who is walking wisely? Are we making foolish decisions with our time? Our thoughts? Oh, that we would pay careful attention to how we walk! Paul says that we should walk *circumspectly,* which means to walk accurately, to walk carefully. This would include being focused spiritually. We might ask ourselves: What am I doing right now with my time? What am I watching on television? What sites am I searching on the internet? What am I listening to? What words am I using with my girlfriends, my children, my husband, my coworkers? What am I thinking? Paul goes on to say we are to walk *not as fools but as wise.* Since we are talking about walking either as fools or as wise then we should define what these terms mean. A *fool* is one who acts unwisely and is deficient in judgment or understanding. Someone who is *wise* is characterized by wisdom, keen discernment, and shows sound judgment. We are not to conduct ourselves as people of the world, but as people chosen by God, conducting ourselves with His wisdom. Foolish was what we used to be before we came to know Christ, as Paul mentions in Titus 3:3: "For we ourselves were also once foolish, disobedient, deceived, serving various lusts and pleasures, living in malice and envy, hateful and hating one another." So how does a fool walk? How does a wise man walk? We're going to consider five contrasts. Let's look at verse 16 together.

Ephesians 5:16
A Wise Man Redeems the Time—A Foolish Man Wastes It

redeeming the time, because the days are evil (Ephesians 5:16).

A wise man will redeem the time. What does it mean to be *redeeming the time*? It means to buy up the time, rescue the time, recover the time, and use it for what is important. Now, the word *time* here is not referring to minutes or hours or even seconds, as we would think to measure time; the word means fixed seasons or a period of time. We don't want to waste our life, we don't want to waste our time, as the foolish do! As we put to good use the seconds, minutes and hours God has given us, then we don't waste the seasons of life. I don't understand women who say they are bored, because there is always something that needs to be done at my home; there is always someone that needs a helping hand or an encouraging word; there is always more time we could spend in the Word, studying, reading and memorizing it; there is always a lost soul that needs the gospel. How can a wise woman be bored?! Sometimes I ask people what they did today or what are they doing today, and I admit that often I am surprised at what transpires in their day. Only what is done for Christ will last.

As I think about this verse, it also makes me wonder about Christians retiring. I've heard my husband say that Christians don't retire. We are always working for the Lord. In fact, I think our later years should be our best for the Lord. My own Dad, who was 95 when I wrote this study, always wanted to be doing something for the Lord. He hated to be idle with his time. My friend, our life is but a vapor. It is the wise child of the Lord who sees her life as fleeting and makes the most of every opportunity for the Kingdom of God! Isn't it interesting that the Psalmist says, "So teach us to number our days, that we may gain a heart of wisdom" (Psalm 90:12)? On the other hand, Ecclesiastes 4:5 says, "The fool folds his hands and consumes his own flesh." The first contrast we see here in Ephesians, is that the wise man redeems the time by making wise choices of managing time, while the foolish man wastes his time by making foolish choices with the time he's been given. Let's continue on with the second contrast of the foolish man and the wise man in verse 17.

Ephesians 5:17
A Wise Man Understands the Will of the
Lord—A Foolish Man Doesn't

Therefore do not be unwise, but understand what the will of the Lord is (Ephesians 5:17).

Therefore, because of the fact that we are to redeem the time, because of the fact that the days are evil, Paul says *do not be unwise, but understand what the will of the Lord is*. The wise person understands what the will of the Lord is because the wise man or woman is walking in the Spirit. Study the Scriptures so that you'll know what the will of the Lord is. In Romans 12:1-2, Paul tells us how we can know the will of the Lord. He says, "I beseech you therefore, brethren, by the mercies of God, that you present your bodies a living sacrifice, holy, acceptable to God, which is your reasonable service. And do not be conformed to this world, but be transformed by the renewing of your mind, that you may prove what is that good and acceptable and perfect will of God." Wise men present their bodies a living sacrifice; they are not conformed to the world, but they are transformed by the renewal of their mind through the Scriptures. Then, and only then, can they prove what is the acceptable will of God. The foolish man on the other hand ignores their responsibility to offer their bodies unto the Lord; they are conformed to the world and all its patterns and they haven't a clue what Scripture says, so they don't know what God's will is. As the Psalmist says in Psalm 14:1, "The fool has said in his heart, 'There is no God.' They are corrupt, they have done abominable works, there is none who does good." The apostle Peter tells us how fools live, in 1 Peter 4:2: "that he no longer should live the rest of his time in the flesh for the lusts of men, but for the will of God." Fools live for the lusts of their flesh, not for the will of God. Proverbs 28:26 states, "He who trusts in his own heart is a fool, but whoever walks wisely will be delivered." The second contrast of the foolish man and the wise man is that the wise man understands what the will of the Lord is, whereas the foolish man doesn't have a clue about the will of the Lord. Paul continues on in verse 18 with another very controversial and vivid contrast between the foolish man and the wise man.

Ephesians 5:18
A Wise Man is Filled with the Spirit—A Foolish Man Gets Drunk with Wine

> And do not be drunk with wine, in which is dissipation; but be filled with the Spirit, (Ephesians 5:18)

Perhaps you are wondering why Paul would interject the subject of drunkenness in his letter to the Ephesians. Drunkenness was a huge problem in the city of Ephesus. In fact, when one would get drunk, it was viewed as the means by which they could experience ecstasy and union with a god, and we have already learned that Ephesus was a city filled with idols. It is supposed that many Christians in Ephesus were becoming drunk in their private lives as well as in their public lives. There is nothing new under the sun, of course, as that is a common problem in our day as well. In fact, recently, I've been surprised to hear of more and more churches serving alcohol at their Bible studies, church gatherings, and even at Christian conferences. In my own hometown, in the past few years, I've known of two pastors who were arrested for drunkenness.

Now, since Paul says that we are not to *be drunk with wine*, it's important that we know exactly what that means. It means that we are not to become intoxicated with wine. Intoxication by wine or strong drink is condemned in the Bible.[107] When one is intoxicated

---

107 The Bible doesn't teach *total abstinence* from wine or strong drink. Sometimes they are commended for physical or emotional uses (e.g.,, 1 Tim. 5:23; Luke 10:34; Prov. 31:6-7). And once the Scripture affirms that it makes the heart glad (cf. Psalm 104:15), although this passage doesn't commend or condemn its use but simply comments on what

it weakens their ability to have physical and mental control of their bodies. Because of this danger, high priests were forbidden to use wine while on duty (Leviticus 10:9; Ezekiel 44:21); kings and princes were forbidden to use it while ruling (Proverbs 31:4); and the children of Israel were kept from it during the wilderness wanderings (Deuteronomy 29:6). Nazarites voluntarily kept themselves from wine (Numbers 6:2-3), as did the Rechabites (Jeremiah 35:1-19), Daniel (Daniel 1:5, 8, 16; and 10:3), and John the Baptist (Luke 1:15). That's also why elders and deacons are not to be given to wine, as Paul says in 1 Timothy 3:3 and 8, and Titus 1:7. Paul's command to Timothy to use wine for medicinal purposes for his stomach suggests that the young pastor had voluntarily and totally abstained from the use of it. Now, the wine in Bible times did not have the same alcohol content as the wine of our day. In the biblical world, water was not safe to drink, just as it's not safe today in some third-world countries. They did not have water purification methods like we do, and so the safest drink was wine, but the alcohol content was minimal.[108] Hence, a good case can be made that although the use of wine is not condemned in Scripture, voluntary abstinence from it is commended.[109] This passage, however, is only condemning

---

it does. Jesus drank wine at meals (e.g.,, Matt. 26:27-29; Mark 14:23) and made water into wine at Cana (cf. John 2:9-10). Once, drinking of wine was an illustration of the refreshment of quenching the spiritual thirst of salvation (cf. Isa. 55:1). Obedience of the nation of Israel would result in abundance of wine (cf. Deut. 7:13; 11:14; Prov. 3:10, etc.) and disobedience would result in a withdrawing of this blessing (cf. Deut. 28:39, 51; Isa. 62:8). It was even used in the worship of God (cf. Exod. 29:40; Lev. 23:13; Num. 15:5-10; 28:14). *Wine* is mentioned 212 times in the Bible; the plural *wines* is mentioned 1 time; and *strong drink* is mentioned 20 times. Wine is no more the cause of drunkenness than food is the cause of gluttony. The contemporary American ban on alcohol among conservative churches is generated more from the 18th Amendment which banned the sales and use of alcoholic beverages in the US, than from the Bible itself. Poor exegesis suggested the so called *Two-Beverage Theory*, i.e.,, one was alcoholic and condemned in the Bible and the other was non-alcoholic grape juice which is condoned in the Bible.

108 Even today, in many places of the world water is impure and the low alcohol content of wine acts as an antiseptic purifying the water it is diluted with.

109 The question must be asked: Is the wine of Biblical times the same as wine or strong drink today? The shekar (Hebrew) and sikera (Greek), translated *strong drink* was of high alcohol content and perhaps refers to types of beer but not distilled liquor (cf. 1 Sam. 1:15; Prov. 20:1; Isa. 5:1); tirosh (Hebrew) and gleukos, is *new wine,* which would normally ferment rapidly so it was diluted with water before drinking (cf. Gen. 27:28, 37; Num. 18:12; Deut. 7:13; 11:14, etc.). The most often terms for *wine* are yayin (Hebrew) and oinos (Greek), which was a boiled grape juice into a thick paste suitable for storage. The

the misuse of wine, not specifically its use.

Being intoxicated is also a problem among those who are addicted to drugs, both legal and illegal. Drugs and alcohol which are consumed in excess both violate the Scriptures' command for a believer to be sober-minded. In Titus 2, Paul commands older men and younger men to be sober-minded; he commands older women to not be drunk and to pass on to the young women that virtue of being sober-minded. Sober-minded means to be self-controlled, to be of sound mind, to have control on all passions. I find it interesting that when John is writing concerning the latter times, he mentions in Revelation 18:23, "… for by your sorcery all the nations were deceived." The word translated as sorcery is the Greek term, <u>pharmakeia</u>, from which we get our English word pharmacy, a word which means to prepare drugs. It seems to indicate that in the latter times the nations will be deceived and given over to drugs. We are certainly getting there, when you consider that more than one out of every ten people in the United States takes some type of mind-altering drug. Here in, Tulsa, Oklahoma, a police officer I know said that 10 percent of all Tulsans drive impaired. This means that one out of every ten drivers I pass on the road is intoxicated with drugs or alcohol! This is not a very comforting thought. Also, since we are dealing specifically here in the text with alcohol, here are some other statistics you might find concerning: 17.6 million Americans now have a problem with alcohol; one person is killed every half-hour due to drunk driving; each year, approximately 16,000 people are killed in alcohol-related crashes; alcohol is a factor in almost half of all traffic fatalities; and every other minute a person is seriously injured in an alcohol-related crash. A mind dulled by drugs and drink is not the will of God for a believer. Jesus says concerning the last days, "But take heed to yourselves, lest your hearts be weighed down with carousing, drunkenness, and cares of this life, and that

---

boiling would remove any fermenting process, until it was mixed with water. When this wine was stored unboiled it was kept in large containers called amphorae and then mixed with water, at a ration of twenty parts water to one part <u>oinos</u>. To drink of pure <u>oinos</u> without diluting it in water, was considered a barbaric act. Unmixed wine during biblical times had an alcohol content of 11% and the strongest wine was mixed with three parts water to one of <u>oinos</u>, which made the alcohol content only between 2.25-2.75%. Obviously, *distillation* of wine to raise the alcohol content higher was unknown. The wine of the OT and NT was not grape juice, but neither was it the high alcohol content (9-11%) wine of today.

Day come on you unexpectedly" (Luke 21:34).

Now I want to be clear that one cannot prove a requirement of abstinence from the Word of God, but one can prove it is not God's will for His children to be drunk! Proverbs 31:6 says, "Give strong drink to him who is perishing, and wine to those who are bitter of heart." When one is dying or going through a critical time in their life there seems to be an allowance for this. Also, Paul told Timothy, in 1 Timothy 5:23, "No longer drink only water, but use a little wine for your stomach's sake and your frequent infirmities." Evidently, Timothy had a stomach problem and Paul told him to drink a little wine—not a lot—for his belly problems. However, we must keep in mind that the wine in biblical times did not have the alcohol content that ours does today. John MacArthur, in his commentary, recommends that we consider asking ourselves some questions before we think about drinking: Is today's wine the same as that in Bible times? Is it necessary? Is it the best choice? Is it habit-forming? Is it potentially destructive? Will it offend other Christians? Will it harm my Christian testimony? Is it right?[110]

Paul says that we should not be drunk with wine, *which is dissipation*. This means drunkenness leads to a life that is void of virtue, a life that is wasted, a life that is debauched, and a life that many times comes with sexual excess. It describes a condition where your mind and body are so dulled from drinking that you are incapable of making wise decisions. "When one is dominated by wine, every area of his life is affected by it. He gets drunk and his wife chews him out for this. So he runs off to his buddies down at the bar for consolation and to drown his problems. Because he does, he has a hangover at work in the morning and this boss gets on him about his sloppy work. Feeling bad about his, he stops at the bar on the way home to get more consolation, comes home drunk and … you fill in the rest. It is a never-ending circle, where each thing he does wrong leads to another so that his entire life is soon dominated by drink. Even his 'solutions' create new and worse problems. Each area of his life is taken over by drink so that he cannot do otherwise."[111]

---

110 MacArthur, *The MacArthur New Testament Commentary: Ephesians*, 235-244.
111 Jay Adams, 115.

Instead of being drunk with wine, Paul says *but be filled with the Spirit.* The use of thr word *but* would indicate that this is a contrast. Paul has already told them they are sealed with the Spirit, in 1:13, and that they should not grieve the Spirit, in 4:30. Now he tells them to be filled with the Spirit. To be filled with the Spirit means to be controlled by the Spirit and the Greek tense means to constantly keep being filled. This is a command, not an option. This also is not some "second blessing" for some super-Christian but is for all of God's children. Instead of being controlled by wine, we are to be controlled by the Spirit. Isn't it interesting that on the Day of Pentecost, when the Holy Spirit came and filled believers, that some thought these Christians were drunk with wine? (Acts 2:13) They weren't drunk with wine, but they were intoxicated with the Spirit. Now, ladies, that's what brings true joy—the filling of the Spirit. "To be filled with the Spirit involves confession of sin, surrender of will, intellect, body, time, talent, possessions, and desires. It requires the death of selfishness and the slaying of self-will. When we die to self, the Lord fills with His Spirit."[112] "To be filled with the Spirit is to live in the consciousness of the personal presence of the Lord Jesus Christ, as if we were standing next to Him, and to let His mind dominate our life. It is to fill ourselves with God's Word, so that His thoughts will be our thoughts, His standards our standards, His work our work, and His will our will."[113] Paul's third contrast is that the wise are filled with the Spirit and fools are drunk with wine. As we are filled with the Spirit, then some exciting things happen, as we see in verse 19.

Ephesians 5:19
A Wise Man Makes Melody in His Heart to God—A Foolish Man Doesn't

speaking to one another in psalms and hymns and spiritual songs, singing and making melody in your heart to the Lord (Ephesians 5:19).

Now this might seem a little odd to us to think about speaking and singing songs to each other. In New Testament times, they would

---

112 Ibid, 251-252.
113 Ibid., 253

take the oral word and speak it to each other, even singing to each other. Paul mentions this in Colossians 3:16: "Let the word of Christ dwell in you richly in all wisdom, teaching and admonishing one another in psalms and hymns and spiritual songs, singing with grace in your hearts to the Lord." One historian writes that "they would form choirs, one of men and one of women, and then they would sing hymns to God composed of many measures and set to many melodies, sometimes chanting together, sometimes taking up the harmony, hands and feet keeping time in accompaniment." What is the difference between psalms, hymns, and spiritual songs? A *psalm* was, originally, a song accompanied by a stringed instrument. The Psalms in our Bible, all 150 of them, were put to music. A *hymn* is a song of praise. Augustine said that a hymn must be sung, it must be praise, and it must be directed to God. Hymns were songs of praise, usually focused on Christ, while the Psalms were focused on God. It is supposed by some that Paul utilized fragments of hymns in his epistles, for example, in 1 Corinthians 13; Ephesians 5:14; 1 Timothy 3:16; and 2 Timothy 2:11-14. This explains how they could admonish one another through these songs, as Paul mentions in Colossians. These songs were not void of meaning, as some of our praise songs are today. *Spiritual songs* were sacred poems, which were neither psalms nor hymns but probably personal testimonies of what God has done.

Notice that Paul encourages us to be *singing and making melody in your hearts to the Lord.* When the early believers sang to each other, they didn't just mouth the words, but they sang from their hearts. If we don't have a song in our heart, then we are just mouthing words. So in thinking about our fourth contrast, the wise sing to others, making melody in their hearts to the Lord, while fools have no song in their hearts but only sadness. What a beautiful picture Paul gives us here as we end with verse 20. The succession is only natural; as we sing to each other, make melody in our own hearts, then we are drawn to give thanks to God for everything.

Ephesians 5:20
A Wise Man Gives Thanks to God—A Foolish Man is Ungrateful

giving thanks always for all things to God the Father in the name of our Lord Jesus Christ, (Ephesians 5:20).

Giving thanks always means we give thanks constantly. And we are to give thanks for *all things*. All things would include blessings, trials, good days, bad days, raining days, hot days, snowing days, feast days, famine days, good food, bad food, people we like, people who rub us wrong, good bosses, bad bosses, and the list goes on—all things! This thanks is to be directed *to God the Father* and it is *in the name of our Lord Jesus Christ*, which means our thanksgiving is consistent with the name of our Lord. We are to pray in His name, which is consistent with His character, and we are to give thanks in His name, which is consistent with His character. The fool does not give thanks, as Paul says in Romans 1:2 and 22: "Because, although they knew God, they did not glorify Him as God, nor were *thankful*, but became futile in their thoughts, and their foolish hearts were darkened. ... Professing to be wise, they became fools." So Paul's fifth and final contrast is that the wise person gives thanks to God always and for all things, while the foolish man is ungrateful.

Summary

A Wise Man Redeems the Time—A Foolish Man Wastes It, (v 16). What about you, dear sister? Is your life characterized by being wise or by being foolish? Are you redeeming the time? What does a typical day consist of for you? Wasting time by surfing endless websites on the web, or redeeming the time by studying or memorizing the Word? Wasting time by gossiping on the phone to your girlfriend, or redeeming the time by caring for your home or investing time in your children. (By the way, speaking of children, I would encourage you as young mothers to be careful about allowing your children to become wasteful in their time. Teach them to be productive, to work, and not to become enslaved to the technology of our day, which has the potential to be damaging to our children.)

A Wise Man Understands the Will of the Lord—A Foolish Man Doesn't, (v 17).What about the will of the Lord? Do you know what it is? Do you know the Word so well that when a decision time comes along you are able to know with certainty exactly what God says about it? Or do you find yourself making foolish decisions because you don't know what God says about what you need to be doing?

A Wise Man is Filled with the Spirit—A Foolish Man Gets Drunk with Wine, (v 18). Are you dulling your mind with drugs or alcohol? Have you bought into the world's way of pleasure? Or are you so intoxicated with the Spirit, and so filled with the joy of the Lord, that you have no need of those things to bring you happiness?

A Wise Man Makes Melody in His Heart to God—A Foolish Man Doesn't, (v 19). Have you been singing lately in your heart and to others? Or are you so dulled in your mind because of drug abuse or alcohol abuse that the only songs you feel like singing are *You Don't Bring Me Flowers Anymore*, or *All By Myself*, or *Alone Again Naturally*?

A Wise Man Gives Thanks to God—A Foolish Man is Ungrateful, (v 20). Last, but not least, are you showing forth wisdom by giving thanks at all times and for all things and all people, or do you complain and express ingratitude throughout the day, thus showing your life is characterized by foolishness?

That song I mentioned in the introduction I learned as a child, more than likely was penned by someone who was wise enough to know what Jesus said in Matthew 7:24-27. "Therefore whoever hears these sayings of Mine, and does them, I will liken him to a wise man who built his house on the rock: and the rain descended, the floods came, and the winds blew and beat on that house; and it did not fall, for it was founded on the rock. Now everyone who hears these sayings of Mine, and does not do them, will be like a foolish man who built his house on the sand: and the rain descended, the floods came, and the winds blew and beat on that house; and it fell. And great was its fall."

Questions to Consider
The Wise Man in Contrast with the Foolish Man
Ephesians 5:15-20

1. (a) Read Ephesians 5:15-20 and list all the commands that you find. (b) Are you obeying these commands? (c) Memorize Ephesians 5:15-16.

2. (a) In the following passages, who do you find giving thanks, and for what are they giving thanks? Job 1; Psalm 34:1-6; Luke 17:11-16; Acts 5:40-41; Philippians 1:3; and 2 Thessalonians 1:3. (b) Are you able to give thanks to God at all times, for all things and for all people? (c) How do you think, as Christians, we can cultivate being more thankful?

3. (a) Paul says in Ephesians 5:17 that we are not to be unwise but to understand what the will of the Lord is. What is the will of the Lord, according to Ephesians 5 alone? (b) How do you think we discern the will of God in our lives?

4. (a) According to the following verses, what should be the Christian's position regarding getting drunk? Proverbs 20:1; Proverbs 23:29-35; Isaiah 5:11-13; Habakkuk 2:15; Romans 13:13; 1 Corinthians 5:11; Ephesians 5:18; 1 Timothy 3:3-8; Titus 1:7 and 2:3. (b) What was or what will be the outcome of those who choose to get drunk, according to Genesis 9:20-29; Genesis 19:30-38; Deuteronomy 21:18-21; Luke 21:34; 1 Corinthians 5:11; 1 Corinthians 6:9-10; and Galatians 5:19-21? (c) Do you think it is a sin to drink alcohol? (Prove your answer biblically.)

5. (a) Make note of the occasions, from the following verses, when God's people were singing or will be singing. Exodus 14:27-15:1; Judges 5:1-31; 2 Chronicles 30:21; Ezra 3:10-11; Nehemiah 12:27-42; Matthew 26:26-30; Revelation 5:8-10; Revelation 14:1-3. (b) What does this tell you about the importance of music for the Christian?

6. (a) Would you say that you redeem the time? (For the brave, keep a log of a typical day or even a week of the things that you do.) (b) Why do you think it is important for God's children to redeem the time, especially as the days are becoming more evil?

7. Choose one verse from Ephesians 5:15-20 to pray for yourself or someone else.

Chapter 18

What Does a Spirit-Filled Marriage Look Like?

Ephesians 5:21-33

The past several years have seen an attack on the family like no other time in my lifetime. More couples in the history of our nation are now living together outside of marriage. We have seen the rapid legalization of same-sex marriage across the United States. In fact, statistics now reveal that 7 out of every 10 people in the United States have no problem with same-sex marriage. Our nation is treating this as if it is some sacred institution, which it is not. We even have commercials endorsing it! If those who are "Christians," who are endorsing this sinful lifestyle, would read and study the Scriptures, they would not find basis for their views, nor would they find any passage, such as the one we have before us in this chapter, that would support the idea of a relationship between a man with a man or a woman with a woman. I heard someone once say that God created Adam and Steve, not Adam and Eve.

For the genuine believer in Jesus Christ, this is not acceptable behavior, because they know that in the beginning God created man and woman, and that relationship is special and sacred. The same God who created man and woman also planned that they would have distinctive responsibilities as husband and wife. What are those responsibilities? Paul will explain those particular responsibilities in the verses that close chapter five of his epistle. But let me say before we begin: even in the Christian world, where heterosexual unions are ordained, we have veered far from what God designed for us regarding a Spirit-filled marriage. We need to understand the responsibilities laid out for us in Ephesians 5:21-33.

Ephesians 5:21-33

submitting to one another in the fear of God. ²²Wives, submit to your own husbands, as to the Lord. ²³For the husband is head of the wife, as also Christ is head of the church; and He is the Savior of the body. [24]Therefore, just as the church is subject to Christ, so let the wives be to their own husbands in everything. [25]Husbands, love your wives, just as Christ also loved the church and gave Himself for her, [26]that He might sanctify and cleanse her with the washing of water by the word, [27]that He might present her to Himself a glorious church, not having spot or wrinkle or any such thing, but that she should be holy and without blemish. [28]So husbands ought to love their own wives as their own bodies; he who loves his wife loves himself. [29]For no one ever hated his own flesh, but nourishes and cherishes it, just as the Lord does the church. [30]For we are members of His body, of His flesh and of His bones. [31]"For this reason a man shall leave his father and mother and be joined to his wife, and the two shall become one flesh." [32]This is a great mystery, but I speak concerning Christ and the church. [33]Nevertheless let each one of you in particular so love his own wife as himself, and let the wife see that she respects her husband (Ephesians 5:21-33).

By way of an outline for this lesson, we'll ask and find answers to four questions:

What Does a Spirit-Filled Person Look Like? (v 21)

What Does a Spirit-Filled Wife Look Like? (vv 22-24)

What Does a Spirit-Filled Husband Look Like? (vv 25-33)

What Does a Spirit-Filled Marriage Look Like? (v 33).

Paul is continuing on with his instructions regarding what a Spirit-filled life looks like, and focuses in verses 21-33 specifically on what a Spirit-filled marriage looks like. Perhaps you have wondered why Paul addresses the relationship between husband and wife to all the saints at Ephesus, and we will get into some of that in our lesson. But briefly, let me say that all marriages at any time in history have had problems. We can look in the Scriptures and see many marriages with problems. For example, Eve tempted her husband to sin; Potiphar's wife tried to commit adultery with Joseph; Sarah had Abraham have sex with Hagar, her handmaiden, so that she might have a child; Hosea had an adulteress wife, Gomer; Abigail's husband was a fool; David's wife, Michal, despised him; Ananias and Sapphira lied together. Doesn't sound like a lot of Spirit-filled marriages, does it? So what does a God-fearing marriage look like?

Let's take a look and see. And let's begin by looking at the Spirit-filled individual in verse 21.

Ephesians 5:21
What Does a Spirit-Filled Person Look Like?

submitting to one another in the fear of God (Ephesians 5:21).

At first glance you might have thought, "See, the Bible says wives and husbands submit to each other." The concept of a mutual submission, in the sense that marital roles are blurred, is not what Paul is commanding, as the context clearly explains: husbands do not submit to the authority of their wives; parents do not submit to the authority of their children; and masters do not submit to the authority of their slaves. The debate has long centered around the term *submit* (Greek, hypotasso), which the so-called evangelical feminists soften to mean a voluntary consideration, instead of a ranking under the authority of another.[114] But upon careful consideration we can see that this statement is really the heading to what Paul is going to address from this point in Ephesians until 6:9, in which he deals with household relationships. In other words, Paul will explain how wives submit by respecting their husbands; how husbands submit by loving their wives; how children submit by obeying their parents; how parents submit by not provoking their children to wrath; how servants submit by obeying their masters; how masters submit by not threatening their servants. This is the obvious intended meaning of Paul's heading statement.[115] We submit to one another *in the fear*

114 The Evangelical Feminists seek their softer definition of hypotasso, claiming that because the verb is in the middle voice it allows for a voluntary submission, i.e.,, to be loving, considerate or self-giving. Secondly they argue the reciprocal pronoun (Greek, allelois; *one to another*) softens the strong language. cf. G. Bilezikian, *Beyond Sex Roles* (Grand Rapids: Baker Book House, 1985), 154; C. S. Keener, *Paul, Women and Wives* (Peabody: Hendrickson, 1992), 168-172). However, the semantic range of the verb *submit* (Greek, hypostasso) simply does not permit the thought of being thoughtful to or considerate of another. And the reciprocal pronoun can't always be pressed to support the Evangelical Feminist view. No, the term means to rank under the authority of another.

115 Obviously this debate within evangelical circles is huge. The *Council for Biblical Equality* promotes a so-called, errant, egalitarian view, arguing for a blurring of gender roles in the church and in the home (e.g.,, Stanley and Patricia Gundry, Roger Nicole, Catherine Clark Kroeger, F. F. Bruce, Gordon Fee, Bill Hybels and Kenneth Kantzer.) The *Council of Biblical Manhood and Womanhood* promotes the hierarchal view (now called the complimentary view) where roles of leadership by men and follow-

of God, the One we stand in awe of and the One to whom we will give an account for everything we have done in our body, good or bad, and this includes the things done in our homes and in our workplaces. I heard someone once say that when we get to heaven we will not be holding our spouse's hand; each of us will give account individually. If we are living a Spirit-filled, God-fearing life, then it will flesh itself out in obedience to God in whatever He has asked us to do. It's like the passage in 1 Peter 3:1-7, where Peter gives the responsibilities of the husband and wife, and then in verse 8 says, "Finally, all of you be of one mind, having compassion for one another; love as brothers, be tenderhearted, be courteous." Yes, we have distinctive roles and responsibilities, but we submit to one another in the sense that we obey what God has said we are to be doing in that role. So what does a Spirit-filled person look like? They submit to whatever God asks them to do in their specific role. Speaking of submission, let's move along to the wife's role and see what a Spirit-filled wife looks like in verses 22-24.

Ephesians 5:22-24
What Does a Spirit-Filled Wife Look Like?

Wives, submit to your own husbands, as to the Lord (Ephesians 5:22).

The Greek word *submit* means to place in an orderly fashion under. We might say the husband is like a five-star general and the wife is like a four-star general, or the husband is like the president and the wife is like the vice-president. This word is also used in Colossians 3:18, where Paul says, "Wives, submit to your own husbands, as is fitting in the Lord." And in 1 Peter 3:1, Peter tells wives they must be subject even to their unsaved husbands: "Wives, likewise, be submissive to your own husbands, that even if some do not obey the word, they, without a word, may be won by the conduct of their wives." Now ladies, this does not mean that a woman is a doormat, or that she can never express an opinion

ing by women, which is the historic way of considering this, are retained. (e.g.,, Gleason Archer, Wayne Grudem, Timothy LaHaye, John Piper, Bruce Waltke, Carl F. H. Henry, D. James Kennedy, J.I. Packer, R.C. Sproul, John Walvoord and John MacArthur.) Of course, Ephesians 5:21 is at the center of the debate.

or an idea. But it does mean she lets her husband make the final decisions in the family. I know this is a hard one for us as women, even for those of us who are older. The reason it's so hard is that it's a part of the curse that we inherited from our mother, Eve, and it's something we will always fight against because of our sinful flesh. When Adam and Eve sinned, they each got cursed for their disobedience. The woman's curse was twofold. Genesis 3:16 says, "To the woman He said: 'I will greatly multiply your sorrow and your conception; in pain you shall bring forth children; your desire shall be for your husband, and he shall rule over you.'" God told Eve that her desire would be to rule over Adam, but that he would rule over her! Women need help to understand how to let their husbands wear the pants in the family, and how to do it graciously; not giving him the silent treatment for days when they don't agree. They need instruction on how to make gracious appeals when they disagree with their husbands' decisions. You might hear from a younger woman, "Well, if my husband loved me the way Christ loves the church, then submission would be a piece of cake." Well, maybe so, but that does not negate our responsibility. I have seen some women make important decisions without consulting their husbands and some go so far as to intentionally defy his wishes. This is an awful indictment on the role of the wife, and it brings shame to the name of Christ!

The Greek rendering here also indicates that this is a voluntary submission, not a forced submission or where the wife is beaten with the submission club by her husband. Just as the church submits to Christ voluntarily because she loves her Lord, so the wife submits to the husband voluntarily because she loves and respects him, and sees it for her good. Notice also that Paul says *your own husbands*—not someone else's—the one with whom she has an intimate relationship; the one she trusts. This submission is also done *as to the Lord*; in other words, she submits to her own husband in order to please the Lord. When wives keep this in mind, then submission becomes a delight. Paul goes on to give a reason why wives are to be submissive to their own husbands, in verse 23.

> For the husband is head of the wife, as also Christ is head of the church; and He is the Savior of the body (Ephesians 5:23).

The reason wives are to submit is because *the husband is the head of the wife*, just like *Christ is the head of the church*. *Head* means he is ruler or authority. We have already learned in Ephesians that Christ is the head of the church, the body (see Ephesians 1:22 and 4:15). Just as Christ leads every aspect of the body, His church, so the husband is to lead and direct his wife. As he has her best interests in mind, as he makes decisions that will include her, as he puts her needs first, then she will delight to submit to him. What woman wouldn't? Now, this does not mean that if your husband doesn't love you like that you don't have to submit, because you will still give an account for your submission or lack of it, and he will give an account for how he has loved you or not loved you. A wife's submission is a huge part of her sanctification.

Now what does it mean *that He is the Savior of the body*? Christ is not mentioned anywhere else is Scripture as being the Savior of the body, but it means He is the Savior of the body of Christ; He saved us and delivered us from our sins. Paul concludes his words on the responsibility of the wife in verse 24.

> Therefore, just as the church is subject to Christ, so let the wives be to their own husbands in everything (Ephesians 5:24).

Just as the church, the body of Christ, sees Christ as her head and sees what He has said to be beneficial for her life and godliness, so also should a wife view her submission to her husbands as the right thing to do, knowing that it will benefit her as she obeys the Lord.

Now before we go on, I do want to say that there is an exception to this command, and that would be if the husband were to ask the wife to do anything that is in direct violation to the Word of God. This is where she would have to graciously decline and obey God rather than her husband. This principle is so clearly set forth in Acts 5:29, where Peter and the other apostles were forbidden to share the gospel, (which is a direct command from God), and they responded by saying, "we ought to obey God rather than men." For example, if a woman's husband asked her to look at pornography with him, a wife would have to decline, as she would have biblical precedent to do so. Ephesians 5:3 is very clear on this: "But fornication and all uncleanness or covetousness, let it not even be named among you, as is fitting for saints." Another example would be in the case of an unsaved husband forbidding his wife to go to church. She might ask him which service (Sunday morning, Sunday night, or Wednesday night, for example) he would like her to attend. This would still allow him to be the head of the house, but also allow her to obey Hebrews 10:25, which says: "not forsaking the assembling of ourselves together, as is the manner of some, but exhorting one another, and so much the more as you see the Day approaching." Wayne Grudem has some helps here, elaborating on what submission does not mean:

1. Submission does not mean putting one's husband in the place of Christ.
2. Submission does not mean giving up independent thought.
3. Submission does not mean a wife should give up efforts to influence and guide her husband.
4. Submission does not mean a wife should give in to every demand of her husband.
5. Submission is not based on lesser intelligence or competence.
6. Submission does not mean being fearful or timid.
7. Submission is not inconsistent with equality in Christ.[116]

So we would say a Spirit-filled wife is a wife who is submissive to her husband with a voluntary attitude, in everything, unless it violates the Word of God. Now, Paul spells out for the husbands what their responsibilities are as they relate to their wives, and what a Spirit-filled husband looks like.

Ephesians 5:25-32
What Does a Spirit-Filled Husband Look Like?

Husbands, love your wives, just as Christ also loved the church and gave Himself for her (Ephesians 5:25).

Husbands, Paul says, *love your wives just as Christ loved the church. Love* here is Greek term <u>agapao</u>, which means to love even

---

116 Wayne Grudem and John Piper, eds., *Recovering Biblical Manhood &Womanhood: A Response to Evangelical Feminism* (Wheaton: Crossway, 1991), 194-195.

if one is undeserving or unloving of love, and it is a love that is to be ongoing. This would be something foreign to a husband in the Greco-Roman world, as men were not expected to love their wives. Women were considered not much more than slaves. For example, a wife could not go out in public without a male escort; couldn't eat with a male guest in her home; and her husband could divorce her for almost any reason, even burning his food. It was the custom of the Jews at that time to pray daily, thanking God that they were not born a Gentile, a slave, or a woman, so that tells you a bit about what they thought of women. So Christ's command here to love a wife was an astonishing thought to a Christian man. Christ comes in and changes even our culture!

It is interesting that the Word of God never directly commands a woman to love her husband, but it does command a husband to love his wife. Titus 2 speaks of older women teaching younger women *how* to love their husbands, but that is the only mention of it. But wives are not off the hook when it comes to loving our husbands, because we are commanded to love our neighbor as ourselves, and we're even commanded to love our enemies! This is not the only place a husband is commanded to love his wife. Paul says in Colossians 3:19, "Husbands, love your wives and do not be bitter toward them." Paul states here in Ephesians that husbands are to love their wives the way *Christ also loved the church*. And how was it that Christ loved the church? He gave Himself for her; He humbled Himself to the point of dying for her. When we consider this, it certainly does away with the notion that a husband can be harsh with his wife or ask her to sin. In my humble opinion, I think the husband has the more difficult sobering responsibility. Paul goes on in the next two verses to elaborate on how Christ loved the church. Some people take these two verses and try to prove ridiculous theology about husbands and their responsibility toward their wives, but we must think accurately about what Paul is saying. Paul gives the reason why Christ gave Himself for the church in verses 26 and 27.

> that He might sanctify and cleanse her with the washing of water by the word, (Ephesians 5:26).

Christ died for the church to *sanctify* her, which means to set her apart for Himself and for service to Him. This is certainly something that a husband cannot do for his wife. Paul also says He *cleanses her with the washing of the Word.* The cleansing with the water would be the baptism of the Spirit, which happens at salvation. Again, this is something a husband cannot possibly do for his wife. Paul speaks of this in Titus 3:5: "not by works of righteousness which we have done, but according to His mercy He saved us, through the washing of regeneration and renewing of the Holy Spirit." And in Hebrews 10:22, we read, "let us draw near with a true heart in full assurance of faith, having our hearts sprinkled from an evil conscience and our bodies washed with pure water." (On a side note, it is interesting to consider that in biblical times a bride would take a bridal bath and go to great lengths to bathe herself before her groom would come to get her and take her to his house and present her to his father.)

Now I have heard some people take this verse and say that the husband is the only one who can wash his wife with the Word of God, and therefore no one can teach her but him. Ladies, this is nothing more than foolish nonsense and pride, and it certainly limits women from learning from pastors, elders, and other women, as commanded in Titus 2. Paul is not saying that, nor is it in the context. Paul goes on to speak of Christ's glorious love for His body, the church, and His desire in her salvation.

> that He might present her to Himself a glorious church, not having spot or wrinkle or any such thing, but that she should be holy and without blemish (Ephesians 5:27).

Again, Paul is talking about the church and not a wife. Christ died for the church in order that He might present her as *a glorious church* to *Himself.* This means a church that is worthy of honor, because she is holy and without spot or blemish. Christ wants His bride to be pure, like a virgin without *spot or wrinkle*, and He wants her to be *holy and without blemish.* Paul has already set this forth in Ephesians 1:4: "just as He chose us in Him before the foundation of the world, that we should be holy and without blame before Him in love." In fact, in Revelation, when the apostle John is speaking of the marriage supper of the lamb, he uses similar imagery. Consider Revelation 19:7-8, "Let us be glad and rejoice and give Him glory, for the marriage of the Lamb has come, and His wife has made herself ready. And to her it was granted to be arrayed in fine linen, clean and bright, for the fine linen is the righteous acts of the saints." Paul goes on to say,

> So husbands ought to love their own wives as their own bodies; he who loves his wife loves himself (Ephesians 5:28).

Just as Christ loves His body, the church, so husbands *ought to love their own wives* as they love *their own bodies*. Loving their wives should be as if they are loving themselves. This is a tall order indeed for the husband, but listen to Paul's logic in the next verse.

> For no one ever hated his own flesh, but nourishes and cherishes it, just as the Lord does the church (Ephesians 5:29).

We don't hate our bodies but we *nourish* them and *cherish* them. This has the idea of feeding it, comforting it, caring for it in its entirety. I mean we get up and we think about what we are going to feed our bodies and what we are going to put on our bodies. If we are cold, we get a jacket; if we are tired, we go to bed; if we are wounded, we get a bandage; if we are sick, we rest or take medicine; if we get dirty, we take a bath. Men don't hate their bodies, and neither does the Lord hate the church. He nurtures and cares for her. In this way, a husband should love his wife just as he loves himself, *just as the Lord does the church*. And then Paul says,

> For we are members of His body, of His flesh and of His bones (Ephesians 5:30).

This might seem a little mysterious to you, but it is simple when you think about what Paul is saying. Christ watches over His church, His body, tenderly and carefully; so should the husband watch over his wife in the same way. Christ cares for us because we are members of His body, as Paul has so beautifully put forth in Ephesians already (Ephesians 1:23; 2:16; 3:6; 4:4; 4:12; 4:16; 5:23). Christ doesn't disconnect Himself from those who are truly of His body. We are eternally connected; He does not divorce us. The husband should consider that, because he and his wife are joined as one, as the next verse states.

"For this reason a man shall leave his father and mother and be joined to his wife, and the two shall become one flesh." (Ephesians 5:31).

This comes from Genesis 2:24 which says, "Therefore a man shall leave his father and mother and be joined to his wife, and they shall become one flesh." Just as the body, the church, is joined together with Christ, so a man and woman are joined together and have become one flesh. To be *joined* together means to be glued together, and it is a reference to sexual intercourse. Paul continues on and says,

This is a great mystery, but I speak concerning Christ and the church (Ephesians 5:32).

Just as the mystery of the union between Christ and the church is amazing and profound, so the union between a man and a woman is amazing and profound.

So what does a Spirit-filled husband look like? He loves his wife as he loves himself, by cherishing her. Wayne Grudem also has some tips for husbands, as he did for wives, by telling us what considerate leadership is not:

1. Considerate leadership does not mean harsh or domineering use of authority.
2. Considerate leadership does not imply equal sharing of leadership in the family.
3. Considerate leadership does not imply lesser importance for a wife.
4. Considerate leadership does not mean always giving in to a wife's wishes.
5. Considerate leadership is not optional for husbands.[117]

We end now with the sum of it all in verse 33, and here we answer the question, "What does a Spirit-filled marriage look like?"

---

117 Ibid, 208-209.

Ephesians 5:33
What Does a Spirit-Filled Marriage Look Like?

Nevertheless let each one of you in particular so love his own wife as himself, and let the wife see that she respects her husband (Ephesians 5:33).

Here's the bottom line, so to speak: Husbands, love your wives; and wives, respect your husbands. Husbands, cherish your wives as you do your body; and wives, fear, honor and obey your husbands.

Summary

What Does a Spirit-Filled Person Look Like? (v 21) They submit to whatever God asks them to do in their specific role. *What Does a Spirit-Filled Wife Look Like?* (vv 22-24) She is submissive to her husband with a voluntary attitude, in everything, unless it violates the Word of God. *What Does a Spirit-Filled Husband Look Like?* (vv 25-32) He loves his wife as he loves himself, by cherishing her. *What Does a Spirit-Filled Marriage Look Like?* (v 33) Husbands love their wives and wives respect their husbands.

Does this describe your marriage? Are you as a wife doing your part to obey God even if your husband is not, and are you doing your part with a joyful heart? Is your submission a sign to others of your growing sanctification? Would your husband rather be on your roof than in the house with you, because you are continually nagging him? Do you want your marriage to look like Christ and the church? Do you want your marriage to be an example to the lost world of Christ's love for His church? Do you want your marriage to be an example of the gospel? Then, my dear sister, be a woman who is submissive to her Lord by being submissive to her husband, with a joyful, willing attitude, and I guarantee that you will stand in vivid contrast to a dark and lost world!

Questions to Consider
What Does a Spirit-Filled Marriage Look Like?
Ephesians 5:21-33

1. (a) According to Ephesians 5:21-33, what are the responsibilities of the husband and what are the responsibilities of the wife? (b) According to the text, why is it essential that we carry out our God-given roles?

2. (a) What are the other responsibilities of the husband and of the wife, according to Genesis 2:18; Proverbs 19:13-14; Proverbs 31:10-31; 1 Corinthians 7:1-16; Colossians 3:18-19 and 1 Peter 3:1-7. (You might want to make two columns, one for the husband's role, and the other for the wife's role.) (b)Write a summary sentence of what the role of the husband should be and another summary sentence of what the role of the wife should be, according to God's Word. (c) Memorize Ephesians 5:33.

3. (a) How does Paul's description of Christ's sacrificial love in Ephesians 5:25-32 help you to understand the sacrificial love that a husband should have for his wife? (b) How can a wife encourage and/or confront her "believing" husband to be the husband that Christ commands him to be?

4. (a) Would you say you are a submissive wife? (Ask your husband if you are brave enough!) (b) What things have you found to be helpful in aiding you to be submissive with a joyful attitude?

5. How would you counsel a woman who is having trouble respecting her husband because of things that he does that do not seem worthy of respect?

6. After looking over all the roles of the wife, what is your greatest need? Please write it down as a prayer request. For those of you who are single, write a prayer request either for yourself as you consider a possible future marriage, or for someone you know who is married and could use prayer. (Please be discreet.)

Chapter 19

Parenting God's Way!

Ephesians 6:1-4

Most believers in our age would admit that the family is in trouble. Divorce rates are soaring; single parents are multiplying; materialism is taking over our lives; we are entertaining ourselves and our kids to death. We are failing to teach our kids work ethics, as well as respect for authority. We are now weaning our children from pacifiers to iPads! Sexual and physical abuse are rampant. It is a rare thing to see a family that lives out what has God set forth for them in His Word.

We are also now faced with the family being perverted in our culture because many "families" now don't have a mom and dad, but they have a mom and a mom, or a dad and a dad. I even read about one couple who had a child and decided not to give it a name or dress it according to its gender so that the child could decide if *it* wanted to be a male or a female! The family is in trouble, indeed, and yet the family was established by God before any other intuition, even before He established the church, and we know how important the church is, because we have been looking at its importance here in Ephesians. So what should the family look like? Paul gives us a little glimpse in the first four verses of Ephesians 6 as he writes concerning the parent-child relationship. Let's read it.

Ephesians 6:1-4

Children, obey your parents in the Lord, for this is right. [2]"Honor your father and mother, which is the first commandment with promise: [3]"that it may be well with you and you may live long on the earth." [4]And you, fathers, do not provoke your children to wrath, but bring them up in the training and admonition of the Lord (Ephesians 6:1-4).

Our outline for this lesson will include two parts:

Children's Twofold Responsibility to Their Parents, with a Twofold Blessing, (vv 1-3)

Parents' Threefold Responsibility to Their Children, (v 4).

Ephesians 5:1-3
Children's Twofold Responsibility to Their
Parents, with a Twofold Blessing

Children, obey your parents in the Lord, for this is right (Ephesians 6:1).

It is interesting that Paul addresses the children in his letter to the saints at Ephesus, as this would indicate they were in the worship service while this letter was being read to the church. I must admit that, while I think Sunday school and children's church do have their advantages, I personally believe children should learn to sit still in church and learn how to listen. There are so many teaching opportunities for parents each time the Word is taught. Ask your child questions on what was taught, or have him write down questions on what he hears. This just furthers your biblical instruction to your child. Now, since Paul addresses *children*, it's important for us to consider the definition of a child. A child is someone who is under the care of their parent. This would not be an adult child; the age would most likely range from early elementary age to late teens or early twenties. This is who Paul is addressing. Next, he gives the responsibilities of the child.

The child's first responsibility to their parents is to obey. What does it mean to *obey*? It means to listen under. A child is to listen to the instruction of the parent and then he or she is to carry it out. They should obey the spoken word. I would encourage you, if you have a child with a listening problem, ask them to repeat to you what you said, and then make sure they carry out your orders and do what they have been told to do. Some children claim to "forget" what a parent has said, so having them repeat what they've been told is a good way to ensure they remember it. We have some wonderful examples of this in God's Word, when we consider that our Lord obeyed His parents in Luke 2:51; Isaac obeyed Abraham to the point of lying down on the altar in Genesis 22; Jephthah's daughter in Judges 11 obeyed her father in a very difficult circumstance. And of course we have some examples of children not obeying their parents, and the results were disastrous, as the rebellious son in Deuteronomy 21; the prodigal son in Luke 15; or Eli's sons in 1 Samuel 2.

Paul goes on to say that children are to obey their parents *in the Lord*, which means because it honors the Lord. Just as a wife's submission honors the Lord, and a husband loving his wife honors the Lord, so a child's obedience honors the Lord. Why should children obey their parents? Paul says because this is the *right* thing to do! This is righteous. As a parent, you are not helping your child to be righteous or helping them do the right thing if you do not help them obey what God says here in Ephesians. If you allow "time out," counting to three, whining, coddling, or any other such nonsense, instead of demanding obedience from your children, you are training them to not obey you. And may I say with love, you are training them in how they will respond to God and to any other authority. Children should obey the spoken word and they should obey with a joyful heart! Can you imagine what kind of world we would have if every child obeyed this command? What sorrow and grief we would all be spared! Paul goes on to give the second responsibility of the child and this one has a twofold blessing with it.

"Honor your father and mother," which is the first commandment with promise: (Ephesians 5:2).

The child's second responsibility to their parents is to honor them. A child who obeys his parents is also honoring his parents. This quote is from Exodus 20:12, which is one of the Ten Commandments, where God says, "Honor your father and your mother, that your days may be long upon the land which the LORD your God is giving you." Interestingly enough, most of the Jewish people would be very familiar with the 10 commandments and would be very familiar with this command. So this would be not only for the child who is under parental authority, but also for a grown child. Now, what does it mean to *honor*? It means to prize, revere, and value. This probably seems foreign in our culture because we are a far cry from this. We put our parents in nursing homes and drug them. But this would be foreign in the biblical world, as families would take care of their parents. We don't treasure our parents and our grandparents, and we don't see caring for them as a gift from God. We want to be rid of them. I know of one nursing facility here in Oklahoma where a doctor actually stated that it was their goal to have residents admitted and gone (dead, that is!) in a year. Paul says that this command to honor parents is *the first commandment with promise*. What is the *promise*? Well, he gives the promise in the next verse, which is a twofold blessing for the child who obeys the command to honor their parents.

> "that it may be well with you and you may live long on the earth." (Ephesians 5:3).

The first blessing or promise is that it will go well with you. This means you will be happy, useful and virtuous. It might be interesting to do a survey of people who dishonor their parents and to see how it fares with them. *The second blessing or promise is that you will live long on the earth.* Proverbs 10:27 states, "The fear of the LORD prolongs days, but the years of the wicked will be shortened." Also consider Ecclesiastes 7:17, "Do not be overly wicked, nor be foolish: why should you die before your time?" I think we have several good examples of this in the word of God. Absalom is a good example of this, as he rebelled against his father, King David, and it cost him his life. In 2 Samuel 18, we read that he got his hair caught in a tree and Joab killed him while he was still alive and hanging in the tree. Or consider Eli's sons, who not only were taking all the prime cuts of meat meant for sacrificing and eating them instead, but also committing adultery with women at the door of the tabernacle! Eli confronted them but to no avail; and we have recorded in 1 Samuel 4:11, "Also the ark of God was captured; and the two sons of Eli, Hophni and Phinehas, died." God took them early in life. It did not go well with them and they did not live long on the earth. Again, it might be interesting to gather some statistics on those who dishonor their parents and to see how long they generally live! Now Paul shifts from explaining the role of the children toward their parents, to explaining the role of the parents toward their children. There are three responsibilities, according to verse 4.

Ephesians 5:4
Parents' Threefold Responsibility

And you, fathers, do not provoke your children to wrath, but
bring them up in the training and admonition of the Lord
(Ephesians 5:4).

The Greek word for *fathers*, is in the plural, and it can refer
to parents and not just the father. When you think of it, it is more
likely that the mother would do the provoking, anyway, since she
is with the child most of the day! Some, however, do think Paul is
addressing fathers, because they are the head of the family, as we
have seen in Ephesians 5:23, where Paul mentioned that the husband
is the head of the wife.

*The first responsibility of the parent to the child is to not
provoke them to wrath.* Paul states something similar in Colossians
3:21: "Fathers, do not provoke your children, lest they become
discouraged." To *provoke* means to aggravate, annoy or inflame
them, and to *provoke them to wrath* means to provoke by harsh
words, angry words, teasing them mercilessly, being overbearing
and making unreasonable demands.

Because I think this is such an important problem in our
parenting, I want to take a moment to share with you from two
authors on ways parents provoke their children to wrath. The first
set of examples comes from Lou Priolo's book, *The Heart of Anger*.
He lists 24 ways that parents provoke their children to wrath:

1. Lack of marital harmony.
2. Establishing and maintaining a child-centered home.
3. Modeling sinful anger.
4. Habitually disciplining while angry.
5. Scolding
6. Being inconsistent with discipline.
7. Having double standards.
8. Being legalistic.
9. Not admitting you're wrong and not asking for forgiveness.
10. Constantly finding fault.
11. Parents reversing God-given roles.

12. Not listening to your child's opinion or taking his or her "side of the story" seriously.
13. Comparing them to others.
14. Not making time "just to talk."
15. Not praising or encouraging your child.
16. Failing to keep your promises.
17. Chastening in front of others.
18. Not allowing enough freedom.
19. Allowing too much freedom.
20. Mocking your child.
21. Physically abusing them.
22. Ridiculing or name calling.
23. Unrealistic Expectations.
24. Practicing favoritism.[118] (Isaac and Rebecca violated this, and it certainly brought nothing but anger and bitterness in Esau and Jacob. Jacob also favored Joseph, and the rest of that story is tragic, even though God meant it for good.)

John MacArthur also gives some of the same examples in his book, *Successful Christian Parenting*, but adds a few others not mentioned above, including:
1. Neglecting things like the essentials: food, baths, clothes, not attending their school functions, and being disinterested in their life.
2. Withholding love.
3. Excessive discipline.[119]

Instead of provoking their children to wrath, parents are to bring them up in the training and admonition of the Lord. The King James Version says "nurture and admonition of the Lord." What does this mean exactly? The *training*, or nurture, would entail discipline, and the *admonition* would involve words of encouragement or instruction. Let's consider these two responsibilities.

The second responsibility of parents is to bring up their children in the nurture of the Lord. The nurture, or discipline, of children is evidence of a parent's love for the child. This is one of

118 Lou Priolo, *The Heart of Anger* (Amityville: Calvary Press, 1998), 30-50.
119 John MacArthur, Jr., *Successful Christian Parenting* (Nashville: Word, 1999), 136-145.

the areas that grieves me as I disciple women. I see them refusing to do what God says regarding the discipline of their children. What hardships they bring on themselves! Parenting is not hard if you will do it God's way. Proverbs 22:15 says, "Foolishness is bound up in the heart of a child; the rod of correction will drive it far from him." Proverbs 23:13 says, "Do not withhold correction from a child, for if you beat him with a rod, he will not die." Let me tell you, ladies, I had a father who believed in discipline and I am not dead! And neither are my six siblings! Proverbs 29:15 tells us, "The rod and rebuke give wisdom, but a child left to himself brings shame to his mother." I don't know about you, but that's the way I feel when I see a child out of control in a public place. It's not the poor child who is to blame; it is the parents. If parents don't discipline their children, then you have to ask, "Do they really love them?" In Hebrews 12:6, we find an interesting verse that tell us that our Heavenly Father disciplines those who are His because He loves them: "For whom the LORD loves He chastens, and scourges every son whom He receives." The writer of Hebrews goes on to say in verse 8, "But if you are without chastening, of which all have become partakers, then you are illegitimate and not sons." Ladies, the Lord loves us enough to discipline us, and if we are not experiencing His discipline, then it proves that we are not His children. If parents do not discipline their children, then it is in serious question whether they love them or not.

Paul mentions the third responsibility of the parent and that is to bring them up in the admonition of the Lord. This means by words of encouragement or instruction. The most encouraging words that parents can give their children are the Words of God. We should train and encourage our children in spiritual things, teaching them biblical principles. We should do that when we sit and when we walk and when we lie down and rise up, as Deuteronomy 6:7 states. We need to be there to listen to their problems and to answer their questions. We should pray with them and for them. We must show them affection and tell them we love them. These are all ways we can show love and encouragement to our children. We must not tear them down by yelling at them and calling them unkind names. For those of you who have grown children, you know what I mean when I say the time slips by too fast. When I was a young mother, I used to think people who said that were foolish, but now that I am on the other side, I say, true, true, true! Those years can never be reclaimed. There are enough children in this world who are unloved, and we need to be different as God's children and bring our children up in the ways of the Lord.

It is interesting that Paul says we bring them up in the training and the admonition *of the Lord*, which is what he said to the children, obey your parents *in the Lord*. In other words, this honors the Lord. Someone once said, most homes nowadays seem to be on three shifts: the father is on the night shift; the mother is on the day shift, and the children shift for themselves. But Paul gives something different for the family who belongs to the Lord.

Summary

What is God's desire for the family? Here it is: *Children's Twofold Responsibility to Their Parents, with a Twofold Blessing,* (vv 1-3). Their responsibilities are to obey their parents and to honor their parents. The blessings promised to them for obeying and honoring their parents are that it will go well with them and that they will live long on the earth. *Parents' Threefold Responsibility to Their Children,* (v 4). They are to not provoke their children to wrath; they are to bring them up in the training of the Lord; and they are to bring them up in the admonition of the Lord.

If you have parents that are living and you are under their authority as a child, are you obeying them? And are you obeying with a joyful heart? If you have parents that are living and you are young or old, are you honoring them by caring for them? Paul is clear in 1 Timothy 5:8, "But if anyone does not provide for his own, and especially for those of his household, he has denied the faith and is worse than an unbeliever." Have you given over your God-given responsibility to the government or to someone else? Do you genuinely look at honoring your parents as a precious gift from God?

As a parent, are you guilty of provoking your child to anger by any of the ways we mentioned in this lesson, or by any other ways we did not mention? Is your child angry? Have you stopped to consider that it might be something you are doing or not something they are doing? What about discipline as a parent? Have you bought into the world's way of discipline—time out, coddling, giving chances, counting to 3, ignoring bad behavior, or, worse, drugging your child so as to not have to deal with his child-like ways? And what about admonition? Are you teaching your child the things of the Lord? They tell us that 1 percent of the child's time is spent under the influence of Sunday school; 7 percent under the influence of the public school; and 92 percent under the influence of the home. That is a huge amount of time that you as a parent have to train your child and not only in the things of the Lord, but things like manners, caring and helping others, and teaching them how to work.

We have seen in Ephesians a beautiful picture of the family: the wife submitting to and respecting her husband; the husband loving his wife as Christ loved the church; the children obeying and honoring their parents; and the parents not provoking their kids to wrath, but teaching them in the ways of the Lord, along with careful and consistent discipline. Is this a picture of your home this past week? If not, what do you need to change so that your home will be one that honors your Master who is in Heavenly Places?

Questions to Consider

Parenting God's Way!
Ephesians 6:1-4

1. (a) What are the responsibilities of children and of parents according to Proverbs 1:8-9; Proverbs 6:20-23; Proverbs 23:22-25; Ephesians 6:1-4 and Colossians 3:20-21? (b) What reasons are given for why these responsibilities should be carried out? (c) Memorize Ephesians 6:1, 2, 3, or 4.

2. (a) According to Deuteronomy 21:18-21 and Proverbs 30:17, what happened to a son who disobeyed his parents? (b) What does this tell you about what God thinks of disobedient children?

3. (a) What do the following verses say about disciplining a child? Proverbs 13:24; Proverbs 22:15; Proverbs 23:13-14; Proverbs 29:15. (b) With these verses in mind, why do you think many believers refuse to do what God commands? (c) What have you found to be helpful in teaching your child to obey the spoken word that you can pass on to others? (d) How can we lovingly help those who are in error regarding parenting God's way?

4. (a) Who in Scripture comes to your mind as a child who disobeyed their parents *or* a parent who provoked their child or children to wrath? (b) What do you learn as valuable lessons for your life as you meditate on their example?

5. (a) What are some ways in which children can honor their parents, whether these children are young or old? (b) What should a child do if a parent asks them to sin? (c) What are some ways in which parents provoke their children to wrath?

6. Is your family a picture of Ephesians 6:1-4? What area(s) do you need help in? Please put your need in the form of a prayer request.

Recommended Reading:
The Faithful Parent, by Martha Peace and Stuart Scott
The Heart of Anger: Practical Help for the Prevention and Cure of Anger in Children, by Lou Priolo
Successful Christian Parenting, by John MacArthur
Shepherding a Child's Heart, by Tedd Tripp

Chapter 20

Employed by the Heavenly Master!

Ephesians 6:5-9

We have come to a topic that more than will likely be a little sensitive and perhaps eye-opening to our 21st century idea of work. Most of you, however, would probably agree with me that in our society today many Americans have no idea what it means to work hard. Many people seem to be lazy and want to do the least amount of work for the most amount of money. Today's statistics for unemployment are staggering; at the time of this writing, 12.3 million people are out of work. Now, I realize that many of those people truly want to work, and that jobs are not as plentiful as they once were, but my friend, some of those numbers are due to people who can work but don't want to work and are just plain lazy. I know because I've met some of them! Some of us have lost the concept of why God gave us work to do. We no longer say, "What can I do for this job?" but "What can this job do for me?" (Of course, that is where we are with most relationships and events today.) In fact, when is the last time you heard someone ask if they were getting paid too much for a job? What we usually hear is, "I'm not paid enough for this job!" We are a society that is driven by greed and laziness and we want to do minimal work for a whole lot of money, and many of us don't want to live within the means that God has provided for us. We have veered far from a biblical view of a God-honoring work ethic, and we are rearing a generation who are worse than we are! The apostle Paul through the Holy Spirit has much to say about work as we cover this most important topic of being employed by our Heavenly Master. Let's see what he has to say.

Ephesians 6:5-9

Bondservants, be obedient to those who are your masters according to the flesh, with fear and trembling, in sincerity of heart, as to Christ; 6not with eyeservice, as men-pleasers, but as bondservants of Christ, doing the will of God from the heart, [7]with good will doing service, as to the Lord, and not to men, [8]knowing that whatever good anyone does, he will receive the same from the Lord, whether he is a slave or free. [9]And you, masters, do the same things to them, giving up threatening, knowing that your own Master also is in heaven, and there is no partiality with Him (Ephesians 5:5-9).

In this chapter we see how Paul continues on with his admonitions regarding household relationships and now deals with the masters and the slaves. Our outline for this lesson will include:

The Responsibilities of the Slaves, (vv 5-8)

The Responsibilities of the Masters, (v 9)

Ephesians 6:5-8
The Responsibilities of the Slaves

Bondservants, be obedient to those who are your masters according to the flesh, with fear and trembling, in sincerity of heart, as to Christ; (Ephesians 6:5).

Now, perhaps you are wondering why Paul would place instructions about slave and master relationships in the midst of his teaching on family relationships. Paul is actually still dealing with household relationships, as foreign as that might sound to us. In the biblical world, many slaves were employed in the home, and often were part of the extended household. At the time, a third of the people in the Roman world at the time of this epistle's writing were slaves, which means there were about 60 million slaves. Many were born into slavery and knew nothing about being free. Every type of work was done by a slave: farming, cooking, teaching, practicing medicine, taking care of children, managing the house, etc. Often it would be hard to distinguish a slave from a master because a slave could have the same responsibilities as a master. (It's really the same in our world today, as employees and employers often have the same responsibilities.) However, there were some differences that are worth mentioning. Slaves had no legal rights and were considered as nothing more than an animal or a tool. They could not do anything on their own without the permission of their master.[120] Often they were put to death, especially if they tried to run away.

Here in verse 5, Paul calls slaves *bondservants*, which means one who is bound to render service to another. That's what a slave was! *And Paul tells us their first responsibility to their masters is to obey.* The Greek word for *obey*, here, is the same as the word used in 6:1, where Paul tells children to obey their parents. It means to listen under, which would indicate obedience to the spoken word. If the master says, "Go weed the garden," the slave obeys. If an employer says, "I want that report by 5:00," the employee is to have it done by 5:00. In our world, we don't want anyone to tell us what to do, not even in the workplace. If we don't like what we're asked to do, we quit, get another job, or collect unemployment. But that would not have been the case in the biblical world, especially since most were dependent on their day's wages to even buy food. If they didn't work, they didn't eat!

Since we are talking about slaves' responsibilities to masters, it is important that we define what a *master* is. A master is one who is supreme in authority; he is a lord. The words *according to the flesh* mean the master or the employer is an earthly master.

The second responsibility of the slave to the master is to have an attitude of fear and trembling. Now, this does not mean they bite their nails and cower in a corner. But it does mean that have deep respect, reverence and fear. Slaves would dread offending their masters because if they did it would mean punishment. Masters would often control their slaves by fear so as to get them to do whatever they wanted them to do. But Paul tells slaves to obey with

---

120 In 2010 John MacArthur published *Slave: The Hidden Truth About Your Identity in Christ*, where he wrote: "It wasn't until the spring of 2007, on an all-night flight to London while reading Slave by Christ by Murray J. Harris, that I realized there had been a centuries-long cover-up by English New Testament translators that had obscured a precious, powerful and clarifying revelation by the Holy Spirit." (John MacArthur, *Slave: The Hidden Truth About Your Identity in Christ* (Nashville: Thomas Nelson, 2010), 1.) He went on to lament the translation of the Greek term doulos as *servant* instead of *slave*. The concept of a *slave* is one who lacks any personal rights whatsoever; but the concept of a *servant* is one who has rights and is gainfully employed by another. Hence Christians are better likened to *slaves* of Jesus Christ and not *servants*.

fear, but not the fear of their master; rather, they are to obey with the fear of offending Christ, as evidenced by the words *as to Christ*.

The third attitude of the slave is that of sincerity of heart. This means a heart that is free from improper motives, a heart that is genuine. This would be someone who is not trying to do his work so that he might gain more money or, in our world, climb the success ladder. He doesn't have secret motives for doing what he does but does it as unto the Lord, which is Paul's point as he says *as to Christ.* If employees would obey this verse, it would certainly do away with complaining about a work situation or a boss.

Now, I will say there is an exception to this command for slaves to obey their masters, and that would be if their master or employer asked them to sin. (This is the same exception for the wife's submission to her husband and the child's obedience to his parents.) We have a good illustration of this in Exodus 1:15-21: "Then the king of Egypt spoke to the Hebrew midwives, of whom the name of one was Shiphrah and the name of the other Puah; and he said, 'When you do the duties of a midwife for the Hebrew women, and see them on the birthstools, if it is a son, then you shall kill him; but if it is a daughter, then she shall live.' But the midwives feared God, and did not do as the king of Egypt commanded them, but saved the male children. So the king of Egypt called for the midwives and said to them, 'Why have you done this thing, and saved the male children alive?' And the midwives said to Pharaoh, 'Because the Hebrew women are not like the Egyptian women; for they are lively and give birth before the midwives come to them.' Therefore God dealt well with the midwives, and the people multiplied and grew very mighty. And so it was, because the midwives feared God that He provided households for them." Pharaoh did not want the people of Israel to multiply any more than they already were, so he commanded the midwives to kill the male babies of the Hebrew women. However, the midwives feared God and obeyed Him over their masters and God blessed them for their obedience. In our world, for example, if an employer would ask you to lie, or ask you for sexual favors in return for a raise, or to lie on the company's income taxes, then the Christian employee must not obey their boss. Paul continues on with the responsibilities of the slaves to the masters in verse 6.

not with eyeservice, as men-pleasers, but as bondservants of Christ, doing the will of God from the heart, (Ephesians 6:6).

The fourth responsibility of the slave is to not do their work with eyeservice. The Greek word <u>ophthalmodoulia</u> means sight-labor. This means working only when the master is watching. Modern-day examples of this might include: Your boss steps out of the office, so you start texting or playing games on your phone. Or you see the boss coming, so you shut down the website you're looking at for entertainment and appear as though you're working on some project for work. Or you're on the phone with your husband or friend, and you see your boss coming, and say, "That's right, Joe, 12:00 sharp for the meeting on the engineering project." Slaves of the heavenly master should realize that the eyes of the Lord are on them at all times, whether their earthly master is watching or not.

The fifth attitude that should be present in slaves is that they should not be men-pleasers. This is an old word that means man-courting, or we might say he's working only to please his master. For the believer, we should do all our work to please God. As Paul says in Colossians 3:22-24, "Bondservants, obey in all things your masters according to the flesh, not with eyeservice, as men-pleasers, but in sincerity of heart, fearing God. And whatever you do, do it heartily, as to the Lord and not to men, knowing that from the Lord you will receive the reward of the inheritance; for you serve the Lord Christ." Paul states the danger of being a man-pleaser in Galatians 1:10, "For do I now persuade men, or God? Or do I seek to please men? For if I still pleased men, I would not be a bondservant of Christ." Man-pleasers are not God-pleasers, and we must keep this in mind when we do our work or when we do anything. In fact, just recently someone was sharing with me how they were uncomfortable because they thought someone knew where they were all times and it was making them nervous. (They were doing things they should not be doing.) I responded to the person by explaining that they should be more concerned that the eye of the Lord was upon them and that He knew where they were at all times!

Instead of being a man-pleaser, Paul says a slave should be a bondservant of Christ who does the will of God from the heart. *This would be the sixth responsibility of the slave, that is, to recognize you are a bondservant of Christ, working wholeheartedly or from your innermost being.* The Christian slave or employee knows that everything he does is for the Lord, and that the eye of the Lord is watching him, and that everything he does will be accounted for, whether it is good or bad. So he works heartily, knowing that the Heavenly Master has a watchful eye at all times. He doesn't even work to receive a promotion. If it happens, fine; if not, he is fine with that, because he knows he has a different Master, a heavenly Master. If all this isn't making us squirm yet, well, Paul goes on to say,

> with good will doing service, as to the Lord, and not to men, (Ephesians 6:7).

The seventh responsibility of the slave is to serve with good will, which means with a cheerful heart, a good attitude, a positive attitude. I think Christians should be the happiest employees. If our minds are truly focused on working for the One who redeemed us with His blood, if we would remember that everything we have is from Him, if we would remind ourselves of His gracious provisions of food, shelter, clothes and the job He gives which provides these things, then why would we not serve with a cheerful heart?! And Paul reminds us again of something he already stated, that we do this *as to the Lord, and not to men.* Why? Because there is a bigger issue at hand, as he reminds them in verse 8.

> knowing that whatever good anyone does, he will receive the same from the Lord, whether he is a slave or free (Ephesians 6:8).

This would be an encouragement to the slaves Paul is writing to because, as a slave, you would have no inheritance. But as a Christian slave, they would have the inheritance of heaven that Paul has so wonderfully reminded them of already in Ephesians 1:11, 14, and 18. Even though their earthly masters don't necessarily see the good they have done, their Master in heaven has seen *whatever good* they have done, and it's His eye that really matters. As Paul puts it in 2 Corinthians 5:10, "we must all appear before the judgment seat of Christ, that each one may receive the things done in the body, according to what he has done, whether good or bad." Just in case the masters think they're off the hook with how they should behave, Paul reminds them that they are not. They also have a sobering charge and responsibility, in verse 9.

> And you, masters, do the same things to them, giving up threatening, knowing that your own Master also is in heaven, and there is no partiality with Him (Ephesians 6:9).

When you read this verse carefully, you come to the conclusion that it is actually the *masters* that have the more sobering responsibilities, as evidenced by the words *do the same things to them.* The masters have to have the same attitudes the slaves have. They also are to obey their Master, the Lord Jesus; they are to have respect for Him; they are to serve with sincerity of heart; they are to realize the eye of the Lord is upon them; they are not to be men-pleasers; they are to do their work wholeheartedly as bondservants of Christ with a cheerful heart. Paul does add a responsibility to the masters, though, and that is *giving up threatening* their slaves. Masters would often beat their slaves, sell their slaves, have sex with their slaves, and since they were considered nothing but trash or tools, why not? But for the Christian master, that was not acceptable. Why? Because their *own Master also is in heaven,* and *there is no partiality with Him. Partiality* means to receive the face. God is not a respecter of persons, and when it comes to the judgment, both slave and master will be treated equally in how they are judged. Some masters or employers think they are off the hook and think much higher of themselves than they should, but God is not more favorable toward a master or an employer than he is a slave or employee. He treats them equally, and expects the same behavior from them.

It is similar to the idea that Peter tells pastors in 1 Peter 5:2-4, where he says, "Shepherd the flock of God which is among you, serving as overseers, not by compulsion but willingly, not for dishonest gain but eagerly; nor as being lords over those entrusted to you, but being examples to the flock; and when the Chief Shepherd appears, you will receive the crown of glory that does not fade away." In other words, just because a pastor is a leader it does not mean he can beat the sheep or lord things over them or serve for dishonest money. Why? Because one day he will give account to the Chief Shepherd! Leadership is held to a higher standard, accountability and judgment. This might be a pastor, a president, a king, a husband or a master. My friend, we must remember the words of our brother Paul in Galatians 3:28, "There is neither Jew nor Greek, there is neither slave nor free, there is neither male nor female; for you are all one in Christ Jesus."

Summary

So *The Responsibilities of the Slaves*, (vv 5-8), are: to obey their masters, respect their masters, serve with a sincere heart, not work only when the master is watching; not be a man-pleaser, work wholeheartedly as a bondservant of Christ, and do their work with a cheerful heart. *The Responsibilities of the Masters*, (v 9), to do these same things, and not threaten their slaves.

Now, perhaps you think this lesson has nothing to do with you; you're not employed and you're not a slave. Sure, you are! Some of you might feel like a slave: a slave to the dishes, to the laundry, to the cooking, to running errands, to feeding the dogs and cats and kids, and other endless things. When you think about it, we are all employed, either by an employer or by the Lord as homemakers. And all who know the Lord are His bondservants! And most of us are in charge of someone or something. Either we are someone's boss or we rule our kids or employ others to do work in our home. More than likely, we have all been in the position of a slave and a master at some point in our life.

As we think about our biblical responsibilities, whether master or slave, let's ask ourselves some thought-provoking questions. Is your service, in whatever role you play, as unto the Lord? Is your attitude one of a cheerful and sincere heart with a view to please Him? Do you do your work as if God were standing next to you? (He is, by the way.) Do you do half-hearted jobs? Are you lazy in your housework, cooking or any other tasks you do? Do you have before your mind's eye that you will receive reward or loss of reward for those things you have done in your body, good or bad?

For those of you who are employers, do you treat your employees harshly by threatening to fire them if they don't straighten up? Do you lead your employees with a sincere and cheerful heart, realizing that the eye of the Lord is upon you? Have you remembered that you are His bondservant? Do you realize that you, too, have a Master in heaven to whom you are accountable?

Whether bond or free, whether master or slave, whether employee or employer, we all should say a hearty "Amen" to the following quote: "Thank God—every morning when you get up—that you have something to do which must be done, whether you like it or not. Being forced to work, and forced to do your best, will breed in you a hundred virtues which the idle never know."[121]

---

121 Quote by Charles Kingsley.

Questions to Consider

Employed by the Heavenly Master!
Ephesians 6:5-9

1. (a) What are the responsibilities of slaves and the responsibilities of masters, according to Ephesians 6:5-9; Colossians 3:22-4:1; 1 Timothy 6:1-2; Titus 2:9-10; and 1 Peter 2:18-21. (b) According to these passages, what are the reasons these responsibilities should be carried out? (c) What happens if they are not carried out? (d) Memorize Ephesians 6:8.

2. (a) Why is it important that we work, according to Proverbs 13:4; 19:15; 20:4, 13; 21:25; 24:30-34; 1 Thessalonians 4:11-12; and 2 Thessalonians 3:10. (b) How would you advise someone who is able to work but chooses not to?

3. (a) Do you think it is right for a Christian to receive aid from the government when they are able to work? (b) What should be the church's responsibility toward those who are unable to work and have need?

4. (a) How would you use the passage we are studying to encourage a believer who has a bad attitude about their job? (b) What tips can you give to others on how to instill a good work ethic in our children?

5. (a) Whether you work inside the home or outside the home, would you say you have the attitudes that Paul commands believers to have in Ephesians 6:5-8? (b) If you are an employer, are you treating your employees with the attitudes that Paul commands in Ephesians 6:9? (c) In what ways can you improve to be a better employee/employer?

6. What is your prayer request after considering question number 6?

Chapter 21

Preparing for Spiritual Battle

Ephesians 6:10-17

Several months ago my husband decided that is was time for us to purchase some guns for the protection of ourselves and our property. Along with the purchase of the weapons, came a class that teaches how to use them. (A good idea, don't you think?) The class was quite lengthy, and we learned not only the different parts of the gun but also how to load the gun, how to clean the gun, and how to use it. A big portion of the time was spent in actually shooting this thing! One of the things that struck me was the instructor teaching us the importance of not letting our weapon out of our sight. I remember him saying that we should carry it through our homes and even consider getting concealed weapons permits so that we could have our weapons on our person at all times. He went on to say, "For example, what if you are in your kitchen or den and an intruder comes into your home, and your gun is in your night stand in your bedroom? I mean, what use is that to you, how can you protect yourself?" I thought to myself, "That makes sense," even though I couldn't imagine carrying a gun around the house! In essence, this is what Paul is saying as he is winding down his letter to the Ephesians. He reminds his readers that they are in a battle and they have a real enemy. Their enemy is not an intruder that might break into their homes, but an enemy that is unseen and always prowling around to steal, kill and destroy them. How are they going to protect themselves? How are they going to battle with this enemy? They must ready themselves to battle this enemy at all times! Let's read what Paul what has to say.

Ephesians 6:10-17

Finally, my brethren, be strong in the Lord and in the power of His might. ¹¹Put on the whole armor of God, that you may be able to stand against the wiles of the devil. ¹²For we do not wrestle against flesh and blood, but against principalities, against powers, against the rulers of the darkness of this age, against spiritual hosts of wickedness in the heavenly places. [13]Therefore take up the whole armor of God, that you may be able to withstand in the evil day, and having done all, to stand. [14]Stand therefore, having girded your waist with truth, having put on the breastplate of righteousness, [15]and having shod your feet with the preparation of the gospel of peace; [16]above all, taking the shield of faith with which you will be able to quench all the fiery darts of the wicked one. [17]And take the helmet of salvation, and the sword of the Spirit, which is the word of God; (Ephesians 6:10-17).

As we consider what it means to be preparing for battle, we'll see:

The Warrior's Source of Power, (v 10)

The Warrior's Enemies, (vv 11-12)

The Warrior's Armor, (vv 13-17)

These are the important closing words Paul has to say to his brothers and sisters in Ephesus, as evidenced by verse 10.

Ephesians 6:10
The Warrior's Source of Power

Finally, my brethren, be strong in the Lord and in the power of His might.

Paul begins the ending of his letter by saying *finally*, which means from henceforth or in the remaining time I have. He is obviously winding down his letter by this word, finally. *My brethren* is a reminder of the fact that they are brothers in the faith. He already referred to them as saints in the opening of the letter (Ephesians 1:1). Paul begins by admonishing his *brethren* at Ephesus *to be strong in the Lord*. To *be strong* means to be strengthened, to become able. God told Joshua three times in Joshua 1 to be strong and of good courage as he was getting ready to go to battle to possess the land God had promised Israel. As we wage war, we must not be wimpy, but we must be strong, and notice that our strength is not of ourselves but it is *in the Lord and in the power of His might*! We cannot muster up enough mental determination. The source of any strength we have is in God, who infuses that strength into us. Paul mentions this in Philippians 4:13 when speaking about contentment in any situation; he says, "I can do all things through Christ who strengthens me." Paul did not muster up some mental determination on his own as he learned contentment, but it was Christ who infused that ability into Him. It is God working through us and in us to conform us to His image. This is what Paul has laid forth from the beginning of the letter to the Ephesians as he has reminded them that it is God who chose them, it is God who redeemed them, and it is God who made them alive, even when they were dead! It is all of Him so that we cannot possibly boast that it is our own efforts! So what is the warrior's source of power? The Lord and His mighty power! In our waging war with our enemy, it is God who helps us, as evidenced by what Paul says again in verse 11.

Ephesians 6:11-12
The Warrior's Enemies

> Put on the whole armor of God, that you may be able to stand against the wiles of the devil (Ephesians 6:11).

By now, maybe the readers of this epistle feel like some of you do; I mean, "How am I going to do all these things Paul has admonished me to do in this letter? Things like walking worthy of my vocation and putting off lying, anger, stealing, corrupt communication, bitterness? How am I going to be kind and tenderhearted and forgiving? How am I going to not grieve the Spirit and put off all those sexual sins? How am I going to redeem the time, be wise, be thankful, submit to my husband, be a good employee or employer, and not provoke my kids?" The answer is really twofold. You are going to do these things and much more by His power and by making sure you are wearing the armor of God!

The words *put on* have the idea of sinking into a garment. The tense here in the Greek means to put on once and for all. You don't take it off to take a spiritual nap! If you do, the enemy will get you! We should always be ready for battle, and we must always have the *whole armor* on, or we will be an open target for the enemy to attack us. It's like Colossians 3, where Paul lists all the put-ons. The idea is the same: it's once and for all that we put on tender mercies, kindness, longsuffering, love, etc. We don't take those virtues on and off, as they are to always clothe a believer. And Paul says, here in Ephesians, that we are to put on the whole armor of God. Not some of it, but all of it, the entirety of it. He will go to explain what that armor is, but the *whole* armor would indicate we are to be fully and heavily armored. This is interesting imagery, as Paul himself was chained to a Roman soldier while there in prison, so he would have this image of armor in his mind. This armor, by the way, is supplied by the Great Warrior, the one who fights for us. You might be wondering, "Why do I need to be clothed with armor?" Paul says clearly why, and it is so we can *stand against the wiles of the devil.* The word *stand* means to face him while maintaining our ground, not yielding, but holding our position and resisting him. When we think of standing it means we don't sit or lie down. Also, someone who is standing is better able to defend their position and hold their ground.

Paul says we stand against *the wiles of the devil,* which means his trickeries, his strategies. Ladies, Satan is cunning, and he knows exactly where to attack the Christian's weak spots. Just today, I met with a gal for the first time, a strong believer, and yet the enemy had gotten her and she knew it. She was weak, she was defeated, and she was in a mess. After further probing, I found out that she had quit reading her Bible and had stopped praying. I told her it was no wonder she was in a mess. She did not have on the full armor of God, and she had laid her weapons down. Peter tells us in 1 Peter 5:8, "Be sober, be vigilant; because your adversary the devil walks about like a roaring lion, seeking whom he may devour." Ladies, he is the master deceiver, and we do not take him seriously enough. John MacArthur gives help here on ways in which the enemy deceives us:

1. He attempts to impugn God's character and credibility, just as he did with Adam and Eve (Has God said? Is God good? Does He care?).
2. He tries to undermine present victory by creating trouble that makes life difficult, thereby tempting us to forsake obedience to God's standard and calling.

3. He attacks believers through doctrinal confusion and falsehood.
4. He attacks God's people by hindering their service to Him.
5. He attacks believers by causing division.
6. He attacks believers by persuading them to trust their own resources.
7. He attacks believers by leading them into hypocrisy.
8. He attacks believers by leading them into worldliness, by enticing them to let the world squeeze them "into its mold.
9. He attacks believers by leading them to disobey God's Word.[122]

Paul continues on to warn the Ephesians of the enemies they do battle with, in verse 12.

> For we do not wrestle against flesh and blood, but against principalities, against powers, against the rulers of the darkness of this age, against spiritual hosts of wickedness in the heavenly places (Ephesians 6:12).

The word *wrestle* is a word that came from the Olympic Games in the Greco-Roman world. It would indicate wrestling with an opponent. That is what we are doing; we wrestle with an opponent, the devil and all his cohorts. It's like Jacob, in Genesis 32:24-25, when he wrestled with God: "Then Jacob was left alone; and a Man wrestled with him until the breaking of day. Now when He saw that He did not prevail against him, He touched the socket of his hip; and the socket of Jacob's hip was out of joint as He wrestled with him." This wrestling is not *against flesh and blood*. This is not a human war; this is something far more concerning, and something we don't think about much. We fight *against principalities, against powers, against the rulers of the darkness of this age, against spiritual hosts of wickedness in the heavenly places. Principalities* and *powers* would be demonic spirits. *Rulers of the darkness of this age* would be all types of hostile spirits. *Spiritual hosts of wickedness* would be demons. The *wickedness* would be all kinds of sexual perversions—Satan worship, the occult, and things like that. *In the heavenly places* would mean that they inhabit the unseen world; they are in the air, and in the sky. Paul has already mentioned

---

122 MacArthur, *The MacArthur New Testament Commentary: Ephesians*, 346-348.

this in Ephesians 2:2: "in which you once walked according to the course of this world, according to the prince of the power of the air, the spirit who now works in the sons of disobedience." Ladies, this is serious stuff, and we need to take heed. Paul says in 2 Corinthians 10:3-5, "For though we walk in the flesh, we do not war according to the flesh. For the weapons of our warfare are not carnal but mighty in God for pulling down strongholds, casting down arguments and every high thing that exalts itself against the knowledge of God, bringing every thought into captivity to the obedience of Christ." So, who are the warrior's enemies? Satan and all his cohorts, evil spirits, and demons, and all kinds of wickedness. Because of who we fight against, then Paul reminds us again of the importance of taking up the whole armor of God.

Ephesians 6:13-17
The Warrior's Armor

> Therefore take up the whole armor of God, that you may be able to withstand in the evil day, and having done all, to stand (Ephesians 6:13).

Once again Paul emphasizes that we must *take up the whole armor of God. Take up* means to lift it up and carry it. You must be covered from head to toe or you will be vulnerable to the attacks of the evil one. The tense here also indicates a sense of urgency. Ladies, if you fail to put on one piece of the armor, you will fall. Paul also says we must have it on so we are *able to withstand in the evil day.* The *evil day* could either mean the entire span of your life, as all of life is evil, or it could refer to the explosion of satanic activity before Christ comes. My friend, we are there, so please pay attention to Satan's ploys, because he wants to kill and destroy us. As Jesus says in Matthew 24:24, "For false Christs and false prophets will rise and show great signs and wonders to deceive, if possible, even the elect." I also will say that I think the more mature we are in our faith, the more difficult the attacks are from Satan. Job, who was attacked by the evil one in ways that most of us could not imagine, was a man who was blameless, upright, feared God and shunned evil. God even told Satan there was no one like him on the earth at that time (Job 1:1, 1:8, and 2:3). Paul goes on to repeat the importance of standing by saying *and having done all, to stand.* And then he says it again in verse 14.

> Stand therefore, having girded your waist with truth, having put on the breastplate of righteousness, (Ephesians 6:14).

This is the fourth time he has told us to *stand,* and so it is of utmost importance that we take this position in battle. Paul then begins to tell us the different pieces of armor the warrior who is fighting this battle must wear. By the way, the pieces of armor that Paul mentions here are in the order that a soldier would have put them on. *The first piece of armor we must put on is girding our waist with truth. Girded* means to fasten around. The girdle or sash was an important piece of armor for the soldier. Because they wore loose, flowing robes, it was necessary to gird them up when they traveled, ran, worked, or fought in a battle. The girdle was made to keep every part of the armor in its place, and to gird the soldier on every side. The Greek tense indicates that this girdle was strapped to oneself. It's not by chance that Paul begins with *truth.* If we are not girded or fastened around with truth we are susceptible to every wind of doctrine and the cunning lies of the enemy. The truth, referred to here, is the knowledge and belief of the truth. It is not only the fact that God is true and all He represents is true, but also that the attitude of truthfulness prevails with the soldier. How can one fight in a war if he is not committed to the purpose for which he is fighting? You must be dedicated and loyal to your goal. The idea of truth is not foreign to this epistle. Consider Ephesians 1:13: "In Him you also trusted, after you heard the word of *truth,* the gospel of your salvation; in whom also, having believed, you were sealed with the Holy Spirit of promise." Or Ephesians 4:15: "But, speaking the *truth* in love, may grow up in all things into Him who is the head—Christ." Also, Ephesians 4:21: "if indeed you have heard Him and have been taught by Him, as the *truth* is in Jesus." And Ephesians 4:25: "Therefore, putting away lying, 'Let each one of you speak truth with his neighbor,' for we are members of one another." And Ephesians 5:9: "(for the fruit of the Spirit is in all goodness, righteousness, and *truth*)" (all emphases mine). If a soldier's waist was not girded, he would be tripped up in the battle; likewise, if you are not girded with truth, you will be tripped up in your battle. Are you girded with truth? Are you willing to live the truth and are you willing to die for the truth?

The second piece of armor is the breastplate of righteousness. This makes sense, because if we do not know the truth, then we do not know how to act out the truth, to live righteously. The *breastplate* was a piece of armor that covered the front and the back, across the chest and from the neck to the thighs, and would protect the heart from wounds made by swords, spears or arrows. Paul calls it the breastplate *of righteousness,* which means integrity, holiness, purity of life. If we are not living a life of righteousness, if we are not taking every evil thought captive to the obedience of Christ and smashing it, we too will fall prey to an attack on our heart. How did Job defeat Satan? The Word tells us there was no one as righteous as Job. That's how his heart was protected from the enemy's attacks, and that's how he was able to face such temptation and not sin (Job 1:22)! He wore the breastplate of righteousness. If you are not living a life of integrity, watch out, my dear friend, for you are exposed to the trickeries of the devil. Even as I wrote this lesson, I found myself grieving over the sins of one who had not worn her breastplate of righteous living and had fallen prey and was being held captive by the evil one. Paul says in 2 Timothy 2:3-4, "You therefore must endure hardship as a good soldier of Jesus Christ. No one engaged in warfare entangles himself with the affairs of this life, that he may please him who enlisted him as a soldier." Just as the soldier in biblical times would be wounded in his heart by a sword without the protection of the breastplate, so will you, my friend, be wounded in your innermost being if you are not living righteously? Those wounds do not go away—ever! Are you wearing the breastplate of righteousness? Do you live a holy life? What do you do when no one is watching? Paul goes on to give the third piece of armor.

> and having shod your feet with the preparation of the gospel of peace; (Ephesians 6:15).

The third peace of armor is having our feet shod with the preparation of the gospel of peace. When a soldier goes to war he has to wear the right foot gear. Soldiers must have the right shoes or they will not be able to fight, much less stand up. Roman soldiers normally wore a half-boot called a caliga, which was studded with sharp nails. They were tied by leather thongs to about half-way up the shin and were lined with wool or fur in the cold weather. *Preparation* means to be ready. In the spiritual realm, we must be ready to fight at all times. The gospel is called the *gospel of peace* because the gospel brings peace between God and man. We were at war with God, but the gospel came to us and we are now no longer at war with God, but we are at peace with God. Paul has already told them in Ephesians 2:14, "For He Himself is our peace, who has made both one, and has broken down the middle wall of separation." We have no fear when the enemy comes, because our feet are firmly planted on the gospel of peace. We were once enemies of God, but now He is our defender. If God is for us, who can be against us? Just as the soldier had to have his shoes on at all times, so we must also make sure that our spiritual feet are firmly planted upon gospel of peace, giving us a firm foothold in the battle with the evil one. Are you wearing the proper foot wear? Have you embraced the gospel? If not, you will stumble and fall. Paul continues on and writes,

> above all, taking the shield of faith with which you will be able to quench all the fiery darts of the wicked one (Ephesians 6:16).

Above all, or in addition to this, take up your *shield*. It's interesting to consider that the first three pieces of armor were worn at all times during a battle, and the last three, the shield, helmet and sword, were picked up or taken up as they were needed. That is why Paul uses the word take up. *The shield of faith would be the warrior's fourth piece of armor.* Now the shield was 4 feet by 2 ½ feet, which was about the size of a small door. The shield was usually made of wood and covered with some type of hide and was preserved by frequent anointing with oil, so that arrows or darts would glance, or rebound, off it. *Fiery darts* would be arrows that were dipped in pitch and then lit on fire. Now obviously, if you were hit with one of these it could be destructive, as it would set your clothes on fire. But if you had your shield, you could quench or distinguish these darts. For the spiritual warrior, he must take up *the shield of faith*. This would be faith in God and who He says He is and what He says He will do. This is probably where most of us give foothold to Satan, because we shake in our faith and wonder if God can really work in our situation. When Satan shoots an arrow of doubt, the believer has the shield of faith in God and who He says He is, and that wards off the Satan's arrow. If you want to ward off the evil one's darts, you must take up the shield of faith; otherwise, he will attack you with all sorts of doubts. I mean, how did all those men and women in Hebrews 11 fight their battles? By faith! In fact, the word faith is mentioned 24 times in Hebrews 11. As Paul says in Hebrews 11:6, "But without faith it is impossible to please Him, for he who comes to God must believe that He is, and that He is a rewarder of those who diligently seek Him." Just as the soldier would be burned or wounded with the fiery darts of the enemy without a shield, so will the soldier of Christ be defeated in battle without a firm, fixed faith built upon the person and work of Christ! Are you holding the shield of faith? Do you believe God is who He says He is? How has this helped you in times of battle? Paul ends with the fifth and sixth pieces of a warrior's armor in verse 17.

> And take the helmet of salvation, and the sword of the Spirit, which is the word of God; (Ephesians 6:17).

The fifth piece of armor is the helmet of salvation. The *helmet* was made of bronze and it fit over the back of the neck and slightly over the shoulder. It was fastened by a band under the chin. Its function would be to protect the head, the nose and the eyes from injury. When Paul says we put on *the helmet of salvation*, he is talking about our hope of salvation, which will help us in our spiritual battles. The helmet defended the head, and so the hope of salvation will defend the soul and keep it from the blows of the enemy when he tries to get the believer to doubt or be discouraged. Just as a soldier would not fight well without a hope of victory, neither will a spiritual warrior fight well without the hope of salvation, which is the security he has in Christ! Are you wearing the proper head gear? Is your hope, as you battle, in some earthly inheritance or is it in your eternal inheritance?

The sixth and final piece of the believer's armor is the sword of the Spirit, which is the word of God. Now, the sword was an essential part of the armor because without it the soldier would not be well-armed. The sword was 6-18 inches long and usually was two-edged, and looked much like a dagger. For the spiritual warrior Paul refers to our sword as *the sword of the Spirit*, which means it has the nature of the Spirit, whom we know is truth. Paul says this sword *is the word of God.* In my opinion, this is a vital piece of armor for the believer! Why? Because Paul says in Hebrews 4:12, "For the word of God is living and powerful, and *sharper than any two-edged sword,* piercing even to the division of soul and spirit, and of joints and marrow, and is a discerner of the thoughts and intents of the heart" (emphasis mine). Every time that Satan tempted Jesus in the wilderness in Matthew 4, Jesus responded with "It is written ...." Jesus knew the Word was his defense against Satan's attacks. If you do not know the Word of God during times of battle and testing, you will fall prey to the devils attacks. He will tempt you to wonder, "Has God said ...?" Women especially are prone to rely on their feelings instead of the solid facts of the Word of God. When Satan tempts us, we should be so grounded that we stand firm on the written Word. Just as the soldier could not ward off the enemy without his sword, my friend, you will not ward off your enemy Satan without the sword of the Word of God. Are you carrying your sword—the Word of God—as you battle, or are you leaning on man's ideas and following the world's counsel? Do you know God's Word? How much of it? When someone says something that is contrary to the Scriptures, can you defend them because you know the Word of God so thoroughly?

Now, just briefly in verse 18, Paul mentions prayer. And even though it is not a part of the believer's armor, it is certainly essential that we are constantly praying for God's strength, His help, and His resources as we battle the evil one. But more of that in our next lesson.

Summary

So what is *The Warrior's Source of Power,* (v 10)? The Lord and His mighty power! Are you fighting your battles in your own strength or in the strength of the Lord?

Who are *The Warrior's Enemies,* (vv 11-12)? It is Satan and all his cohorts of evil spirits and demons and all kinds of wickedness.

Do you believe in the devil? Do you take him seriously? Are you ignorant of his devices? Do you know yourself well enough to know where Satan attacks you the most?

What is *The Warrior's Armor*, (vv 13-17)? It is the girdle or sash of truth, the breastplate of righteousness, feet that are shod with the preparation of the gospel of peace, the shield of faith, the helmet of salvation, and the sword of the Spirit, which is the word of God. Is there any piece of the armor missing from your armor?

Are you serious about waging war, my friend? Are you standing ready for war, or have you laid your weapons down? Are you prepared to fight? Oh, that we could echo with Brother Paul on the day that the Lord receives us to His glory and Kingdom: "I have fought the good fight, I have finished the race, I have kept the faith" (2 Timothy 4:7).

Questions to Consider

Preparing for Spiritual Battle
Ephesians 6:10-17

1. (a) As you read Ephesians 6:10-17, what words or phrases do you notice that are repeated? (b) Why do you think Paul repeats certain words or phrases in this section on the believer's armor?

2. (a) List each piece of the armor that we, as believers, should put on. (b) What importance does each piece play in the war against our spiritual enemies? (c) Why do you think it is important that a believer put on the whole armor of God and not just a portion of it? (d) Memorize Ephesians 6:11.

3. (a) Paul states in Ephesians 6:11 that we are to put on the whole armor of God, in order that we might fight against the wiles of the devil. What do you learn from the following passages that help you to understand the seriousness of this enemy we battle? Matthew 4:1-11; Acts 5:1-3; Acts 26:18; 2 Corinthians 4:3-4; 2 Corinthians 11:3; 2 Corinthians 11:13-15; 2 Thessalonians 2:9-11; 2 Timothy 2:24-26; 1 Peter 5:8. (b) After looking over these passages would you say that you seriously consider the working of Satan in your life to defeat you? (c) What are some ways in which Satan tricks or deceives the believer?

4. Paul has been using the metaphor of walking up to this point in his epistle to the Ephesians. (See Ephesians 2:10; 4:1; 4:17; 5:2; 5:8 and 5:15). Why do you think he now changes the position of the believer from walking to standing in Ephesians 6:10-14?

5. (a) How do your personally wage spiritual warfare? (b) What are some practical things you have found to be helpful in the midst of battle?

6. (a) How are you doing in waging war against your spiritual enemies this day? (b) Have you put on the whole armor of God? (c) Is there a piece of the armor that you have laid aside? (d) What is your prayer request as you fight your spiritual battles?

Chapter 22

Paul's Final Prayer, Faithful Friend, and Farewell Words

Ephesians 6:18-24

Someone once said, "All things must come to an end."[123] Basically, that is a true statement. The Scriptures talk about a number of things that come to an end: the end of all flesh; the end of the earth; the end of the year; the world; and the end of time. As people of this world, many of us look forward to the end of certain things: the end of a day; the end of a school year; a job; a nightmare; a diet; an illness; the end of a bad relationship; the end of a season, and many more things we might enjoy reaching an end.

And of course, sooner or later books come to the end. Each of the 66 books of the Bible has an ending. For example, Genesis ends with Joseph dying and being embalmed and put in a coffin; Judges ends with everyone doing what is right in their own eyes; Nehemiah ends with him asking God to remember him for his good; the Psalms end with "Praise the Lord"; Ecclesiastes ends with the fact that God will bring every work into judgment, whether it is good or bad; Malachi ends with the Lord smiting the earth with a curse; Matthew ends with a command to share the gospel; Luke ends with everyone continually praising God in the temple; James ends his book by calling us to go after the erring brother; and John ends 1 John with a command to keep ourselves from idols. All of the 66 books of the Bible have an end, and they are rather interesting to read. We have now come to the end of one of Paul's prison epistles, his epistle to the Ephesians. What does the end look like? What is on Paul's mind as he ends this letter? Let's discover the end together as we read Paul's final words.

---

123 A supposed proverb from the 1300s.

Ephesians 6:18-24

praying always with all prayer and supplication in the Spirit, being watchful to this end with all perseverance and supplication for all the saints— [19]and for me, that utterance may be given to me, that I may open my mouth boldly to make known the mystery of the gospel, [20]for which I am an ambassador in chains; that in it I may speak boldly, as I ought to speak. [21]But that you also may know my affairs and how I am doing, Tychicus, a beloved brother and faithful minister in the Lord, will make all things known to you; whom I have sent to you for this very purpose, that you may know our affairs, and that he may comfort your hearts. [23]Peace to the brethren, and love with faith, from God the Father and the Lord Jesus Christ. [24]Grace be with all those who love our Lord Jesus Christ in sincerity. Amen (Ephesians 6:18-24).

In this lesson, we'll consider:

Paul's Final Prayer, (vv 18-20)

Paul's Faithful Friend, (vv 21-22)

Paul's Farewell Words, (vv 23-24)

Now, even though prayer is not a piece of the armor, it certainly is an important part of the battle that we fight, because without prayer we are in trouble indeed! So let's consider Paul's Final Prayer, and as we do we will also see his admonition for us to pray.

Ephesians 6:18-20
Paul's Final Prayer

praying always with all prayer and supplication in the Spirit, being watchful to this end with all perseverance and supplication for all the saints— (Ephesians 6:18).

Before we start talking about prayer we should define what prayer is. Prayer is the act of worship whereby we talk to God. As Paul begins this brief section on prayer, he is not saying prayer is a piece of the armor that we are to wear, but because of the context we can conclude that prayer is essential as we wage war against our enemies. We must be praying at all times, watching at all times, persevering in prayer at all times, because without prayer we can't win any battle. We must be praying while we are warring! Even our Lord, when He was wrestling in the Garden of Gethsemane before the cross, prayed over and over to His Father to deliver Him from the cross. He even rebuked the disciples for not watching and praying! The text doesn't say it, but I imagine when Jesus was in the battle with Satan in the wilderness (Matthew 4). He communicated much with the Father, since the passage tells us that He was led by the Spirit into the wilderness to be tested, and afterwards angels came and ministered to Him. It must have been quite a battle! Since we are to put on the whole armor of God, then it only makes sense, since it is *His* armor that we are wearing, that we should be in communication with Him as we battle! One man put it well, "Satan trembles when he sees the weakest saints upon their knees."[124]

Paul begins by telling them that they are to be *praying always*, which means at all times.[125] It is very similar to what he says in 1 Thessalonians 5:17, where he tells the church at Thessalonica to "pray without ceasing." We should pray at all times, not just during a spiritual battle, even though that would seem to be an occasion in which we should be more prayerful with greater fervency. There should always be a prayer upon our lips, whether we are having good days or bad days, times of trouble or times of blessing. We should have an attitude of prayer during any season of life. We should also pray at all times, in all places and occasions, and with all kinds of prayers. We should pray formal prayers, informal prayers, long prayers, short prayers, out-loud prayers, silent prayers, private prayers, and public prayers. Paul uses another term for prayer here, *supplication*, which just means earnest praying. These are prayers that are fervent, red-hot, and gut-wrenching. This would seem to indicate that during battle these are the types of prayers we should offer up. We have a great example of this in Colossians 4:12: "Epaphras, who is one of you, a bondservant of Christ, greets you,

---

124 Words by William Cowper.
125 It is possible that the two participles (i.e.,, *praying* and *watching*) suggest the practical means of putting on the whole armor of God. In other words, they culminate the paragraph of Ephesians 6:10-17. Although such a view is possible it seems the object defined here (i.e.,, *supplication for the saints*) speaks of a focus on others instead of self-protection.

always laboring fervently for you in prayers, that you may stand perfect and complete in all the will of God." His prayers were red hot for these saints. Wouldn't it be great if there was a saint among us that would pray like that for our individual churches? Epaphras is a rebuke to us, because many of us are lazy in our praying, but he is also an encouragement to us, because prayer is a ministry of the saints that is much neglected, yet certainly something we can all be doing.

And Paul adds that these prayers are *in the Spirit*, which means they are aided by the help, the power, and the influence of the Spirit. The Holy Spirit assists us and guides us as we pray. As Paul says in Romans 8:26-27, "Likewise the Spirit also helps in our weaknesses. For we do not know what we should pray for as we ought, but the Spirit Himself makes intercession for us with groanings which cannot be uttered. Now He who searches the hearts knows what the mind of the Spirit is, because He makes intercession for the saints according to the will of God." If you have ever been earnest in prayer about something, then you know what Paul is saying. Sometimes our hearts are so heavy that we do not know how to pray or what to pray for in a given situation or for a certain person, and so we groan or cry out to God. It is a comfort to know that the Spirit of God assists us as we pray and intercedes for us in the groaning of our hearts!

So we pray at all times with supplication aided by the Spirit, and as we do this, Paul says, we must be *watchful to this end*, which means we must be alert at all times. We must be watchful before prayer, during prayer, and after prayer. We must also watch for times to pray and watch for things that would keep us from praying. We must be alert to the temptation to get up off our knees and become sluggish, thinking, "Okay, I've done my praying for the day!" We must not get up off our knees and be lazy! We must be in an attitude of prayer at all times. We have the reminder from our Lord when He warned the disciples in Matthew 26 that they must watch and pray, lest they enter into temptation. If we are indifferent to what is going on and are not on the alert in prayer, we will be discouraged and defeated.

Paul ends his admonition about prayer by saying that we should pray with *all perseverance and supplication for all the saints.* This means we never stop praying and we never lose heart, and we don't just pray for ourselves but for all the saints. I know many times I get discouraged when I pray for something over and over and over again and I feel like my prayers are hitting the ceiling. I wonder, is God listening? Does He hear my cries? And yet I know the principle of persevering in prayer, and so I keep crying out to Him to answer my petitions, knowing that He knows the beginning from the end and He has a plan that is much better than mine! And Paul gently reminds us that prayer isn't just about us; it is also about others. We should be praying for other *saints* who are also in the midst of a battle and that, my friend, is *all the saints* alive today! They are all in the midst of some type of battle. Sometimes we think we are the only ones wrestling and fighting and praying, and yet the Scriptures tell us that, "No temptation has overtaken you except such as is common to man" (1 Corinthians 10:13). We all have tests and trials, even though sometimes we think we are the only ones struggling. We should not be so self-consumed that we forget that others are hurting and need our prayers. I love the example of our Lord in Luke 22:31-32, when he tells Peter, "Simon, Simon! Indeed, Satan has asked for you, that he may sift you as wheat. But I have prayed for you, that your faith should not fail; and when you have returned to Me, strengthen your brethren." Jesus knew that Peter was going to be in the midst of a battle with Satan, and He tells him not only that He prayed for him but also what He actually prayed for Him. What an encouragement! James says, "Confess your trespasses to one another, and pray for one another, that you may be healed. The effective, fervent prayer of a righteous man avails much" (James 5:16). It is interesting that Paul encourages the Ephesians to pray for all the saints, because the next thing he mentions is a prayer request for himself!

> and for me, that utterance may be given to me, that I may open my mouth boldly to make known the mystery of the gospel (Ephesians 6:19).

Paul doesn't say, "And pray for me that I might get out of this horrid place," or "pray for me that I might have a decent meal," or "pray for me that I might not have to be chained to this soldier anymore," or "pray for me that I might not get sick." He doesn't ask them to pray about any of those things; instead, he asks for prayer for boldness to speak the gospel! He asks that *utterance may be given to me, that I may open my mouth boldly to make known the mystery of the gospel.* What a rebuke to us! My dear friend, being in prison in Paul's day was nothing like being in prison in our day! Paul spent about 25 percent of his life in prison! They say that Roman imprisonment was preceded by being stripped naked and then flogged, a humiliating, painful and bloody ordeal. Bleeding wounds went untreated; prisoners sat in painful leg or wrist chains. Mutilated, bloodstained clothing was not replaced, even in the cold of winter. We know that in Paul's final imprisonment, he asked for a cloak, presumably because of the cold. Most cells were dark and unbearably cold. The lack of water, cramped quarters, and sickening stench from few toilets made sleeping difficult and waking hours miserable. Male and female prisoners were sometimes incarcerated together, which led to sexual immorality and abuse. Prison food, when available, was poor. Because of the miserable conditions, many prisoners begged for a speedy death and others simply committed suicide. And Paul spent 25% of his time there! But he asks his friends to pray that he might *open* his *mouth boldly* to share the gospel, which means that he would open his mouth freely, not holding anything back. Paul wanted to declare the gospel while bound in prison. He refers to it as *the mystery of the gospel,* which he has mentioned several times in this epistle (Ephesians 3:3, 4, 9). This was his desire, as well, when he wrote to the church at Philippi. He says in Philippians 1:12-14, "But I want you to know, brethren, that the things which happened to me have actually turned out for the furtherance of the gospel, so that it has become evident to the whole palace guard, and to all the rest, that my chains are in Christ; and most of the brethren in the Lord, having become confident by my chains, are much more bold to speak the word without fear." Evidently, Paul was bold in sharing his faith, and some even embraced the gospel because of it. As he comes to the end of Philippians, he is able to say, "All the saints greet you, but especially those who are of Caesar's household" (Philippians 4:22). This is an encouragement to my own heart, when I consider that even the apostle Paul asked for prayer for boldness. It tells me that he had fears and discouragements just as we do when it came to sharing his faith. He lacked boldness, just as we do, but he secured the prayers of his fellow saints so that he would be bold! For Paul, this boldness could mean death; in fact, sharing the gospel is what ultimately landed him in prison, as he says in verse 20.

> for which I am an ambassador in chains; that in it I may speak boldly, as I ought to speak (Ephesians 6:20).

Paul says, this is why I am here in prison, this is why I am in these *chains*, which means coupling chains bound to a guard. But I am chained, Paul says, because *I am an ambassador* for Christ. An *ambassador* was a representative through whom God spoke. Paul says, in 2 Corinthians 5:20, "Now then, we are ambassadors for Christ, as though God were pleading through us: we implore you on Christ's behalf, be reconciled to God." Now, ladies, this is a sobering statement! Preaching the gospel is what landed Paul in prison, and now he prays for boldness to preach some more?! Is he a fool?! Yes, for Christ's sake, he is! (See 1 Corinthians 4:10.) And again, he asks that he'd be able to *speak boldly*, and he says I know this is how *I ought to speak*. I should not cower in fear. I should not fear those who can kill my body, but I should fear Him who can destroy my soul and body in hell! (See Luke 12:15.) Paul's final prayer is for boldness to share the gospel! Paul now shifts from his final prayer to write about his faithful friend, Tychicus.

Ephesians 6:21-22
Paul's Faithful Friend

> But that you also may know my affairs and how I am doing, Tychicus, a beloved brother and faithful minister in the Lord, will make all things known to you; (Ephesians 6:21).

Paul wants them to know how he is doing and so he does this through his faithful friend, *Tychicus*. I am sure that the saints at Ephesus were concerned for Paul's welfare, as they knew his imprisonment was not a piece of cake and that it could lead to his death at some point. Remember, there were no phones, email, texts, or twitter in those days, and so letters that were carried by hand were the only means of communication for Paul. Perhaps you're wondering who his faithful friend, Tychicus, is? Tychicus was from the province of Asia and had traveled with Paul on this third missionary journey. Evidently he had spent some time with Paul in Rome and was sent by Paul to take these letters to their destination. Paul calls him *a beloved brother*, which means he was a dear brother. Paul also calls him a *faithful minister*, which means he was a trustworthy and reliable companion in ministry with Paul. It is interesting that Paul uses this word, *faithful*, when telling Timothy whom he should disciple in the things of Christ (2 Timothy 2:2). "And the things that you have heard from me among many witnesses, commit these to faithful men who will be able to teach others also." Paul goes on to say,

> whom I have sent to you for this very purpose, that you may know our affairs, and that he may comfort your hearts (Ephesians 6:22).

Paul is sending Tychicus to the Ephesians so that Tychicus can let them know how Paul is doing, as he has just mentioned in verse 21, but also so that he can comfort their hearts. I imagine it would be encouraging to the saints at Ephesus to know that Paul is remaining steadfast in the faith, that his spirits are good, and that he is trusting in the providence of God. He also, perhaps, would comfort the saints at Ephesus by encouraging them to remain steadfast, as well, and generally encouraging in the things of Christ. That truly is a faithful friend—one who is a dear brother, a faithful minister, and an encouragement in the things of Christ! Paul now ends with some final words, in verses 23 and 24.

Ephesians 6:23-24
Paul's Farewell Words

> Peace to the brethren, and love with faith, from God the Father and the Lord Jesus Christ (Ephesians 6:23).

The ending here is very similar to most of Paul's letters. He ends this letter by sending them greetings of *peace*, which is harmony among others and is something that is impossible apart from Christ. In fact, he goes on to say that it is *from God the Father and the Lord Jesus Christ*. It is interesting that Paul begins this epistle with a greeting of peace in 1:1; he mentions Christ is our peace in 2:14, 15, and 17; he encourages us to keep the bond of peace in 4:3; he tells us in 6:15 that our feet should be shod with the preparation of the gospel of peace; and now, in 6:23, he closes with this same idea of peace.

The second thing he mentions is *love with faith*, which means love united with faith. Love with faith could be referring to Paul's love for the Ephesians, or it could be referring to the Lord's love for them, which is the more likely interpretation, because it is God's love which saved us and gives us the ability to have faith, or to believe. Paul has mentioned this several times in this epistle. In Ephesians 2:4-5, he says, "But God, who is rich in mercy, because of His great love with which He loved us, even when we were dead in trespasses, made us alive together with Christ (by grace you have been saved)." And in Ephesians 5:2, he says, "And walk in love, as Christ also has loved us and given Himself for us, an offering and a sacrifice to God for a sweet-smelling aroma." Grace is next on the lips of the apostle Paul, which is how he ends most of his epistles.

> Grace be with all those who love our Lord Jesus Christ in sincerity. Amen (Ephesians 6:24).

Grace is God's divine influence upon our heart; it is His unmerited favor toward us. Grace has been a theme throughout this epistle (Ephesians 1:2; 1:6; 1:7; 2:5; 2:7; 2:8; 3:2; 3:7; 3:8; 4:7; 4:29; 6:24). Paul started this epistle with a greeting of grace and he ends with grace. Ephesians is certainly a book which focuses in on the grace of God, because it is most certainly God's grace alone that saves any of us. Paul says that this grace is for *those who love the Lord Jesus Christ in sincerity*. In other words, they love Him with no hypocrisy. This is a love that is undying. Genuine faith will produce genuine love for God. Love for God is something we really can't mask. We either love Him or we don't. And our love for God is proven by our obedience, as Jesus says in John 14:15, where He tells us that if we love Him we will keep His commandments. John also tells us in 1 John 5:3 that keeping God's commandments is not a burden. Paul say in 1 Corinthians 16:22. "If anyone does not love the Lord Jesus Christ, let him be accursed. O Lord, come!" Oh, how can we not love the one who loved us first, chose us, died for us, redeemed us and will one day bring us home to be with Him forever in heavenly places?! And with that, Paul ends with *Amen*, which means so be it!

Summary

Paul's Final Prayer, (vv 18-20), is for boldness to share the gospel! But before he shares that prayer request for himself he admonishes them to pray at all times, for all saints, with all perseverance. Are you in the habit of praying at all times? When you need help with an unruly child or a difficulty in your marriage, do you pray? When you are timid in confronting an erring brother, do you pray? When you lose your car keys or something else of value, do you pray? When you need insight into the Word, do you pray? Are you alert in prayer? Do you pray for others who are going through a spiritual battle? For whom do you pray? Do you know what is going on in the lives of those you love and serve so that you can intercede for them? Are you only praying for yourself? Do you pray for your spiritual leaders? They are fighting battles that need your prayers! Since Paul's final prayer is for boldness to share the gospel, then I am compelled to ask, are you bold in sharing the gospel? When is the last time you shared the gospel? When is the last time you asked someone to pray for you that you would be bold to share the gospel?

Paul's Faithful Friend, (vv 21-22), was Tychicus, who was a dear brother, a faithful minister, and an encouragement in the things of Christ! Do you have a friend like Tychicus? Or, a better question might be, are you a faithful friend to someone else, like Tychicus was to Paul?

Paul's Farewell Words, (vv 23-24), are for peace, love with faith, and grace, which all come from a relationship with Christ. Do you possess the peace, love, faith, and grace that come from knowing Christ alone? Paul leaves us a great example of how to end well by reminding us of the faith, the grace, the love, and the peace that come only from our Master who is in Heavenly Places!

Questions to Consider

Paul's Final Prayer, Faithful Friend, and Farewell Words
Ephesians 6:18-24

1. (a) Why is it important that we pray, according to Ephesians 6:18-20? (b) Why do you think it is important for *you* to pray? (c) Memorize Ephesians 6:18.

2. Paul says we are to persevere in our praying, in Ephesians 6:18. What encouragement can you take from Matthew 26:36-46 and Luke 18:3-7 as you persevere in prayer?

3. (a) What do you learn about Tychicus in Acts 20:4-5; Ephesians 6:21-22, Colossians 4:7-8; 2 Timothy 4:12; and Titus 3:12? (b) How does Tychicus compare with some of the others who were with Paul at one time, according to 2 Timothy 1:15; 2:17-18; 4:10; and 4:14? (c) What qualities would you look for in someone with whom you would minister?

4. Read over all of Ephesians and write down any new truths you have learned as well as changes you have made as a result of this study.

5. Looking back at lesson 1, what was your answer about what you hoped to gain from this study? Did you achieve it?

6. Write out a praise or thanksgiving to God for what He has taught you through this study, as well as a prayer request that includes what your plan of action will be to obey what you have learned.

About the Author

Susan Heck, and her husband Doug have been married for 40 years. She has been involved in Women's Ministries for over 30 years. This includes teaching Bible Studies, counseling, and leading Ladies with the Master women's ministry at Grace Community Church in Tulsa, Oklahoma. (www.gccoftulsa.net)

Susan is a certified counselor with the National Association of Nouthetic Counselors. (www.nanc.org) She is the author of "With The Master" Bible Study Series for women. Previously published books in that series are,

- With the Master in the School of Tested Faith:
  A Ladies' Bible Study on the Book of James

- With the Master on our Knees:
  A Ladies' Bible Study on Prayer

- With the Master in Fullness of Joy:
  A Ladies' Bible Study on the Book of Phillipians

- With the Master Before the Mirror of God's Word:
  A Ladies' Bible Study on First John

She is also the author of four published booklets:

- Putting Off Life Dominating Sins

- A Call to Scripture Memory

- A Call to Discipleship

- Assurance: Twenty Tests for God's Children

Susan's teaching ministry is an outgrowth of her memorization work on the Bible. She has personally memorized 23 books of the New Testament word-for-word (The Gospel of Matthew, The Gospel of John, Romans, Second Corinthians, Galatians, Ephesians, Philippians, Colossians, First and Second Thessalonians, First and Second Timothy, Titus, Philemon, Hebrews, James, First and Second Peter, and First, Second, and Third John, Jude, Revelation), one book of the Old Testament (Jonah), and several other portions of Scripture.

Susan and her husband have two grown children and seven grandchildren. Both children and their spouses are in full-time ministry. Because of the enthusiasm of ladies who attended Susan's Bible studies, she has been invited to speak to ladies' groups both nationally and internationally. (www.withthemaster.org) Susan's teachings can be heard on radio at World View Weekend: www.worldviewweekend.com/profile/brannon-howse